Disability, Gender and Violence over the Life Course

This is the first book to explore the interplay of disability, gender and violence over the life course from researcher, practitioner and survivor perspectives. It gives due weight to the accounts of disabled children and adults who have survived institutional or individual violence, evidencing barriers to recognition, disclosure and reporting.

Written by disabled and non-disabled women from around the world, *Disability, Gender and Violence over the Life Course* addresses the dearth of voices and experiences of disabled women and girls in empirical research, policy and practice on issues of violence, victimisation, protection, support and prevention. Divided into three parts – Childhood, Adulthood and Older Life – this collection offers diverse perspectives on the intersectionality of disability, age, ethnicity, sexuality and violence that have hitherto been absent.

This book will be an invaluable resource for students and practitioners of multiple fields of practice and academic studies, including health and social care, nursing, social work, childhood studies, gender studies, disability studies, safeguarding and child protection, equality and human rights, sociology and criminology.

Sonali Shah graduated with a PhD in Occupational Psychology and Disability in 2002. Since then she has developed a series of innovative projects, supported by prestigious awards and university fellowships on disability issues, human rights and social change. She is author of 3 research monographs and 12 journal articles. Sonali has grown up as a British Indian disabled woman.

Caroline Bradbury-Jones is a registered nurse, midwife and health visitor. She holds a position as Reader in Nursing at the University of Birmingham, UK where she leads the Risk, Abuse and Violence Research Programme. Her research focuses primarily on violence against women and girls. Her funded research has included the study of access to maternity services for disabled women who have experienced intimate partner violence.

Interdisciplinary Disability Studies

Series editor: Mark Sherry
The University of Toledo, USA

Disability studies has made great strides in exploring power and the body. This series extends the interdisciplinary dialogue between disability studies and other fields by asking how disability studies can influence a particular field. It will show how a deep engagement with disability studies changes our understanding of the following fields: sociology, literary studies, gender studies, bioethics, social work, law, education, or history. This ground-breaking series identifies both the practical and theoretical implications of such an interdisciplinary dialogue and challenges people in disability studies as well as other disciplinary fields to critically reflect on their professional praxis in terms of theory, practice, and methods.

For a full list of titles in this series, please visit www.routledge.com/series/ASHSER1401

A Sociological Approach to Acquired Brain Injury and Identity
Jonathan Harvey

A Feminist Ethnography of Secure Wards for Women with Learning Disabilities
Locked Away
Rebecca Fish

Forthcoming:

International Perspectives on Teaching with Disability
Overcoming Obstacles and Enriching Lives
Edited by Michael S. Jeffress

Disability, Gender and Violence over the Life Course
Global Perspectives and Human Rights Approaches
Edited by Sonali Shah and Caroline Bradbury-Jones

Film, Comedy and Disability
Understanding Humour and Genre in Cinematic Constructions of Impairment and Disability
Alison Wilde

Disability, Gender and Violence over the Life Course

Global Perspectives and Human Rights Approaches

Edited by
Sonali Shah and
Caroline Bradbury-Jones

Routledge
Taylor & Francis Group

LONDON AND NEW YORK

First published 2018
by Routledge
2 Park Square, Milton Park, Abingdon, Oxon OX14 4RN

and by Routledge
711 Third Avenue, New York, NY 10017

Routledge is an imprint of the Taylor & Francis Group, an informa business

British Library Cataloguing in Publication Data
A catalogue record for this book is available from the British Library

Library of Congress Cataloging in Publication Data
Names: Shah, Sonali, 1973– editor. | Bradbury-Jones, Caroline, editor.
Title: Disability, gender and violence over the life course : global perspectives and human rights approaches / edited by Sonali Shah and Caroline Bradbury-Jones.
Description: 1st Edition. | New York : Routledge, 2018. |
Series: Interdisciplinary disability studies | Includes bibliographical references and index.
Identifiers: LCCN 2017060127 | ISBN 9781138085190 (hardback) | ISBN 9781315111452 (ebook)
Subjects: LCSH: Victims of violent crimes – Social conditions. | People with disabilities – Crimes against – Social aspects. | Human rights.
Classification: LCC HV6250.4.H35 D55 2018 | DDC 362.4 – dc23
LC record available at https://lccn.loc.gov/2017060127

ISBN: 978-1-138-08519-0 (hbk)
ISBN: 978-1-315-11145-2 (ebk)

Typeset in Bembo
by Florence Production Ltd., Stoodleigh, Devon, UK

Contents

List of figures and tables

Figures

Tables

Notes on contributors

Karen Soldatic is an Australian Research Council Discovery Early Career Research Award (DECRA) Fellow. Karen's DECRA, entitled 'Disability Income Reform and Regional Australia: The Indigenous Experience', draws upon two previous fellowships: British Academy International Visiting Fellowship (2012) and The Centre for Human Rights Education, Curtin University (2011–2012) where she remains an Adjunct Fellow. Karen's research on global welfare regimes builds upon her 20 years' experience as an international, national and state-based senior policy analyst and practitioner.

Christine Jones is Senior Lecturer at the University of Strathclyde in Glasgow, Scotland. Her research focuses on state interventions in family lives and the impact of these on family relationships. She has a particular interest in the experiences and outcomes of children who have been abused and neglected and who enter public care. She has written on the sibling relationships of children in long-term foster care and adoption, post-adoption contact, the views of deaf and disabled children and young people of the child protection system and barriers to permanence for disabled children.

Julie Taylor is Professor of Child Protection, Institute of Clinical Sciences, University of Birmingham, in partnership with Birmingham Women's and Children's NHS Foundation Trust. She is a nurse scientist specialising in child maltreatment working with multidisciplinary teams nationally and internationally to position child maltreatment as a public health concern. Julie's research programme is concentrated at the interface between health and social care and is largely underpinned by the discourse of cumulative harm and the exponential effects of living with multiple adversities. She is the author of nine books and over 100 academic articles on child abuse and neglect.

Ashley Thompson graduated in 2010 from the University of Edinburgh with a BSc Hons in Nursing Studies where she developed a particular interest in the health and wellbeing of children and young people. She has worked for Barnardo's, Action for Children and Roots of Empathy, supporting children and young people with various specialist support needs. She is currently working for Shakti Women's Aid as the Children and Young Peoples Team

Leader, working with Black Minority Ethnic children and young people who have experienced domestic abuse, honour-based violence, forced marriage and female genital mutilation. She is an active member of the Edinburgh Violence Against Women School Prevention group and the Scottish Government Forced Marriage Network and is committed to improving the lives of children and young people affected by gender-based violence.

Mridul Wadhwa has worked in the gender-based violence sector in Scotland since 2005 mainly with Black Minority Ethnic (BME) women experiencing domestic abuse and forced marriage. She was involved in the development and delivery of forced marriage training commissioned by the Scottish Government. She has been involved in supporting survivors of forced marriage as well as advising public sector professionals on best practice in Forced Marriage cases. She currently works for Rape Crisis Scotland as training and volunteer coordinator for the Rape Crisis National Helpline and is an associate of the College of Policing, England, and Wales.

Freyja Haraldsdóttir is an Icelandic politician and a disability rights activist. She was elected to the Icelandic Constitutional Assembly in 2010 and chosen to become a deputy Member of Parliament of the Althing in 2013. Before going into politics, she was an advocate in support of providing people with disabilities with personal assistants. Outside of her political career, she worked at Independent Living Centre from 2010 to 2014 as a director. After leaving the ILC, she co-founded the company Tabú whose goal is to create safe spaces for women with disabilities in Iceland.

Aizan Sofia Amin is Senior Lecturer in the Psychology and Human Well-Being Research Centre at Universiti Kebangsaan Malaysia for Social Work Programme. She is also a registered counsellor certified by Board of Counsellors of Malaysia. She gained her PhD in Disability Studies from the University of Glasgow UK, focusing on the lived experiences of Malaysian women with physical impairment. She has also been appointed as a member of the National Council for Persons with Disabilities by the Ministry of Women, Family and Community Development Malaysia. During her 2-year term, she will supervise the implementation of national policy and a national plan of action, and recommend changes to existing laws and propose new legislation to ensure the full participation of people with disabilities in the community. She is a Malaysian disabled woman with physical impairment. She lost her leg to cancer at the age of 16. Since then, she has been an active advocate of the rights of disabled people in Malaysia, increasing public awareness of the struggles encountered due to a lack of resources and negative societal attitudes.

Theresa Lorenzo is Professor in Disability Studies and Occupational Therapy in Faculty of Health Sciences at University Cape Town (UCT). She gained experience in community-based disability and development programmes in the rural and urban communities in South Africa, which has involved the training of community rehabilitation workers. She joined UCT's occupational therapy department in 1996 and has worked with a Primary Health Care non-government organisation in building students' capacity to work with civil society organisations in addressing the needs of disabled people and their families. She initiated the Disability Studies Postgraduate Programmes at UCT in 2003 to bridge the gap between activism and scholarship. Her research experience has focused on addressing poverty, inequality and employment of disabled youth and women, including monitoring and evaluation of inclusive development.

Harsha Kathard is Professor in Communication Sciences in the Department of Health and Rehabilitation Sciences, Faculty of Health Sciences at the University of Cape Town. She has a Doctorate in Education and is committed to generating knowledge that develops and transforms health professional education. She actively participates in research and social responsibility projects on service delivery with emphasis on population-based approaches, disability, identity and inclusion, and enhancing classroom communication.

Lois Llewellyn (psuedonym) is an independent researcher with a masters in disability studies. Her work focuses on the relationship between disabled people and God.

Bridget Penhale is currently Reader in Mental Health of Older People at the University of East Anglia (UEA), UK. She has been qualified as a social worker since 1981, and has specialised in work with older people since 1983. She worked as social worker and manager for some 15 years, before becoming an academic – at the University of Hull (UK) in 1996, Sheffield in 2004 and currently at UEA, Norwich since October 2010. Bridget has published widely (12 books, 23 book chapters and several journal articles) on decision-making and mentally incapacitated adults and extensively on elder abuse. Previously Chair of the British Association of Social Worker's Community Care Sub-Committee, she is Vice-Chair of Action on Elder Abuse and independent co-chair of the Hull Domestic Violence Forum, a multi-agency network to develop responses to domestic violence (predominantly of women). She is a member of the UK National Social Care Research Ethics Committee and a Board member of the International Network for the Prevention of Elder Abuse (INPEA). In 2010 she received the International Rosalie Wolf Award for her work in the field of elder abuse research and practice.

Anne-Sophie Parent has been Secretary General of AGE Platform Europe since 2002, a network of 120 organisations representing 40 million seniors across Europe, in consultative status with the United Nations Economic and Social Council, and participatory status to the Council of Europe. AGE aims to promote the rights of older people at European Union (EU) and United Nations (UN) level, and voice the interests of the 190 million inhabitants aged 50+ living in the EU. Anne-Sophie represents AGE in the European Pensions

Forum, European Health Policy Forum, the Advisory Board of Assisted Ambient Living Joint Programme, the Societal Advisory Board of the More Years Better Lives Joint programme. She is also member of the Expert Group of the EU-UNECE Active Ageing Index project, and the Advisory Board of the New Pact for Europe. She currently chairs the Financial Services Users' Group set up by the European Commission, and sits in the Euro Retail Payment Board set up by the European Central Bank in which she is leading an informal group on accessibility of retail payments.

In 2016, she was elected Secretary General of the newly established European Covenant on Demographic Change, a large network bringing together sub-national public authorities, non-for-profit and profit actors who wish to join forces to promote age-friendly environments to support active and healthy ageing in close cooperation with the World Health Organization.

Introduction

The context of the book

Sonali Shah and Caroline Bradbury-Jones

Disability and violence are global human rights issues that cut across gender, race, age, sexuality, geographical, religious, socio-economic status and cultural boundaries. They can be viewed as socially produced and culturally constructed and can manifest at different or multiple, generational locations over a person's life course (childhood, youth, adulthood and older age). Disability and violence have a bi-directional causal relationship in that the onset of impairment can be caused by exposure to violence, or violent actions by a perpetrator can be stimulated by a victim's impairment. While both issues were once considered to be private problems hidden from public view, increasingly they are recognised as public issues, warranting public attention and intervention including legal rights and financial support from the public purse. Moreover, both are gendered; they have impacts across the life span; and they effect women and girls across the world. Hence this book! We are interested in intersectionality – in other words, how these issues interact and specifically, what impact this has for women and girls. First, we are going to explore the key concepts that we draw upon as the foundation for the book.

Unravelling the issue of disability

In this book we use the term 'disabled people', 'disabled adults' and 'disabled child/disabled children'. We do not use 'people with disabilities', 'child/children with a disability', 'adults with disabilities /a disability'. We consider disability to be an integral part of an individual's identity, not something negative that should be detached from them. Further, in line with the social model of disability, the editors and chapter authors of the book consider disabling barriers to be the product of the interaction between society and the individual with an impairment, and not purely the impairment. In this book, disabled people (women and men, boys and girls) are identified according to the United Nations Convention of Persons Disabilities (UNCRPD) as:

> those who have long-term physical, mental, intellectual or sensory impairments which in interaction with various barriers may hinder their full and effective participation in society on an equal basis with others.

With 50 binding articles, the UNCRPD (UN 2006) is the first international treaty to afford disabled people full civil rights and fundamental freedoms in all aspects of life. Three of these articles are particularly relevant to this book: Article 6 which pays particular attention to the situation of disabled women and girls and calls for actions to ensure they are able to exercise and enjoy their human rights; Article 15 which seeks to protect disabled persons from abuse, violence, torture or scientific experimentation by taking appropriate measures (administrative, legal and judicial); and Article 16 which also aims to protect disabled people from abuse, exploitation and violence, including gender-based violence – inside and outside the home.

However, despite the national and international disability legislation like the UNCRPD, people with different impairments and life-limiting illnesses experience significant inequalities and multiple discrimination in different areas of their lives and across the life span as they interact with different social structures and public policies from birth to death. In developed and developing countries, disabled people experience poorer educational, employment and health outcomes compared with their non-disabled contemporaries. Although 80 per cent of the world's disabled population is currently of working age, they continue to be disadvantaged in all sectors of the labour market, experiencing unemployment, underemployment or unequal pay.

With inequalities in education and employment it is not surprising that disabled people are more likely to experience poverty, which has in itself been cited as a cause of impairment (Priestley, 2001; World Health Organization (WHO), 2011). The Organization for Economic Co-operation and Development (OECD) survey of 29 countries showed that disabled people of working age were more likely to be in poverty compared to non-disabled counterparts in all countries except three (Norway, Slovakia and Sweden) (OECD, 2009). World Health Survey data indicate that households with a disabled member spend more capital on health care than those with no disabled member (Mitra *et al.*, 2011). Although extra expenditure on disability-related costs could mean households have worse living conditions and fewer assets compared to households with no disabled member, this is not always the case. In South Africa for example, the supply of disability-related grants means that the income for households with a disabled member is often greater than those with no disabled member (Leob *et al.*, 2008).

Disability as a gendered issue

Disabled people make up 15 per cent of the world's global population (WHO, 2011). However, the prevalence of impairment across this globe is higher for women compared to men – 19.2 per cent and 12 per cent respectively according to the World Report on Disability (WHO, 2011). Unlike disabled men and non-disabled women, disabled women can experience both disablism and sexism by systems and structures at micro, meso and macro levels. As systematic norms are created by those in positions of power, the more marginal characteristics an individual has, the greater the gap between their own social position and those deemed as socially acceptable (Barile, 2010). The organisation of social structures, processes and systems means that disabled women, compared to non-disabled women, are particularly susceptible to employment inequalities such as glass ceiling advancement, lower wages and occupational segregation (Shah, 2005; WHO, 2011). With the loss or absence of employment and economic power comes a drop in social status, a loss of identity, a general sense of powerlessness and vulnerability. Such a situation contributes to social isolation, poverty and to violence against disabled women. We have already mentioned poverty and, from a gendered perspective, it is worse for disabled women in comparison to men across the globe. This is unsurprising given the economic, educational and social disadvantages they encounter as a consequence of living at the intersection of disability and gender.

Disabled women and girls have experienced invisibility both by disability rights movements and women's movements. This has increased their marginalisation and vulnerability to violence and discrimination across the life course, in multiple areas of their lives. Traditionally, disabled women have been subjected to social infantilisation, being conceptualised as weak, passive and dependent. The disabled female body has not been seen as beautiful or sexual, but as fragile, weak and unfit to be someone's sexual partner (Fine and Ashes, 1988). This can be illustrated by the 2007 case of Ashley X, a 6-year-old disabled girl whose parents had obtained medical and legal consent from respective professionals for her to have surgical and hormone treatment to restrain her growth and sexual development.

The Ashley case demonstrates how the assumption that disabled women cannot be sexual beings is an example of the intersection of disability and female oppression. As a group, disabled women and girls have traditionally been exposed to disempowering messages about their reproductive choices from babyhood, having limited exposure to sexual knowledge and opportunities while growing up due to being excluded from the cultural spaces where these exchanges take place, or being constrained by high levels of surveillance (Nosek et al., 2001; Shakespeare, 2000; Shakespeare et al., 1996). The disabled female has historically been asexually objectified by media, medical and legal discourse, conceptualised as undesirable sexual partners or mothers (Kallianes and Rubenfeld, 1997; McFarlane, 2004; Priestley, 2003). They have been actively discouraged and sometimes physically prevented from exercising their reproductive capacities and becoming parents (Thomas, 1997; Waxman, 1994). This has created a culture of healthcare and maternity services where organisational, physical and attitudinal barriers may impact negatively on disabled women's maternal and reproductive health. WHO (2016, www.who.int/mediacentre/factsheets/fs352/en/) reports that disabled women continue to encounter barriers to having needs met. For instance, they are less likely to be targeted by health promotion and prevention activities, such as screening for breast or cervical cancer, than non-disabled women. Research with disabled women in developing countries such as Ghana or Uganda, have reported that disabled women's reproductive health needs receive little attention due to the prevailing assumption that disabled women are not sexually active and less likely to marry or have children then non-disabled women (Ahumuza *et al.*, 2014).

Disabled women and the issue of abuse and violence

Many disabled feminist scholars (e.g. Morris, 1991; Thomas, 1999) have noted that dominant definitions of violence focus on the experiences of violence by non-disabled women but fail to represent those of disabled women. Research on violence against women, particularly from psychological, criminology and sociological perspectives, has consistently failed to recount experiences of disabled women and girls in their analysis. For instance, UK-based criminologist researchers Michele Burman and Susan Batchelor have missed opportunities to capture the voices of disabled women and girls in their extensive and important work relating to themes of violence, crime and justice. As suggested by Roulstone and Mason-Bish (2012) in their edited collection *Disability, Hate Crime and Violence*, crimes against disabled people have not been investigated with the same rigour and sense of urgency as those against non-disabled people across the life course. This can be attributed to a number of factors, not least the exclusion of the disability experience from mainstream discourse on violence, justice and support.

Although disabled women and girls can experience the same types of abuse as their non-disabled contemporaries – physical, sexual and emotional, they are likely to be subjected to additional abuse triggered by the objectification and manipulation of the disabled female body, and perpetrated by people who are supposed to 'care' for them, such as personal assistants or carers in institutions, parents, health care workers (Sobsey and Doe, 1991). Professional, social and institutional practices have often been taken for granted as a normal part of disabled people's everyday lives and not considered to be 'abusive practices' in the same way that they would if experienced by a non-disabled child/adult. Professionals may not necessarily recognise scars of disabled child abuse and misdiagnose them as being related to the child's impairment (Brandon *et al.*, 2011; Hibbard and Desch, 2007). This diagnostic overshadowing can thwart the enactment of necessary child protection and support (as illustrated for example, in Chapter 2 of this book by Jones and Taylor). It also causes disbelief when victims do seek help and disclose their experiences of violence. Being silenced and unsupported has psycho-emotional impacts that the victims can carry with them for the rest of their lives. It is important to stress that it is not a child's impairment that provokes abuse, but rather the context in which disabled children are placed and the practices they are coerced to endure.

Mainstream definitions of violence are usually based on the potential per-petrater being a male intimate partner, therefore organisations and services have been designed to focus on this. However as disabled women and girls can be victims of disablist abuse where the perpetrater is not necessarily an intimate partner and not necessarily male (as explored in Chapter 7), they may experi-ence difficulty getting help. In this regard, adopting a feminist disability lens would be useful to explore the experiences of violence for disabled women and girls with multiple identities. Feminist disability theory is the integration of feminist materialism and disability theory (essentially the social model approach). Such a tool is useful to inform the understandings of the social, political and cultural nature of disability and gender, and its interconnections with structures and systems, to understand disabled woman's lived experiences of differing forms of oppression (i.e. sexism and disablism). It would also provide insights to understanding how disabled women and their experience as female is linked to the broader political oppressions of disablism.

The pervasive stereotyping that disabled women are asexual and dependent beings (Nosek et al., 1997) increases their vulnerability to abuse by different perpetrators (including carers, family members and health professionals). It also has the potential to influence professionals' views that violence towards disabled women and girls as less serious than it is for non-disabled contemporaries (Kennedy, 1996). This will be a growing problem as the global population survives into old age, as has been suggested in the Madrid International Plan of Action on Ageing (Sidorenko and Walker, 2004). It postulates that older women will be exposed to practices and relationships that increase their vulnerability to multiple levels of discrimination in relation to elder abuse, neglect and manipulation, often exacerbated by lack of legal protection and barriers to accessing services and support.

Disabled women and girls are at a higher risk of violence than non-disabled populations. They are more likely to be placed in potentially vulnerable situations and exposed to potentially risky practices and dependent relationships that cultivate types of abuse that are signifcantly more diverse in nature and specific to being disabled. These forms of violence include chemical restraint, medical exploitation and institutional abuse (Howe, 2006), which simul-taneously increase the powerfulness of the perpetrators and the powerlessness of the disabled women. Unlike non-disabled women, disabled women are vulnerable to abuse from the health care providers and personal assistants who are important to their independence at different points in their lives. Reviews by Jones et al. (2012) show that those defined as disabled are 50 per cent more likely than non-disabled people to experience violence. Jones et al. (2012) evidence the increased prevalence of violence for disabled children and maltreat-ment as being three times that of non-disabled children. In terms of gender, Sullivan and Knutson (2000) and Kelly et al. (1991) suggest that disabled girls are more prone to sexual violence than disabled boys while the opposite is true for physical violence. Further, disabled girls are likely to be sexually abused before their eighteenth birthday. In this regard, violence against disabled people across the life course is not only a human rights issue but also a significant social and public health problem.

This book addresses the subject of disablist violence, violence that is specific to being disabled and that non-disabled women/girls do not experience. This includes actions that simultaneously increase the powerfulness of the perpetrators and the powerlessness of the disabled women. Curry *et al.* (2001) highlight examples of disablist violence as including the misuse of medication, isolating individuals from family and friends, removing assistive mobility devices from the disabled persons' reach and sexual touching/unwanted fondling while providing personal care. However, these practices and actions may not be recognised as abuse, either by professionals or by disabled people themselves, but rather misdiagnosed and normalised as part and parcel of the victim-survivors' impairment.

Across the globe, the risk of violence for children with impairments or life-limiting illnesses, during their lifetimes, is three to four times greater compared to their non-disabled contemporaries. They are likely to experience more than one type of violence across their lifetime starting from an early age (Jones *et al.*, 2012; Sullivan and Knutson, 2000). Violence against disabled children tends to be more severe than for non-disabled children (Akbas *et al.*, 2009), while severity is correlated with the impairment type (Stalker and McArther, 2010). Accounting for gender, Sobsey *et al.* (1997) found that significantly more disabled girls than disabled boys were likely to experience sexual abuse, while the opposite is true for physical abuse. Disability and violence have a bi-directional causal relationship in that the onset of impairment can be caused by women and girls' exposure to gender discriminatory practices such as child marriage, child pregnancy or female genital mutilation. On the other hand, violent and abusive actions by a perpetrator can be stimulated by a victim's impairment, coupled with the negative societal constructions of disability.

A plethora of international evidence suggests that women and girls with impairments are more susceptible to systemic and individual violence across their life course compared to their non-disabled contemporaries (Thiara *et al.*, 2011). Studies conducted in Europe, North America and Australia have shown that over half of all disabled women have experienced physical abuse, compared with one-third of non-disabled women (United Nations (UN), 2006). Nearly 80 per cent of disabled women have been victims of psychological and physical violence, and are at a greater risk of sexual abuse than non-disabled women (European Parliament, 2006). This high proportion of disabled women and girls exposed to and experiencing violence over their lives could be associated with a number of factors, starting with the societal contention that the life of a disabled child is a wrongful life and an economic burden to the family and society (Priestley, 2003). Such a view can impact the inter-action and quality of attachment between parent and disabled child, and thus it is this that determines the child's risk to violence not their impairment (Howe, 2006).

Other factors include: professionals' tendency to misdiagnose effects of abuse as being a consequence of impairment; the objectification and manipulation of the disabled female body over the life course by different professionals; the cultural devaluation of disabled people and their constrained exposure to appropriate sexual health knowledge and education while growing up; increased levels of surveillance and dependency on others for intimate personal care. Cockram (2003) suggests that the fact disabled women and girls have to depend on others for basic personal and social needs not only places them at greater risk of abuse compared to non-disabled females, but also reduces opportunities to disclose.

Limited violence prevention support and intervention for disabled females at different points of the life course can leave them feeling disempowered and doubting their rights to protection and support. Thomas (2007) refers to this cumulative damaging impact on disabled people's self-worth as 'psycho-emotional disablism' and suggests that it creates long-term 'barriers to being'.

Intersectionality and violence

Dominant definitions of violence have historically been based on the experience of the White non-disabled female. Feminists campaigned for the need for a gendered analysis of the concept. Thus 'violence' became 'domestic violence' and was conceived as a manifestation of the unequal power relations between men and women, which has led to the discrimination and oppression of women and their subordination in relation to men. According to the United Nations (UN), violence against women and girls is defined as:

> Any act of gender based violence that results in, or is likely to result in, physical, sexual or mental harm or suffering to women, including threats of such acts, coercion or arbitrary deprivation of liberty, whether occurring in public or in private life.

In the United Kingdom, the concept of domestic violence is informed by Women's Aid, a national charity working to end violence against women in the United Kingdom. With a network of 350 domestic and sexual violence services across the United Kingdom, Women's Aid (2007) defines domestic violence as:

> Physical, psychological, sexual and financial violence that takes place within an intimate or family-type relationship and forms a pattern of coercive and controlling behavior. This could include forced marriage and so-called 'honour' crimes. Domestic violence often includes a range of abusive behaviors, not all of which are inherently violent.

A life course approach

Life story or biographical methods are making an important contribution to the field of disability studies and, in particular, uncovering the hidden childhood histories of disabled people (Shah and Priestley, 2010). Bringing victim-survivors' self-told histories into the light has been considered paramount for service providers and planners to ensure policies and practices are developed to protect and support disabled children. As Jenny Morris (1997: 257) pointed out:

> We need to know much more about the experiences of disabled children and young people, and such research must offer an opportunity for their accounts to be heard. Only when this happens will policy and practice be driven more clearly by the interests of disabled children themselves.

The life history method not only generates personal narrative, but also has a potential to offer a unique understanding of development across time (both biographical and historical) and space (Chase, 1995), and the interplay between the individual and the broader social structures and interdependent relationships (Bertaux, 1981). It also favours a social model lens and allows a space for non-medicalised narratives to be voiced by disabled women. It allows for the focus to move beyond the 'life experiences of disabled people' and towards the 'experiences of disability in people's lives', responding to Finkelstein's reminder that 'disabled people are not the subject matter of social interpretation of disability' (Finkelstein, 2001: 1), but that their experiences can provide unique evidence of the ways disability manifests itself. This can also reveal the network of social relations, institutions and practices that, while being part of life as a disabled child, increase their vulnerability to violence and barriers to support.

We specifically use the life course lens to encourage individual biography and semi-structured narration about experiences across different periods of time, cultural and social spaces to examine specific life transitions, trajectories and turning points, influenced by the structural and the individual. From a social model sense, this lens allows us to uncover how disability and violence manifests and which came first. It also reveals stories of resistance and resilience, and moments of agency that contribute to positive change in the lives of disabled females at different points in their lives.

Bringing it together: about this book

This book gives due weight to the accounts of disabled children and adults who have survived institutional or individual violence, evidencing barriers to recognition, disclosure and reporting. In turn, this provides important insights for mainstream child protection, violence support services and criminal justice systems to recognise disablist violence, avoid diagnostic overshadowing and support victim-survivors to speak out and not be silenced. Written by disabled and non-disabled women across the globe, this collection addresses the dearth of voices and experiences of disabled women and girls in mainstream research on violence, victimisation, protection, prevention, and disability. This participation of all women and girls in meaningful disability dialogue will help achieve the goal 'nothing about us without us'. It will also raise an awareness of the need to include disablist violence in official definitions of gender-based violence and child abuse.

The stories told in this book are not only the stories of disabled women and girls, but those who have intersectional identities – identify as homosexual, identify as transgender, are of minority ethnic or religious background, and are of different ages. Living with multiple identities, or what Maria Barile (2010: 172) refers to as 'marginal characteristics', contributes to unique experiences of oppression and disadvantage. This experience of intersectional discrimination is a form of discrimination not experienced by White non-disabled heterosexual women who, due to increasing social, political and economic advancements nationally and internationally, can have a social position closer to the non-disabled White male than women with one or more minority identities.

The book is divided into three parts, reflecting three generational periods of the human life course i.e. childhood, adulthood and older life. Each part includes perspectives of researchers, practitioners and survivors from different countries. Part one focuses on childhood, starting with a contribution from Karen Soldatic (Chapter 1) who, using one person's narrative, explores the intersectional experience of family violence for indigenous mothers with disabled children in Australia. Next Christine Jones and Julie Taylor offer a reconceptualision of disclosure of abuse relating to disablism in theory and practice, from a combined England and Scotland perspective (Chapter 2). Ashley Thompson and Mridul Wadhwa bring a practitioner perspective, reflecting on their experiences as practitioners taking a holistic approach to responding to forced marriage for children and young people who are Black Minority Ethnic (BME) survivors with learning disabilities in Scotland (Chapter 3).

Part two of the book focuses on disability and violence in adulthood, from practitioner, researcher and survivor perspectives. From Iceland, Freyja Haraldsdóttir highlights the importance of creating safe spaces for the empowerment of disabled women and disabled trans-sexual people (Chapter 4). Turning to the issue of sexual abuse, Aizan Sofia draws on her PhD study to discuss sexual abuse in healthcare settings among Malaysian disabled women (Chapter 5). Theresa Lorenzo and Harsha Kathard also present empirical data to show how disabled women negotiate violence in contexts of poverty in South Africa (Chapter 6). This is followed by a survivor perspective, offered from Lois Llewellyn (pseudonym) on the 'aftermath' of sexual, physical and psychological violence at different points of her life (Chapter 7).

The third and final part of the book focuses on older people. Bridget Penhale addresses the issue in a critical discussion of elder abuse, ageing and disability (Chapter 8), and AGE Platform Europe present a review of the risk of abuse for disabled people in older life, and the European and international human rights frameworks needed for protection (Chapter 9). Through this exciting collection of contributions, this book offers a unique perspective on the intersectionality of disability, gender and violence, viewed from a life course perspective.

References

Ahumuza, S., Matovu, J., Ddamulira, J. and Muhanguzi, F. (2014) 'Challenges in accessing sexual and reproductive health services by people with physical disabilities in Kampala, Uganda', *Reproductive Health*, 11(1), p. 59.

Akbas, S., Turla, A., Karabekiroglu, K., Pazvantoglu, O., Keskin, T. and Boke, O. (2009) 'Characteristics of sexual abuse in a sample of Turkish children with and without mental retardation, referred for legal appraisal of the psychological repercussions', *Sexuality and Disability*, 27(4), pp. 205–213.

Barile, M. (2010) 'An intersectional perspective on violence: A new response', in Driedger, D. ed., *Living the edges: A disabled women's reader*. Toronto: Inanna Publications and Education, pp. 171–185.

Bertaux, D. (1981) 'From the life history approach to the transformation of sociological practice', in Bertaux, D. ed., *Biography and society: The life history approach in the social sciences*. London: Sage, pp. 29–45.

Bradshaw, J. S. (1989) *Healing the shame that binds you*. (Cassette Recording No. 1–55874–043–0). Deerfield Beach, FL: Health Communications.

Brandon, M., Sidebotham, P., Ellis, C., Bailey, S. and Belderson, P. (2011) *Child and family practitioners' understanding of child development: Lessons learnt from a small sample of serious case reviews*. Research Report DFE-RR110.

Chase, S. E. (1995) 'Taking narrative seriously: Consequences for method and theory in interview studies', in Josselson, R. and Lieblich, A. eds, *The narrative study of lives: Vol. 3. Interpreting experience*. Thousand Oaks, CA: Sage, pp. 1–26.

Cockram, J. (2003) *Silent voices: Women with disabilities and family and domestic violence*. Nedlands, Western Australia: People with Disabilities (W.A.), The Ethnic Disability Advocacy Centre and the Centre for Social Research, Edith Cowan University.

Curry, M. A., Hassouneh-Phillips, D. and Johnston-Silverberg, A. J. (2001). 'Abuse of women with disabilities: An ecological model and review', *Violence Against Women*, 7, pp. 60–79.

European Parliament (2006) European Parliament resolution on the situation of people with disabilities in the enlarged European Union: The European Action Plan 2006–2007 (20062007 (INI)).

Fine, M. and Asch, A. eds. (1988) *Women with disabilities: Essays in psychology, policy, and politics*. Philadelphia, PA: Temple University Press.

Finkelstein, V. (2001) 'The social model of disability repossessed', retrieved January 2007 from www.leeds.ac.uk/disability-studies/archiveuk/finkelstein/soc%20mod %20repossessed.pdf.

Hibbard, R. A. and Desch, L. W. (2007) 'Maltreatment of children with disabilities', *Pediatrics*, 119(5), pp. 1018–1025.

Howe, D. (2006) 'Disabled children, maltreatment and attachment', *British Journal of Social Work*, 36(5), pp. 743–760.

Jones, L., Bellis, M., Wood, S., Hughes, K., Bates, G., Eckley, L., McCoy, E., Mikton, C., Shakespeare, T. and Officer, A. (2012) 'Prevalence and risk of violence against adults with disabilities: A systematic review and meta-analysis of observational studies', *The Lancet*, 380(9845), pp. 899–990.

Kallianes, V. and Rubenfeld, P. (1997) 'Disabled women and reproductive rights', *Disability & Society*, 12(2), pp. 203–222.

Kelly, L., Regan, L. and Burton, S. (1991) *An exploratory study of the prevalence of sexual abuse in a sample of 16-21 year olds*. Child Abuse Studies Unit. London: PNL.

Kennedy, M. (1996) 'Sexual abuse and disabled children', in Morris, J. ed. *Encounters with strangers. Feminism and disability*. London: The Women's Press, pp. 116–134.

Loeb, M., Eide, A., Jelsma, J., Toni, M. and Maart, S. (2008) 'Poverty and disability in Eastern and Western Cape Provinces, South Africa', *Disability and Society*, 23(4), pp. 311–321.

McFarlane, H. (2004) *Disabled women and socio-spatial 'barriers' to motherhood*. PhD thesis, University of Glasgow.

Mitra, S., Posarac, A. and Vick, B. (2011) *Disability and poverty in developing countries: A snapshot from the World Health Survey*, Discussion Paper.

Morris, J. (1991) *Pride against prejudice: Transforming attitudes to disability*. London: Women's Press.

Morris, J. (1997) 'Gone missing? Disabled children living away from their families', *Disability & Society*, 12(2), pp. 241–258.

Nosek, M., Howland, C. and Hughes, R. (2001) 'The investigation of abuse and women with disabilities: Going beyond assumptions', *Violence Against Women*, 7(4), pp. 477–499.

Nosek, M., Howland, C. and Young, M. (1997) 'Abuse of women with disabilities: Policy implications', *Journal of Disability Policy Studies*, 8(1–2), pp. 157–175.

O'Reilly, A. (2003) *The right to decent work of persons with disabilities*, Skills Working Paper, 14, Geneva: International Labour Organization, pp. 31–33

Organisation for Economic Co-operation and Development (2009) *Sickness, disability and work: Keeping on track in the economic downturn*. Paris: OECD.

Priestley, M. ed. (2001) *Disability and the life course: Global perspectives*. Cambridge: Cambridge University Press.

Priestley, M. (2003). *Disability: A life course approach*. Cambridge: Polity.

Roulstone, A. and Mason-Bish, H. eds. (2012) *Disability, hate crime and violence*. London: Routledge.

Shah, S. (2005) *Career success of disabled high-flyers*. London: Jessica Kingsley.

Shah, S. and Priestley, M. (2010) 'Home and away: The changing impact of educational policies on disabled children's experiences of family and friendship', *Research Papers in Education*, 25(2), pp. 155–175.

Shakespeare, T. (2000) 'Disabled sexuality: Toward rights and recognition', *Sexuality and Disability*, 18(3), pp. 159–166.

Shakespeare, T., Gillespie-Sells, K. and Davies, D. (1996) *The sexual politics of disability: Untold desires*. London: Cassell.

Sidorenko, A. and Walker, A. (2004) 'The Madrid International Plan of Action on Ageing: From conception to implementation', *Ageing & Society*, 24(2), pp. 147–165.

Sobsey, D. and Doe, T. (1991) 'Patterns of sexual abuse and assault', *Sexuality and Disability*, 9(3), pp. 243–259.

Sobsey, D., Randall, W. and Parrila, R. K. (1997) 'Gender differences in abused children with and without disabilities', *Child Abuse & Neglect*, 21(8), pp. 707–720.

Stalker, K. and McArthur, K. (2010) 'Child violence, child protection and disabled children: A review of recent research', *Child Violence Review*, 21(1), pp. 24–40.

Sullivan, P. M. and Knutson, J. F. (2000) 'Maltreatment and disabilities: A population based epidemiological study', *Child Violence and Neglect*, 24(1), pp. 1257–1273.

Thiara, R., Hague, G. and Mullender, A. (2011) 'Losing out on both counts: Disabled women and domestic violence', *Disability & Society*, 26(6), pp. 757–771.

Thomas, C. (1997) 'The baby and the bath water: Disabled women and motherhood in social context', *Sociology of Health & Illness*, 19(5), pp. 622–643.

Thomas, C. (1999) *Female forms: Experiencing and understanding disability*. London: McGraw-Hill Education.

Thomas, C. (2007) *Sociologies of disability and illness. Contested ideas in disability studies and medical sociology*. Basingstoke, UK: Palgrave Macmillan.

United Nations (2006) *Convention on the Rights of Persons with Disabilities*. New York: United Nations General Assembly.

Waxman, B. (1994) 'Up against eugenics: Disabled women's challenge to receive reproductive health services', *Sexuality and Disability*, 12(2), pp. 155–171.

Women's Aid (2007) 'What is domestic violence?', retrieved from www.womensaid. org.uk/domestic-violence-articles.asp?section=00010001002200410001&itemid=1272&itemTitle=What+is+domestic+violence.

World Health Organization (2011) World report on disability. *WHO Library Cataloguing-in-Publication Data*.

Part 1

Childhood

Chapter 1

Indigenous mothering and disabled children in regional Australia

A narrative study

Karen Soldatic

Introduction

Examining the role of family violence in the lives of Aboriginal and Torres Strait Islander Australians is a contested area of research. The term 'family violence' is used in this chapter rather than 'domestic violence' or 'intimate partner violence' (Walsh *et al.* 2015). As Wilson *et al.* (2017) discuss, family violence offers a much broader framework in which to understand gendered patterns of violence in the lives of Indigenous women and their children, as it acknowledges the broader familial and kinship networks of Indigenous society and the ways in which settler colonial violence has led to the destruction of culture and family breakdown.

It is well recognised within the research that 200 years of European invasion and colonial settlement have resulted in a significantly higher prevalence of disability among Aboriginal and Torres Strait Islander Australians (Hollinsworth 2013; Gilroy and Emerson 2016). As Walter and Saggers (2007) point out, across all indicators of social exclusion, deprivation and poverty, Indigenous Australians are by far the most disadvantaged group in Australia. Inequality for Indigenous Australians entails more than economic exclusion, encompassing broader indicators associated with familial connection, community participation and cultural wellbeing (Walter 2016). It also translates into very high rates of disability throughout the life course (Australian Bureau of Statistic (ABS) 2012; Gilroy and Emerson 2016). These high rates of disability are only likely to compound the structural position of absolute poverty for Indigenous Australians, as disability and poverty are closely related in Australia (see Soldatic and Sykes 2017). These national statistics strongly suggest the importance of disability supports and services for Indigenous Australians living with disability, and that disability will often be present in some way when considering family violence (Dowse *et al.* 2013).

Family violence in Indigenous Australia also needs to be considered in the historical context of settler colonial governance with European invasion. Settler colonial governance involved a range of highly gendered practices as the control of Indigenous women's bodies, sexuality and reproduction was seen as a central component of settler expansion (Atkinson 1990; Brock 1995). Such processes, as Atkinson (1990) illustrates, have led to the destruction of Indigenous culture and the breakdown of family, kinship and community.

In Australia, much like Canada and the USA, the policy of forced child removal required the manufacturing of a racialised discourse about Indigenous mothers and their practices of mothering and care to justify the severing of the intimate maternal connection (Swift 1995). As Cutcher and Milroy (2010: 156) discuss, 'Aboriginal women were constructed as 'promiscuous' and 'nomads' and it was largely assumed by white Australia that notions of family and motherhood were tenuous and short-lived for Aboriginal women'. Indigenous mothers as 'bad mothers' guilty of neglecting their mothering responsibilities to their children remains a dominant public narrative in many settler societies (see Lake 1992), and such ascriptions become heightened in public discussions surrounding maternal payments and entitlements (see Cutcher and Milroy 2010). Despite national recognition of the intergenerational trauma caused by these longstanding policies, today Indigenous mothers endure the highest rates of child removal (Australian Institute of Family Studies 2016; see also Human Rights and Equal Opportunity Commission 1997). For Indigenous women, the experience of family violence is embedded in these historical practices of violent settler colonial expansion, and it often shapes their decision-making in relation to remaining in violent relationships and households (Atkinson 1990).

Given this historical context, it should not be surprising that mothering a disabled child is particularly fraught for Indigenous mothers as they navigate disability service and healthcare systems for their children (Salmon 2011). Highly racialised, moralising codes often lay the blame for their child's impairments on the mother's own behaviour, rather than recognising the impact of intergenerational trauma and poverty caused by settler colonial invasion (Salmon 2011). As Canadian researcher Amy Salmon (2011) has documented, Indigenous mothers of disabled children walk a tightrope between enduring further racialised stigmatisation of being a 'bad mother' and securing a disability diagnosis so that their child can receive the supports and services they require for a life of flourishing and opportunity. Reporting family violence in this context can often undermine their efforts to shore up resources and supports for their disabled child (Hedwig 2013). These daily complex negotiations of racialised tensions create additional strains and tensions for Indigenous mothers. Yet, as Salmon suggests, the experience of childhood disability for Indigenous mothers is often a paradox; it can be both enabling and disabling. Salmon's (2007, 2011) work in the Canadian context has shown that, in some instances, engagement with the disability service system enables Indigenous mothers a deeper understanding of the needs of their disabled child. Salmon also suggests that for many Indigenous mothers of disabled children, the disability service system often enables access to vital supports for their own mothering through contact with disability advocates who work alongside them to advance their rights.

Appropriate distribution of disability supports and services is a significant issue for Indigenous mothers and their disabled children. The distribution of disability supports and services across Australia is very uneven; there are marked distinctions between rural and remote towns, regional centres and large cities (Soldatic 2017). While the vast majority of the Australian disabled population reside in urban areas where there is a higher distribution and availability of specialist support and services (Productivity Commission 2011), there is a higher incidence of disability in regional areas as a proportion of the population (ABS 2015). In regional and outer regional areas, the Aboriginal and Torres Strait Islander population with disabilities is 1.6 times that of non-Indigenous Australians with disabilities (ABS 2015). Therefore, we need to consider issues of space and place (Habibis and Walter 2015), and the ways in which this lack of disability service provision outside of large urban centres may, in fact, create unique vulnerabilities in relation to family violence for Indigenous mothers and their disabled children. All this research suggests that in order to fully understand the real issues of family violence for Indigenous mothers and their disabled children we need to begin to distil the intersectional interplay of Indigeneity, disability, poverty and location in settler colonial Australia.

Methodology: the telling of Indigenous women's stories

This chapter draws upon Indigenous narrative history methodologies to illustrate the significant issues faced by Aboriginal mothers and their disabled children living in a white racist society (Smith 1999). This entails positioning the lives of Indigenous people through their own rich narratives, through research processes that are inclusive and authentic in their dialogue (Smith 1999). Such a methodological approach is grounded in an ethical orientation committed to the redistribution of social power within the western scientific academy (Gilroy and Emerson 2016) and situated within knowledge production strategies that aim to decolonise Indigenous ways of knowing, being and doing. Indigenous narratives, particularly those of Indigenous women, can be transformative through the oral re-enactment of past injustices, giving clarity to their current meaning and impact (Martin 2008).

The research reported in this chapter undertakes such an approach through presenting the life narrative of an Aboriginal mother and her disabled child and their experiences of family violence. This iterative process entails the non-Indigenous researcher first 'knock' and then wait to be invited to enter (Martin 2008). The life narrative is Tracy's retelling of her journey of being an Indigenous mother of a child with a congenital impairment, forced to move from a small regional town to a large urban centre and back again. Tracy told her story to me (the author) over a period of 6 years from our first meeting (November 2011) as part of a broader national research project on Disability in Rural Australia (DP110102719), and subsequent research projects (Centre for Social Impact 2015, and ARC DECRA Fellowship 2016–2019). When we first met in the small town at the top end of Western Australia, Tracy had recently returned to this regional community after being forced to move to the state capital city (Perth), more than 2,400 kilometres away, as primary maternal health services for women thought to be carrying a child with a severe congenital impairment were not available in the regional town.

Issues of trust, respect and unequal power relations are always at the forefront of research that involves a non-Indigenous researcher and an Indigenous research participant (Johnson *et al.* 2007). Tracy and I were introduced by the local disability advocacy service where Tracy first sought support for her son and issues of family violence. Contact with Tracy has always been facilitated by the local disability advocate who has supported Tracy over these years. The interviews have therefore involved the disability advocate, too, who at times would offer points of clarification on some key issues, yet the story is Tracy's own. Such a process, as Indigenous scholar Karin Martin (2008) suggests, is critical to ensure that Indigenous women's ways of knowing, being and doing the research are transformative for Indigenous women; that is, through the process of telling and retelling their stories, they are able to reflexively engage with their own past to distil understanding, meaning and impact.

Tracy and I have conducted an open-ended in-depth dialogue over 6 years about her experiences being an Aboriginal mother of a disabled child and the life story presented here is the outcome of three core interviews over this period. Tracy agreed to this longstanding research relationship as she feels:

> Yeah, every bit – like me tellin' my story helps someone else as well. 'Cause I know I'm not the only one and there's probably someone that's going through the same as me or probably worse.

Tracy's life narrative is presented under section headings based on the relocations she has had to make from the rural to urban and back to a rural town in order to access disability and healthcare services and to make herself and her children safe from violence.

Findings: Tracy's story

Birthing disability: racism, prenatal care and rurality

When I was pregnant with little Adrian [pseudonym] I'd been up here for 8 years already, so we'd moved back to Perth, y'see. But only because they didn't have any of the resources or facilities or anything here to help him when he was born.

Is it 21 or 22 weeks or something? Yeah, I'd missed that and it wasn't by my fault, I actually asked, I requested for an ultrasound at 22 weeks. And the doctor that was there at the time said 'no, you don't need one' and I said 'well, I think I should have one' and he said no. Basically made me feel guilty and said 'look, they cost money you know. Every time you have a scan that costs money'. I was like okay, so I didn't bother going back. And I didn't find out till the new doctor, my own doctor had come back 'cause she'd been out of town.

And she'd been away for about 3 months and this old guy he was there, so he basically made me feel guilty and I didn't feel like, I didn't want to go back. I waited till she got back and by that time I was almost due. She said 'I really need you to do a scan because you missed the 22 weeks'. I said 'I didn't miss it, I came here and the doctor didn't make an appointment'. She said 'what?' Okay, so anyway we done the scan and that same day they called and drove up to my house and said 'Dr [. . .] said that she needs to see you right now' and I thought 'oh my god, what's wrong with me?' I was scared. Then I got there and yeah, she told me that I'd only got – how many weeks did I have? I only had 8 weeks to go. And she said, 'oh, you need to have . . .'. She basically said that Adrian has just got too much fluid on the brain, saying all these long words and I was just sitting here stunned like 'what the hell are you talking about?' Like hydrocephalous, I was like I've never heard that in my whole entire life ever, y'know. So they ended up, I end up finding out what that was, she said 'I want to fly you down to Perth tomorrow'. I was like 'what?' It's 3 o'clock in the afternoon right now and you're telling me I've got to get ready to fly down to Perth tomorrow morning. She goes 'you need to Tracy, it's really important, your baby might die'.

So, they brought him on 6 weeks prem [premature] ended up having him and then we were in Princess Margaret Hospital, Perth, for 3 months. It was like never ending, we had our own room, there was a few complications in the first two operations, then the third one worked so we could finally go home but by that time, I'd chucked my house in up here [rural town] because it was too much to come backwards and forwards, and yeah I'd gone and chucked the house in, 'cause it's too much to pay for the kids all the time. So, we ended up all going down to Perth and I ended up chucking my house in [in rural town] because it was just too much.

They told me he'd never walk, he got up and walked. Nearly 2 years ago, on the 10th of November actually, that'll be tomorrow. It'll be 2 years exactly since he's been walking. He just got up and started walking one day. After I was told he would never sit up, first of all I was told he'd never live and he did. Then I got told that he'd never be able to do anything independently. He walks around, you can hear him now, he walks up and down this house, he just goes in the fridge, he'll grab his juice box, he's independent. He taught himself [to swim]. When he got in that pool he was scared, then he slowly started getting himself into it and holding his head up like this at first, so I wouldn't fill it up too high, and all of a sudden just went under the water and thought 'oh, I have to hold my breath' 'cause he was coughing and spluttering and everything, but he taught himself that he had to hold his breath underwater.

Relocation, homelessness and vulnerabilities to violence

Well the day they discharged us from the hospital, I just stood outside the hospital with four kids and I had nowhere to go. I thought 'where am I going?' They're saying 'you can go home now'. And we're saying 'where's home? We don't have a home, we're homeless now'. So, we ended up standing there for a while and I thought I can't go to mum's because she had boarders in her house, she's got people boarding with her to help pay the rent because the rent was really high in [suburb in Perth]. And I thought well I can't sort of, I don't know where I'm going to be sleeping and I thought can't stay with anyone else because I don't talk to anyone in my family, can't get along with my family, y'know, not like a lot of Aboriginal people, they're close and they all live together. I never grew up with my family, so I don't know them and it was awkward, y'know. And then one of my aunties said that I could stay there but she ended up getting really sick so I couldn't stay with her in the end because she needed a carer to move in, so yeah that fell through. And that's when dad said 'well, you can stay with me for a while', like my own dad. And we ended up staying there. Y'know we were just all crowded in one little two-bedroom unit and y'know my dad was trying to help but we were all crowded in one little house in [suburb in Perth], my dad's house, and he's a heavy drinker as well so we were putting up with people coming through the house drinking all the time as well. So, we had no accommodation, nowhere else to go.

And then mum was homeless. So, mum was sleeping in the car with my stepdad and my baby sister. Then mum finally got another house in [suburb in Perth] so she ended up moving in there, she said 'come and stay with me'.

I ended up moving in with her but me and my brother don't get along, well we didn't get along back then. And he ended up threatening me with one of his little weapons he had in his room, so I packed up again, dragging my bags down the street, raining, had nowhere to go with four kids, a sick child who just got out of hospital. I stood there in the street and I thought 'well what do I do?' I was upset, I said 'I can't live here and be fighting with him all the time', it's too stressful so I had nowhere to go and my kids were scared of him.

So, I thought well we got to go and I ended up ringing [violence non-governmental organisation], and it was the long weekend mind you, and it was a Friday afternoon and I thought 'if I don't get these people to help me now, what am I going to do over the long weekend?' And I was stuck and I stood there at the phone box and I said to them 'please, I've got nowhere to go, it's raining, I've got a kid that's had three major operations on his brain'. I said 'when I left the hospital I had nowhere to go, I'm homeless, I got nowhere to live' and I told them what happened to my brother and everything.

They finally sent a taxi, a taxi was driving round the streets everywhere in [suburb in Perth] looking for me, on back streets. They finally found me, he goes 'are you Tracy?' I said 'yeah'. He said 'they've just sent an order through, a fax thing, to head office to order us to pick you up and take you to a motel'. I was like 'really, oh my god', I couldn't believe it, I was like 'holy shit, I can't believe they actually helped me'. And we got there and I thought I had Friday, Saturday, Sunday night there and then Monday morning I had to pack everything up 'cause I thought Tuesday morning we gotta leave because they could only pay for the long weekend and gave us a food voucher and everything.

We got to the motel room and sat there and thought 'okay, Tuesday morning, where do I go?' and Tuesday morning had to get out by 10 o'clock because that's the motel's policy so I packed everything up in this bag again, it was that heavy, god, and my son he was only, what was he? I think he was only 10, 10 or 11, no he was 12. My son was 12 years old and he had to be like the man, y'know he carried the heavy bags, he was complaining and carrying on because he was tired and hungry, I had no money, y'know I had nothing and I thought we got to walk to the middle of the city now, with everyone staring at us with bags and blankets and pillows and a pram. I thought 'my god'. So, I walked straight through the middle of Perth, went straight to government child welfare office and I sat in there for 5 hours with screaming kids that were hungry. They weren't screaming but they were crying because they were hungry. And I said 'can anyone just give me a food voucher? I'll go for a walk, I'll take my kids with me but can I just leave my bags here?' 'Oh no, we can't do that, you have to wait till you see your caseworker'. So, we sat there for like 5 hours, I had no milk for my son and they finally had the decency to get some milk for my son because I wasn't breastfeeding, I was that stressed out I'd dried up, I couldn't even produce no milk, that's how stressed out I was.

Precarious, unprotected and inaccessible housing

I got into a refuge there and that took like 3 hours of paperwork, of getting there, y'know settling the kids down and they had nothing to eat so the refuge mob got them something to eat and we had our own room and we were there for about, it would've been about 6 or 7 weeks. And they said, 'look, you're not a battered wife so you don't need to be locked up, you don't need to be on a curfew like these women are. So, we feel awkward that you're being here but you're not hiding from anyone'. They said 'you're homeless, so we'll put you out into one of the community houses'.

They also have houses in the community, they own them. So, we stayed in a little two-bedroom unit in [suburb in Perth], so we packed up again and stayed there for about 6 weeks and in the meantime I had his [disabled child just born, Adrian] father just abusing me and coming to the unit all the time drunk. I said 'you left me in [northern regional town], you had nothing to do with me, you didn't support me through all of this, y'know when your son was having major surgery, you come in there drunk and stinking of alcohol and embarrassing me. And then half the time you weren't there anyway when he was sick'. And so he sort of put me through a hell of a lot while I was there and they found out and they said 'look, you need to hurry up and get a house because we can't deal with this, y'know'. And I said 'well, can you please do me up a support letter?'

They offered me a house, the housing department offered me a house in the middle of an industrial area where there were trucks and industrial factories and the stairs to the front were this high. Now he can't, the doctor said he will never walk, so how is he supposed to get up stairs this high by the time you get a wheelchair or he starts trying to walk? So, they said that's ridiculous, we're looking at long term. And the man at department, the boss, had the cheek to turn around and say to me 'well, you should just take any house, this is not Perth y'know'. And I said 'excuse me, I was born and bred in Perth, don't talk to me like that, you're talking to me like I've just come from a country town. I was born here in Perth'. He goes 'well what are you going back here then?'

And he was judging me for moving to Perth and I said 'well if you would've read my file properly, you'd understand that this child needs treatment and he's been through three major surgeries'.

Escaping violence, returning to the rural

I put in for a transfer about 4 years ago because I'd met someone in Perth and I went through heaps and heaps of domestic violence, he was bashing me, in front of this boy and all. He didn't care that my son had a disability. I was with him for 4.5 years. He flogged, bashed me, put me in hospital and my kids, my older kids had to fight for me and stick up for me. Y'know to see a 10-year-old try and stick up for you and jump in the middle of two adults fighting, it was just too much, and to see me knocked out on the ground, imagine what they were thinking, that I was probably dead or something, y'know. So, I had to get out of that situation and I said to them, 'look I put in for a transfer years ago'. 'Oh yeah but it takes a long time to get a house back in [northern regional town]' and I said 'well, I need to get out here before he kills me'. I had DCP [Department of Child Protection] on my doorstep all the time, threatening to take my kids, y'know they were willing to take my kids but they weren't willing to help me get rid of him or to help me take that step to get out of that life because I had nowhere to go. My mum died, I couldn't rely on her.

The child welfare department rang up one afternoon and said 'we need to see you right now'.

Ending up going to DCP, they paid for my taxi fare amazingly. And I got there and they said 'we've just bought your tickets to go to [northern regional town] on Thursday'. 'Are you telling me I've got tonight, tomorrow and Thursday morning to get everything prepared and just leave my house?' And they said 'well you have to because if you don't we're going to take your kids because your partner is getting out of prison tomorrow. So, if he gets out tomorrow, he's going to come straight to your house and look for you isn't he?' And I said 'yeah, like he always does'.

Finally, I got this place and I said 'I'll take it. I don't care'. I don't care that there's one bedroom for him but I didn't care, I said 'he can sleep with me'. So, I put in for another transfer so I can get a bigger house, not so much a bigger house but an extra room so he can have his own room because he can't sleep with me forever. And he's nearly 9 years old so I'm trying to collect support letters at the moment so I can get the housing department to get me another place. I don't care if I have to wait a year, 2 years, if I get all the support letters in, I've already put the transfer papers in. But I have to get the medical, I've got a medical thing there for the paediatrician to fill out for me today and I've got to hand that in.

At our second, third and fourth meetings, two (2013), four (2015) and six (2017) years later, Tracy was still awaiting a transfer to an appropriate disability accessible house that was large enough for all her family, which now included her young sister whom she had cared for since the death of their mother. The house remains inappropriate, not just from an accessibility perspective for her disabled son, Adrian, but for other issues surrounding health and hygiene, as the following illustrates from our meeting in 2013.

The water comes flooding out of the bathroom into the hallway all the time. And now in the hallway some of the tiles are lifting. So, I'm having to chuck in clothes and towels and − so the water doesn't come out into the hallway − and now I'm having to wash clothes, like five or six loads a day, because I'm having to bank up all these clothes because there's one, two, three, four of us having showers every day. So here I am having to clean this horrible cupboard out now. It's that mouldy and stinks.

Forced to relive the trauma of violence: resisting violence

Over time, Tracy had developed a number of personal strategies to actively move on from and resist forms of violence. This not only included moving to the rural town to move away from her previous partners in the main city centre (Perth), but also developing strategies to resist enduring structures of bureaucratic collusion to that violence. As Tracy illustrates below, as an Indigenous mother of a disabled child, she is forced to continually relive her experiences of violence by repeating them in order to receive the supports she requires.

I'm having to explain my whole life all over again. Yeah last year was pretty full on with all the Strong Families meetings and meeting new people from different departments, I had to tell my story all over again and then all over again. And then sort of 'oh this is such and such new person' so I'd have to start all over again. It just got so tiring, 'cause I'd have to start all over again. And then you've got idiots in the housing department going 'why did you come to [northern regional town]?' It was just so ridiculous, y'know like. 'Did you think that you were just going to move to XXX and get a house?' I said 'no'. He said 'well, it is a holiday town'. 'So what are you saying? I've just come here for a holiday?' He says 'well why did you come back?' And I said 'I'm not here because I'm a fucking tourist, I come here because this was, I lived here before I moved to Perth'. He goes 'oh, I didn't know that', I said 'no, you didn't know that because you didn't read my file, you didn't take the time, over the last 3 days, you didn't take the time to think "I got a meeting, we've got a XXX meeting on Friday, maybe I should take the time to read this girl's file"'. He didn't even say anything and he goes 'well how do I justify to people that you've come to Perth and I'm giving you a house before them on the priority list?' I said 'you don't have to justify yourself to anyone', I said, 'you take people's cases individually. You don't have to justify yourself to no one. I'm just putting my case forward and you say yes or no, simple as that'. And I said 'what are you judging me for? I've come here, I've been through hell and back, man, I've lost my mother, I've been through 4 years of domestic violence'. I said 'that's why I'm here, 'cause I don't wanna die or have my children taken away from me'. He's like 'oh, I didn't know the situation'. I said 'exactly, I have to explain myself all over again'. Here we go again.

Even with [welfare department], you have to explain what sort of a disability your child's got, the level of care, and then they've got the cheek to ask us to fill out those forms every couple of years, 'uh hello, 2 years ago, he's still the same, y'know he's not going to change'. Like ask a stupid question, I mean it's not but y'know it is to us. I think they don't recognise there's certain special needs or certain disabilities in this town, they think 'oh, that's a lovely holiday town'. 'Oh surely there can't be people with disabilities living in that town 'cause it's for tourists'. Y'know, it's not true. You come here and there's so many kids disadvantaged.

Diminishing disability services in regional areas

Escaping family and intimate partner violence in urban cities and moving to small regional towns mean that opportunities to access disability appropriate supports and services are substantially diminished. As Tracy outlines below, the costs are very real for disabled children, and often this will impact upon developmental opportunities for the child. However, as Tracy's story illustrates, safety within the family home is the core priority to ensure overall wellbeing for all family members. Thus, Tracy's narrative highlights the significant dilemmas faced by mothers of disabled children who are required to move to escape violence.

In Perth he has the hip and spine clinic, the sleep unit, the cerebral palsy unit will sometimes have other things going on and they'll invite us – generally, because it's through them privately, PATS [Patient Assistance Travel Scheme] won't cover me for the air fare [from the regional town to Perth].

It's just sad really, sad that he's missing out on all the supports he had in Perth. Soon as he started at school [in Perth], I could see his world opening up, his eyes, he was more alert 'cause he'd been getting hydrotherapy every Friday. Every Friday was swimming day. Every Thursday was music day. Every Wednesday he was there was physio and outside day, y'know they'd put them on the trampoline and through the tubes and help them walk along planks and everything. Just normal everyday stuff plus more.

That's the thing in Perth, we had music programmes going on too but they don't have them here. So, I see that he's sort of missing out a bit here but I'm sort of, I'm more content being up here. It's heaps better being up here but I'm just sort of sad that he misses out a little bit. He misses out on hydro, they don't have hydrotherapy classes up here.

Now [in rural town] every Tuesday, they'll have a water day for him because they know what he's like. There's some days where he'll just start kicking up and he's tired and there's days when he just doesn't want to be around anyone. So, they've made it now that Tuesday is water day for him, they'll just fill up a little pool, let him run amok in the water and then there's days where they'll let him sit in the sand in the shade and he loves sand. They send him home, he's got hair full of sand, oh true.

Holiday programmes, oh school holidays are the worst. There's no school so he's upset because he likes going to school. There's programmes going but because there's no carers where they're running the programmes, he can't go.

The power of disability advocacy

As this section outlines, disability advocacy for her disabled child's broader welfare, provided for the first time, the possibility of long-term interventions and support to escape violence and protect her children and family. With the active support of disability advocacy, Tracy was finally empowered to resist violence and simultaneously tackle the racist institutional structures that had long colluded to keep Aboriginal women and mothers, in relations of family violence.

I know how to talk for myself, but I think it's important too to have people who back up and advocate for you as well.

It took for Red Cross – [support worker] when she was working there – I told 'er my situation. I didn't know they can help too but I just walked in there one day and just – broke down you might as well say. She was like, 'Do you wana come in 'ere and talk? Do you need someone to talk to?' And I said, 'Yeah I do actually'. I said, 'I don't know what I'm doing'. I'm just walking around everywhere and I don't know where to go or who to ask for help. I went in there, explained to her my situation had a good cry and then she said, 'Well look here, we'll try and arrange for a Strong Families meeting'. And I said, 'What's that?' I didn't even know what they were. So, I went into Red Cross and if I didn't find really, you know, I don't know, I would have been struggling. I still would have been struggling. I probably would have eventually, you know, got a house but it took for someone like her to support me. Drive me everywhere, come to all the meetings, collect all the support letters, do everything.

Because I've linked up with more people. Like I said, it took for me to make that first step after I broke down and everything wasn't working and everything was falling to pieces and I had nowhere to live and everything else – it took for me to take that first step and go to Red Cross and I got help from that one person. I was just lucky, she was the one who helped kick it all off. And then I got to meet different people and I got to know my Local Area Coordinator better and then got to meet all these other agencies, people, and I know who they all are now. It took for me to get [Red Cross support worker] to do that first kick-off for me, that first bit of talking. Now I'm confident enough to just walk in there and talk to them myself. So, it is better.

They did it because of Adrian and they knew all the supports I had in place and they had people arguing for me. So, I had people arguing for me. And they knew that the more people I get involved, then they know that I've got witnesses to what they're saying, what they're doing you know, I've learned that now. When I was in Perth, I knew nothing. I thought, 'Oh yeah just live in a house, move out, whatever. You don't need no one to help you, you just talk for yourself' but it's not like that.

Discussion: disability and family violence

Tracy's narrative is an important insight into the ways in which disability significantly shapes, and is shaped by, the experience of family violence for Aboriginal mothers and their disabled children. Tracy's story helps us to understand how the intersection of race, mothering and disability may open up vulnerabilities to gender-based family violence, and the longstanding impacts that can result for families who live in rural, isolated locations. Indigenous mothers of disabled children who have experienced family violence are placed in a position where they are required to recall the violence to relevant authorities as part of a strategic battle to advocate for their children. There is always some process, form or person that demands the traumatic experience is revisited as a way to reassert colonial power over the lives of Indigenous women. Interestingly, it was the release of the violent partner from prison that propelled the state to move Tracy, her disabled child Adrian and her other children back to the rural town where they lived before the identification of the risks involved in her pregnancy with Adrian. Most significantly, the family's homelessness came about due to the unforeseen, yet necessary, migration from the rural town to Perth in order to access health services and disability supports. This ultimately placed Tracy and her children at the greatest risk of differing forms of gender-based family violence.

Tracy's and Adrian's experience of family violence was thus deeply associated with issues of Indigenous intergenerational poverty, caused through processes of settler colonisation and invasion that entailed the dispossession of Indigenous peoples of their lands and cultural, familial and kinship networks. It is well recognised in the international literature about non-Indigenous mothers and their disabled children escaping family violence that, often, strong familial and social networks are vital to enabling pathways of escape (Walsh *et al.* 2015). As Tracy was propelled to travel over 2,400 kilometres for Adrian's birth, they had few real resources they could safely and securely rely on. Tracy did not have deep familial ties or kinship connections in the city and those that were available were often strained, fraught with their own personal histories of economic deprivation and housing insecurity. White settler colonial policy continues to displace Indigenous families.

Conclusions

Tracy's narrative has revealed that, despite multiple constraints created through deep structural inequalities, the possibilities created through disability advocacy support enabled her to rebuild her life and opportunities for her disabled son. As she noted in her dialogue, it was often because of Adrian that she received support from a range of disability and health professionals – who would assist her and complete the mounds of official paperwork, attend meetings alongside her and even drive her to appointments. Over time, this allowed her to build her strength to advocate for herself and for Adrian. Disability advocacy worked as a central mechanism for Tracy to not only escape long-term physical violence, but also to build a new life for herself and her children. The power of disability advocacy was that, once informed of her rights and the available supports, Tracy was able to assert her role as a mother of a disabled child.

Key messages from this chapter

- A higher proportion of disabled Aboriginal and Torres Strait Islander Australians than non-Indigenous disabled people live in regional areas, and lack of specialist healthcare and disability services in regional areas necessitates movement to urban centres.
- Women need housing support in order to resist and escape family violence, and this housing must be accessible for disabled children.
- Disability advocacy can enable Indigenous mothers to assert their rights as mothers as well as the rights of their disabled children.

Acknowledgements

This chapter draws on a research project investigating disability in rural and remote Australia which was funded by an Australian Research Council Discovery grant: DP 110102710 – Disability in Rural Australia (2011–2014), and The Centre for Social Impact Internal Research Grant (2015). Additional funding for this chapter has also been provided by the Australian Research Council DECRA DE160100478 for the longitudinal analysis and write up of the research.

References

Atkinson, J. (1990) 'Violence in Aboriginal Australia: colonisation and gender', *Aboriginal and Islander Health Worker Journal*, 14(2), 5–21.
Australian Bureau of Statistics (ABS) (2003) *Disability, ageing and carers, Australia: summary of findings*, cat. no. 4430.0, Canberra: ABS.
Australian Bureau of Statistics (ABS) (2012) *Australian social trends, March quarter 2012*. Canberra: ABS.
Australian Bureau of Statistics (ABS) (2015) *Disability, ageing and carers, Australia: summary of findings*, cat. no. 4430.0, Canberra: ABS.
Australian Institute of Family Studies (2016) 'Child protection and Aboriginal and Torres Strait Islander children', CFCA Resource Sheet, Canberra: Australian Government.

Brock, P. (1995) 'Aboriginal families and the law in the era of assimilation and segregation, 1890s–1950s', in D. Kirkby (ed.), *Sex, Power and Justice: Historical Perspectives of Law in Australia*. Melbourne: Oxford University Press, 133–149.

Cutcher, L. and Milroy, T. (2010) 'Mispresenting Indigenous mothers: maternity allowance and the media', in S. Goodwin and K. Huppatz (eds), *The Good Mother: Contemporary Motherhoods in Australia*. Sydney: University of Sydney Press, 153–174.

Dowse, L., Soldatic, K., Did, A. and van Toorn, G. (2013) *Stop the violence: addressing violence against women and girls with disabilities in Australia*, background paper. Sydney: UNSW Australia.

Gilroy, J. and Emerson, E. (2016) 'Australian indigenous children with low cognitive ability: family and cultural participation', *Research in Developmental Disabilities*, 56, 117–127.

Habibis, D. and Walter, M. (2015) *Social inequality in Australia: discourses, realities and futures*. Melbourne: Oxford University Press.

Hedwig, T. (2013) *The cultural politics of fetal alcohol spectrum disorders and the diagnosis of difference*, unpublished thesis, University of Kentucky.

Hollinsworth, D. (2013) 'Decolonizing Indigenous disability in Australia', *Disability & Society*, 28(5), 601–615.

Human Rights and Equal Opportunity Commission (1997) *Bringing them home: report of the National Inquiry into the Separation of Aboriginal and Torres Strait Islander Children from Their Families*. Sydney: Human Rights and Equal Opportunity Commission.

Johnson, J., Cant, G., Howitt, R. and Peters, E. (2007) 'Creating anti-colonial geographies: embracing Indigenous peoples' knowledge and rights', *Geographical Research*, 45(2), 117–120.

Lake, M. (1992) 'The politics of respectability', in G. Whitlock and D. Carter (eds), *Images of Australia*. St Lucia: University of Queensland Press, 75–93.

Martin, K. L. (2008) *Please knock before you enter: Aboriginal regulation of outsiders and the implications for researchers*. Brisbane: Post Pressed.

Productivity Commission (2011) *Disability care and support: inquiry report, no. 54*, Melbourne: Australian Government.

Salmon, A. (2011) 'Aboriginal mothering, FASD prevention and the contestations of neoliberal citizenship', *Critical Public Health*, 21(2): 165–178.

Smith, L. T. (1999) *Decolonising methodologies: research and indigenous peoples*. London: Zed Books.

Soldatic, K. (2017) 'Neoliberalising disability income reform: what does this mean for Indigenous Australians living in regional areas?' in D. Howard-Wagner, M. Bargh and I. Altimarino-Jimenez (eds), *Indigenous rights, recognition and the state in the Neoliberal Age*. Canberra: ANU E Press.

Soldatic K. and Sykes, D. (2017) 'Disability and poverty', in K. Serr (ed.), *Thinking about poverty*, 2nd edn. Sydney: Federation Press.

Swift, K. (1995) *Manufacturing 'bad mothers': a critical perspective on child neglect*, Toronto: University of Toronto Press.

Walsh, J., Spangaro, J. and Soldatic, K. (2015) 'Global understandings of domestic violence', *Nursing and Health Sciences*, 17(1): 1–4.

Walter, M. (2016) 'Social exclusion/inclusion for urban Aboriginal and Torres Strait Islander people', *Social Inclusion*, 4(1), 68–76.

Walter, M. and Saggers, S. (2007) 'Poverty and social class', in B. Carson, T. Dunbar, R. Chenall and R. Bailie (eds), *Social determinants of Indigenous health*. Sydney: Allen & Unwin.

Wilson, M., Jones, J., Butler, T., Simpson, P., Gilles, M., Baldry, E., Levy, M. and Sullivan, E. (2017) 'Violence in the lives of incarcerated Aboriginal mothers in Western Australia', *Sage Open*, 1(1), 1–16, http://dx.doi.org/10.1177/215824 4016686814.

Chapter 2

Disclosure of abuse by disabled children

An emergent international model of telling, listening and acting

Christine Jones and Julie Taylor

Introduction

Research suggests that disabled children face a significant increased risk of maltreatment compared to their non-disabled peers (Sullivan and Knutson 2000) and face particular challenges regarding the disclosure of abuse and seeking justice (Jones *et al*. 2012). The intersectional nature of their vulnerabilities (disabled, young, abused, often economically disadvantaged) renders them a population in significant need of protection. The consequences of maltreatment are known to be experienced across the life course creating a need for prevention and early intervention. If we can identify barriers to and facilitators of positive disclosure, we can begin to identify interventions, processes and practices that might be more effective and less patchy than what we see currently. This chapter contributes towards making this a reality.

Background

Some 95 million children in the world are classified as disabled, of whom around 13 million are 'severely' disabled, that is, have significant difficulties in functioning (World Health Organization (WHO) 2011). There are an estimated 950,000 disabled children living in the United Kingdom (UK), approximately 7.3 per cent of British children (Blackburn *et al*. 2010), which is in line with other countries in the global north. Figures for disabled children seem to be higher in the global south, especially in countries of low economic resource (WHO 2011), but statistics are not reliable. Data is collected differently and to different extents within and across countries, making international comparisons impossible.

The United Nations Convention on the Rights of Persons with Disabilities (UNCRPD) (Article 16) mandates governments to:

> take all appropriate legislative, administrative, social, educational and other measures to protect persons with disabilities, both within and outside the home, from all forms of exploitation, violence and abuse . . .
>
> (UNCRPD 2006, p. 12)

Although there is a limited pool of quality research, we know that disabled children experience a three to four-fold increased risk of abuse compared to their non-disabled peers (Sullivan and Knutson 2000; Jones *et al.* 2012). The nature of the abuse disabled children experience may also differ, starting at an earlier age (Sullivan and Knutson 2000), being more violent (Akbas *et al.* 2009) and affecting boys disproportionately (Sobsey *et al.* 1997; Sullivan and Knutson 2000; Kvam 2004). Prevalence varies as far as we know, but children with some types of impairment experience higher rates, including those with behavioural disorders, learning disabilities, sensory impairments and concentration problems (Sullivan and Knutson 2000; Kvam 2004).

Before proceeding we will touch briefly on terminology used within the chapter. Child maltreatment is a broad term that encompasses a range of childhood experiences including physical and emotional ill treatment, sexual abuse, neglect and exploitation (WHO 2016). Within this chapter we have chosen to use the generic term 'abuse' rather than maltreatment as it is more widely used in the UK and, therefore, assumed to be more acceptable to the victims/survivors of abuse. When referring to individual circumstances, specific types of abuse are identified where appropriate.

Disability is also a contested term, with different meanings to different communities. We recognise that some deaf people, for example, will identify with the term disabled while others will not, but for ease of reading we use the term disabled throughout. The UNCRPD (2006, p. 4) uses the following definition:

> Persons with disabilities include those who have long-term physical, mental, intellectual or sensory impairments which in interaction with various barriers may hinder their full and effective participation in society on an equal basis with others.

We draw upon the social model of disability and make a distinction between impairment, that is, lost or limited functioning experienced by an individual, and the barriers that disabled people face because of the way societies are organised and run (Union of the Physically Impaired Against Segregation (UPIAS) 1976). Following Thomas' (2004, 2007) social relational understanding of disability we recognise the significance of 'impairment effects', meaning the everyday impact of living with particular conditions. For example, some disabled children have restricted speech and/or language; others have profound intellectual impairments, which limit their understanding. Other people may use such impairment effects to exploit the child, an act of *disablism*.

Disclosure of abuse is not easy for anyone, but we contend that disabled children experience significant barriers in timely recognition, accessing helpful support or effective response to any sort of disclosure they may make. Abuse of disabled children is underreported and often invisible, surrounded by myths and stereotypes. These perpetuate the silence around the abuse of disabled children. In this chapter we aim to explore current evidence and theories relating to disclosure of abuse in order to drive forward knowledge relating to disabled children's disclosures.

Empirical and theoretical developments in the field of disclosure of abuse

Much of the knowledge that has developed around disclosure of abuse has come from studies of non-disabled populations. In this section we provide an overview of empirical studies and theoretical developments. Early empirical research on disclosure of abuse focused primarily on 'formal disclosures' as part of forensic investigations (McElvaney 2017) and these criminal investigations were typically associated with sexual abuse. More recently attention has been paid to informal disclosures but there remains a disproportionate focus on disclosure of sexual abuse with less known about disclosure or non-disclosure of other forms of abuse or neglect (Cossar et al. 2013).

Rates of non-disclosure of abuse are believed to be high. For example, research has estimated that at least 60 per cent of child sexual abuse victims withhold disclosure (Alaggia 2010) and around one-fifth of victims never disclose (Kogan 2004; Hebert 2009). Where disclosures are made, they may occur several years after the onset of abuse (Allnock and Miller 2013). Initial disclosures are typically made to friends and family members (Kogan 2004; Vincent and Daniel 2004) with formal disclosures most often made to teachers (Allnock and Miller 2013).

Delays or barriers to disclosure and facilitators of disclosure are discussed in the literature and are understood within an ecological framework as being related to individual, family, community and cultural factors (Alaggia 2010). Age and developmental factors have been the focus of research. There is some evidence that disclosure rates increase as the child's age and understanding increase (Kogan 2004; Hershkowitz et al., 2005; Lippert et al. 2009; Cossar et al. 2013) and that older children wait longer to disclose sexual abuse (Goodman-Brown et al. 2003). There are mixed findings regarding gender and disclosure. For example, Lippert et al. (2009) report that boys are less likely to disclose sexual abuse than girls, yet Goodman-Brown et al. (2003) found no gender difference in the ultimate rate of disclosure.

The relationship of the child and caregivers to the abuser may be important, that is, children are more likely to disclose abuse by non-family members (Goodman-Brown et al. 2003, Kogan 2004, Hershkowitz et al. 2005). Jensen et al. (2005) report children's sensitivity to adult emotional reactions to telling and how this can encourage or discourage further disclosure. Fear of harm or repercussions for self, the perpetrator or others can inhibit disclosures (Jensen et al., 2005). In other circumstances a wish to protect others from potential abuse can trigger a disclosure (Allnock and Miller 2013). There are mixed findings regarding the effect on disclosure of abuse severity, duration and frequency. There is some evidence that escalation of abuse may lead to disclosure (Allnock and Miller 2013). Cossar *et al.* (2013) convey some of the subtleties of social interactions that make it difficult for a young person to recognise when experiences are abusive or neglectful, such as the situation where a parent is unpredictable, abuse is episodic, and the relationship is sometimes good or where there are unclear boundaries between discipline and physical abuse. Some triggers for disclosure have been identified, including escalation of abuse or realisation that the abuse was wrong,

Cultural issues may inhibit disclosure, for example, taboos about sexuality. Shame is identified as common to most victims of child sexual abuse and an obstacle to disclosure for many (Hershkowitz *et al.* 2007; McElvaney *et al.* 2012). Alaggia (2004) suggests that children who have been marginalised and disempowered because of race, ethnicity or poverty may be deterred from disclosing abuse. Although no reference is made by Alaggia to disabled children, this issue is also likely to apply to them.

Some attention has been paid to the particular disclosure challenges faced by disabled children. Disabled children are far less likely to disclose abuse and more likely to delay disclosure than their non–disabled peers (Hershkowitz *et al.* 2007). Attitudes and assumptions about disability and impairment abound and it has been suggested that this creates challenges for disabled children around disclosure (Sobsey 1994; Briggs 2006). This can be compounded by inefficient sex, relationship and personal safety skills education for deaf children or those with special educational needs (Suter *et al.* 2009; Franklin *et al.* 2015). There is also evidence of a reluctance to believe that disabled children are abused, or of underestimating or minimising the harm they may experience as a result of maltreatment (Marchant 1991; Westcott and Cross 1996; Taylor *et al.* 2015). Moreover, there is often the possibility that a child's impairment could mask child protection concerns, with people attributing the manifestations of abuse to a physical or mental condition (Murray and Osborne 2009; Ofsted 2009). Shah *et al.* (2016), in their study of violence perpetrated against disabled girls, explain the impact of stereotyping, objectification and marginalisation of disabled people on the experiences of abused disabled children. They identify a number of barriers to disclosure specific to disabled children including reliance for care on an abuser and fear of this being withdrawn; lack of adequate communication support available to children with communication impairments to enable disclosures; and framing of disclosures as paranoia related to over-medication. Hernon *et al.* (2015) have also emphasised the need for practitioners to develop skills in relation to the protection of disabled children in order to identify abuse rather than just relying on children's capacity to report harm.

From the empirical research on disclosure of abuse (by non-disabled children) some attempts have been made to theorise disclosure. These have typically involved the development of typologies of disclosure. Alaggia (2004) attempted to develop a comprehensive typology of disclosure of child sexual abuse that included: purposeful, accidental, elicited, behavioural, withheld and triggered disclosures. While this categorisation conveys a breadth of disclosure types, it does not fully explain the significance of these. Some categories make reference to motivation, some to mode of elicitation and others to forms of communication.

Some authors have focused on the completeness of the disclosure. For example, Lippert *et al.* (2009) categorise disclosures as full or partial. McElvaney (2013) differentiates disclosure as delayed disclosure, partial disclosure and non-disclosure. Alnock and Miller (2013) refer to disclosures and attempted disclosures. They use the categories direct, indirect, partial, accidental, prompted, assisted, non-verbal and behavioural. Several of the typologies include non-disclosure as a category given how common this is. Lippert *et al.* (2010) also refer to credible disclosures, leaving open the possibility for children's reports to be categorised as 'unbelievable or unreliable disclosures'.

While these typologies raise awareness of the range of modes of disclosure (or non-disclosure) that adults may encounter, they do little to explain why some disclosures are effective in ending abuse and others are not. Cossar *et al.* (2013), who have conducted one of the few studies of disclosures by children of multiple forms of abuse and neglect, acknowledge that telling can result in both positive and negative responses from professionals. There is a body of literature within the field of forensic investigation of child sexual abuse that focuses on the credibility of the disclosure as an indicator of effectiveness (Lippert *et al.*, 2009). The concept of credible disclosure is problematic as the implication within it is that effectiveness is the responsibility of the teller.

There is little emphasis throughout the literature on the purpose of disclosure. This again may reflect the predominance of research on forensic investigation of child sexual abuse where, perhaps, the purpose is taken for granted to be ending abuse and seeking justice. The danger, however, is that attention is focused on the adult agenda of criminal investigation with less emphasis on understanding the meaning of disclosure from the child's perspective. Allnock and Miller (2013) identify multiple reasons for disclosures beyond stopping abuse including receipt of emotional support and protection of others. This suggests a need for a more child-centred understanding of disclosure.

Many of the typologies implicitly differentiate a teller and a listener, for example, including references to elicited or prompted disclosures. They fail, however, to make fully explicit the role of the listener or recipient of the disclosure. Definitions that move beyond descriptions of what is disclosed, by whom and to whom and to what degree seem to offer more insight. For example, emphasis has been placed by some academics on disclosure of sexual abuse as a dialogical or relational process (Jensen *et al.* 2005; Reitsema and Grietens 2015). Jensen *et al.* (2005) describes a set of circumstances supportive of disclosure that include provision of an *opportunity* to talk, a *purpose* for speaking, and a *connection* or activator for the talk.

Reitsema and Grietens (2015) highlight some limitations to current conceptualisations of disclosure. They suggest that disclosure is too frequently conceived as a single event, rather than a process over time and is conceived as a one-way process of telling rather than an interaction between the teller and the listener. They propose as an alternative a more dialogical approach, emphasising relational aspects, and emphasise that disclosure happens over time and over the life course (Reitsema and Grietens 2015). This is likewise reflected in Allnock and Miller's (2013) term 'disclosure journey'.

The narrow focus in previous research on the universal child and greater attention to disclosure of sexual abuse has resulted in gaps in understanding of the experiences of diverse types of abuse and the impact of intersectionality on children's experiences. While there is academic awareness of the problem of abuse of disabled children, much of the theorising around disclosure of abuse has ignored their perspective.

We now wish to draw on our own recent work on protection of disabled children in the UK to further develop understandings of the dynamics of disclosure in the context of disabled children. Our work problematises notions of (re)telling and listening, taking account of individual impairment and a disabling society and attempts to get nearer a child-centric model of disclosure that respects children's rights to protection and recovery from abuse (United Nations Convention on the Rights of the Child (UNCRD) 1989).

Methods employed in two UK studies

We draw on data from two of our studies. The first (Study A) was commissioned by the commissioned by the National Society for Prevention of Cruelty to Children (NSPCC) and sought the accounts of deaf and disabled people who had experienced abuse or neglect in childhood. The second (Study B) was commissioned by the Scottish Government and focused on child protection professionals' experiences of interventions with disabled children and their families.

Table 2.1 Summary of research studies

Study A	Help-seeking behaviours of deaf and disabled children and young people following maltreatment (Taylor *et al.* 2015; Jones *et al.* 2017).	Direct accounts of help seeking from deaf and disabled young people who had experienced abuse in childhood from across the UK (n=11)
Study B	Disabled children and the child protection system (Taylor *et al.* 2014; Stalker *et al.* 2015; Taylor *et al.* 2016).	Interviews with a range of practitioners and child protection committees in Scotland about their experiences and accounts of practice (n=61)

Findings

From these studies a number of barriers to disclosure emerged that were particularly challenging for disabled children who experienced abuse or neglect. We will focus here on three aspects:

1   The challenges of telling.
2   The challenges of listening.
3   The challenges of acting on disclosures.

The challenges of telling

There are challenges for all children and young people in telling someone about abuse. We suggest that these challenges are not only exacerbated for disabled children but can be used by perpetrators to avoid detection. This was a concern expressed by professionals in Study B.

> It is easier to abuse a child who has a disability. Who are they going to tell? What are they going to say? Can they say anything? How is that going to be brought to light . . . especially complex disabilities.
>
> (Study B)

The challenges of telling include understanding the experience as abusive; being aware of its seriousness; and a compromised disclosure environment.

Many of the children and young people in Study A did not understand that what was happening to them was abusive and tolerated these experiences.

> I'd grown up around it for like ages it was like all I know and I just thought it was normal.
>
> (Study A)

> I was naive . . . I didn't feel that it was wrong or terrible. I didn't feel offended. I thought it was ok.
>
> (Study A)

Although they may not have understood what was happening, some recognised that the behaviours were nonetheless distressing.

> When you're immersed in an abusive environment as a child, you don't realise that it's abuse, I didn't know it was abuse, I just knew I was unhappy, I knew I didn't like how I was being treated, but I didn't realise it was abuse, I didn't know it was wrong, or that it shouldn't have been happening to me.
>
> (Study A)

Disclosure can be particularly difficult for children with intellectual impairments and communication impairments. This was sometimes recognised by professionals.

> I think our rate of detection is probably quite poor because I think of all the personal care and things that a child has, I would suspect that the rate of sexual abuse and stuff is probably higher than we actually detect. It's hard enough in the average population without them being disabled where they can't talk and tell us.
>
> (Study B)

But there was a tendency in Study B to assume that disabled children would either speak out or had enough people around them to ensure adequate protection.

> Presumably [a deaf child] could tell somebody [if she was being abused].
>
> (Study B)

Deaf children faced particular challenges in our studies. It was clear that professional interpreters were not always made available to children and young people with communication difficulties. Often instead informal communication support was provided through parents or foster carers. This could have the effect of children operating within a restrictive or impoverished communication environment which hindered disclosure of abuse, either because of embarrassment by the child or because the carer was implicated in the abuse. We came across cases where abusers were able to use their role as 'interpreter' to intimidate children and hide abuse.

> There's been a number of children where I've seen professionals having huge difficulty about deciding whether it might be a child protection issue or related to a diagnosis of autism . . . what is autism, what is child protection and what is both and what is neither, it is very, very confusing sometimes.
>
> (Study B)

While shame and self-blame are common to the experience of abused children, they can be particularly present for disabled children living within a society that devalues their experience.

> I think with me, I would've needed somebody who was quite intuitive to be able to get that kind of information out of me in the first place, because I wasn't . . . because I felt it was all my fault, it would have been very hard to get that information out of me.
>
> (Study A)

but it was hidden, you know, people didn't know. I felt ashamed because I was being told, you know, that I was bad, it was all my fault, so I didn't want to tell people, I thought it was my fault, I thought I was a bad person.

(Study A)

Social isolation was a feature of many participants' childhoods in Study A and acted as a barrier to disclosure. Often children were not exposed to informal peer education about sex or personal safety that would have given them an opportunity to compare what was happening to them with more developmentally appropriate relationships.

I was isolated so I didn't get to spend time with other children and their families, because then I would've seen that actually this is very different to how my family is.

(Study A)

The challenges of listening

It was striking that the disabled participants in Study A often made multiple disclosures. Seven of the 11 participants had made clear disclosures of abuse in childhood in order to seek help. Disclosures were made to a range of trusted people including teachers, school friends, relatives, foster carers, a neighbour and a priest. However, disclosures did not lead to abuse being stopped, even in one case where a formal child protection investigation was undertaken. Telling was, therefore, not the key issue in the disclosure process but listening and acting on disclosures. Three main barriers to hearing disclosures were evident from the studies. First, not all practitioners or professionals have the ability to contemplate that someone would harm a vulnerable child. Second, disabled children are often seen as unreliable witnesses. Third, there is lack of 'voice' of disabled children within services.

There appeared to be a cognitive dissonance regarding abuse of disabled children, especially in relation to sexual abuse. Listening requires belief, but some individuals, lay and professional, just cannot contemplate the notion that a disabled child would be abused.

I told my foster mother what happened. 'Uncle [name] touched me on the breasts!' She said, 'Don't be stupid!'. I tried to tell her that he did touch me. She just said, 'Don't be stupid!' She was annoyed with me.

(Study A)

We also heard numerous accounts where professionals did not recognise that abuse may be a factor in the disabled child's presenting signs.

I still don't understand how my teachers didn't see any signs of abuse . . . things like in the summer, I would never take my jumper off because I always had bruises on me . . . because I didn't have privacy at home, so I was too afraid to have a bath properly . . . I knew that I smelt really bad, I knew that . . .

(Study A)

When I first started showing signs of mental illness I think someone should have sat down and asked me why 'cause it's not a normal thing for an 8-year-old to do.

(Study A)

This cognitive dissonance could lead to signs being explained in terms of impairment rather than signs of abuse.

We work with children who have behavioural problems that can't be put down as part of the condition they have, but equally it might be them trying to communicate that something else is going on.

(Study B)

There were also examples of dismissed accounts. Where disclosures were made, these were not always handled in a sensitive and supportive manner by adults, leaving children feeling disbelieved and disempowered. Some children became skilled at maintaining a silence about their experience over many years. The apparent ease with which the credibility of disabled children could be called into question acted as a further barrier to protection. Our data suggested previously uncategorised types of disclosure that could be described as thwarted, silenced, dismissed or minimised.

One deaf woman who disclosed her abuse to her parish priest recalled:

the priest told me that I shouldn't tell stories like that and he must've spoke to my father who was 'big' in the Catholic society there and the priest came to my house and said to my parents that I was a liar and I was telling stories and they took me to a retreat to repent.

(Study A)

One young woman explained that when she was 12 she told her parents' best friends that she was having sex with her father (she did not know how else to explain what was happening). The friends, who had been surrogate auntie and uncle to her, looked at her with 'sheer disgust' and never spoke to her again. They would cross the street whenever they saw her. Another's mother told her:

> You deserve it, you know, you used to be such a happy lovely little girl and now you're this awful, sullen monster and . . . if you don't pull your socks up, I don't think I can love you anymore.
>
> (Study A)

Much emphasis was placed by professionals on the credibility of the account with disclosures by disabled children being too easily dismissed as unreliable accounts, particularly where there was a learning disability or communication impairment.

It was apparent from both studies that children's rights were not always respected and the invisibility of children within services was notable. In some cases, services were absent from their lives, in others, provision was inadequate or inappropriate. Particular concerns were raised in relation to the quality of some foster care placements and the lack of professional interpreting services and communication support.

> I did have counselling but with a woman who couldn't sign. She would use a laptop to communicate with me. She typed, 'How are you?'. I thought it was strange. I typed back 'I am ok'. She said, 'Do you want to talk about anything?' . . . It wasn't possible because we couldn't communicate with each other.
>
> (Study A)

Case conferences are one way where children's voices can be heard, but as we heard in Study B:

> It's not good at all. Certainly of any of the ones I've been to in the 6 years, I've been here, [children] certainly haven't attended a case conference. I've certainly been to case conferences but not one where a child with disability has been represented.
>
> (Study B)

As well as making clear disclosures, participants attempted to communicate their distress and seek help through challenging internalising and externalising behaviours and attempted suicides. The data suggest that disclosures are often made but not recognised as such as they do not follow the expected form. However, these expressions of distress were often assumed to be related to the child's temperament or even their impairment rather than an indication of abuse.

> I wonder . . . if that little boy who's been seen five times previously, I wonder whether because of his difficulties, his disclosures were being minimised because people really weren't understanding him.
>
> (Study B)

Non-verbal disclosures may be the only recourse for some disabled children with communication impairments and this requires skills of the listener. Public service practitioners disclosed that due to a gap in practitioner knowledge about effective communication methods, practitioners were more likely to miss distress 'cues' that would otherwise be picked up more efficiently in non-disabled children and young people. Practitioners are much more likely to rely on the behaviour of children and young people as indicators of distress as a result of neglect and/or abuse.

> I think that's the difficulty with children who have a disability that certainly with children that don't have a disability they are telling us what their life experience is like through their behaviour, so that very much informs our assessment.
>
> (Study B)

This was raised by professionals who gave the following example:

> there was a joint meeting held between police and social work . . . it was decided that they would do [the interview] just using verbal communication. We got some help from school to their advice but they weren't at the joint interview and the joint interview was done and it was quite sad in a way you know, this wee [small] boy had said very clearly his foster carer's son-in-law had punched him and hit him and was very specific about where on his body he got hit yet the police spoke to the foster carer and the son-in-law and would take no further action and it felt as though it was mainly due to the boy having complex needs.
>
> (Study B)

There was also some evidence of disabled children's needs not being considered when specialist facilities were designed.

> the video recorded interview unit in [Scottish city] doesn't fit a powered wheelchair . . . we discovered that when we took somebody there in a wheelchair that couldn't get through the door!
>
> (Study B)

The challenges of acting on disclosures

Most models of disclosure assume that disclosure leads to positive action, that is, the abuse being successfully addressed. However, this was rarely so in the accounts provided in Studies A and B. Action was often not a consequence of telling and listening for disabled children. The reasons for this appear to be complex. In Study B we modelled 34 case examples against the factors influencing assessment (e.g. burden of proof, third party accounts) and the factors influencing the threshold for action. Thresholds for action were found to be high and decision-making was highly contextual.

From our study of professional practice (Study B) evidence suggested that public service practitioners assume that disabled children and young people have additional support and access to services in place than non-disabled children. This leads to a tendency by public service practitioners to rely on 'others' to pick-up any signs of risk of significant harm.

> There is a tendency to think that if there's a child with additional needs or are disabled then they have already got that extra support there . . . and they would expect somebody else to pick it up.
>
> (Study B)

A number of negative outcomes of 'unsuccessful' disclosure were evidenced from the study of disabled people's experiences (Study A). These included silencing of children and maintenance of abuse that can lead to both risk-intensification and re-traumatisation. Children and young people in Study A talked about their frustration and distress at disclosures being discounted as they saw it.

> They came to visit me and they then stopped coming. For 4 years, I suffered and it was all over within 2 or 3 weeks. I felt what was the point in telling them what happened to me.
>
> (Study A)

> They never charged him or took him to the court. Never. No charge or court. Nothing. The police said that I had to forget about it. There was nothing more that they could do about it. He was free to walk. I was so upset.
>
> (Study A)

Injustice was, therefore, also a consequence of lack of action following a disclosure. Professionals in Study B expressed concerns that disabled children are more likely to be dismissed as not being credible and that their stories are less likely to be heard.

> disabled children don't make good witnesses, . . . they are not classed as reliable witnesses . . . And that is scary because you know these children are at a huge amount of risk.
>
> (Study B)

> Because of the young persons' needs . . . the police were basically saying, 'well we couldn't really interview them'. I think that's really been the most

frustrating thing, that [the child] couldn't be used as evidence because of their disability.

(Study B)

We contend that the tendency described above, to be dismissive, to conflate impairment effects with those of abuse, to restrict the physical and social and emotional environments where children could disclose, all are forms of disablism. While creating the conditions to enable disclosures may be particularly challenging in the case of disabled children and young people, it is imperative that we find ways to make this possible in order to effectively protect disabled children from human rights abuses.

Discussion: a new model of disclosure of abuse

From our research on protection of disabled children, we have identified five key purposes of disclosure of abuse by disabled children and adults, which we have called The Five Rs of Disclosure (Table 2.2). The emphasis is on the meaning of the disclosure for the victim/survivor.

These five categories are not mutually exclusive. Disclosures may have one or more purpose or intended outcome. They may also take on particular relevance at different points across the life course. The challenge for professionals is to develop a child-centric approach to understanding and responding to disclosures of abuse.

Table 2.2 The Five Rs of Disclosure

Purpose of the disclosure of abuse by victims/survivors: the Five Rs of Disclosure

---

Rehearsal – To test the readiness of the listener to hear the full extent of the abuse. This is a tentative disclosure of partial information in order to gauge the likelihood of a positive and constructive response from the recipient of the disclosure.

Recovery – To seek help with the physical, psychological and emotional effects of abuse. Recovery may be sought at the time that abuse is being perpetrated or many years after the abuse has ceased. This involves recognition of the harm done by abuse and the need to address this trauma.

Rescue – To create a set of circumstances that will lead to the cessation of abuse. This requires recognition on the part of the victim/survivor of the abuse nature of their experience.

Redress – To seek justice for the abuse experienced through the legal system or through informal means. This may include punishment of the perpetrator or compensation for the victim/survivor.

Rehabilitation – To produce a long-lasting change in the abuser. The onus is on the perpetrator's need to cease the abuse rather than the victim/survivor's need to protect him/herself.

From our recent studies of disclosure of abuse by disabled children and adults and the broader research literature on disclosure more generally, we propose a new model for understanding disclosure of abuse by disabled children. In the case of initial disclosures to professionals, it is often a teacher in receipt of the information and when this moves into an investigation, it is mostly legal and social work professionals supporting and responding to disclosures. One concerning feature of disabled children's experiences of abuse is that they are often in contact with numerous professionals such as teachers, nurses, disability specialists and social care practitioners yet abuse goes undetected. This model focuses particularly on these professionals.

One limitation of the broader research literature on disclosure is that it focuses primarily on disclosure by the child rather than failure by the adult to recognise, acknowledge and intervene. We frame our model, therefore, as a relational and situated process. We use the term situated to refer to the efforts made by children to identify the right time and place to disclose, to seek out these opportunities. It also refers, though, to the ability of the recipient of the disclosure to create such opportunities or maximise these if it becomes apparent that a child is seeking an opportunity to talk. The model also takes account of life course and developmental aspects of disclosure and has at its foundation disabled children's rights.

We pay particular attention to the relevance of the features of the model to the experiences of disabled children, but suggest that this model could also have wider applications to other marginalised groups if, for example, disablism was replaced with racism or hetero-normativity. We will now outline the model. We will then explore the particular relevance of the model to the experience of disabled children and adults who have experienced abuse or neglect in childhood.

Our model places emphasis on the professional's role in (a) preparing the ground for disclosures, (b) maintaining an openness to 'hearing' or detecting disclosures whether verbal or non-verbal and responding in a way that does not shut down the disclosure and (c) acting on the disclosure in a way that validates the victim/survivor, demonstrates an understanding of their perception of the situation and their motivations or needs to disclose and upholds the safeguarding responsibilities of the professional. We frame disclosure as an interactive process, not only between the teller and the listener but also between individual experience and societal structures.

This sort of approach, we suggest, is more likely to lead to a virtuous cycle of disclosure that will ensure the disabled child feels able to reveal more details incrementally having been reassured of the integrity of the listener. The model is framed in terms of protection of disabled children but could be used to understand disclosure potential in both disabled children and adults.

While the motivations to disclose described earlier may not differ greatly from those expressed by non-disabled children or adults, there are likely to be particular challenges with implementing such a model in the context of

Figure 2.1 A virtual cycle of relational disclosure: protecting disabled children

a disabling society. Shah *et al.* (2016) suggest the extent to which disabled children are listened to and believed when attempting to disclose may be linked to public perceptions that disabled children are less damaged by abuse as they do not fully understand what has happened to them. This expression of disablism requires urgent attention if children's right to protection is to be realised.

Typically, an emphasis in preventative programmes is placed on increasing the competence of children to disclose rather than the competence of adults to read cues and interpret partial or non-verbal disclosures. This puts disabled children at a significant disadvantage and is disabling in itself. Education aimed at adults with the goal of enabling them to detect abuse and subtle cues is needed and within such education disability awareness needs to be fully integrated. Shah *et al.* (2016) recommend that prevention programmes should include real-life case studies of disabled survivors to increase the visibility and understanding of their particular experiences. Franklin and Smeaton (2017), in their study of people with learning disabilities who experience sexual exploitation, conclude that children need to build up a relationship over an extended period and to discuss their lives in order to recognise certain experiences as abusive and to be able to disclose. This suggests that preventative education should not be delivered in isolation, but should be part of a programme of longer-term engagement with children about identifying risk and raising awareness and self-esteem.

Conclusions

We offer this emergent model as a starting point for future research. We would also like to suggest other fruitful areas to be pursued through empirical work. Little is known about the process of disclosure in cases other than child sexual abuse or in particular populations of children. Such studies suggest that factors influencing disclosure of other forms of abuse may differ. For example, a process of normalisation of emotional abuse in the lives of marginalised populations may undermine an individual's ability to recognise a situation as abusive and, therefore, seek help. Family-based neglect is also likely to be experienced from birth and, therefore, normalised, making it difficult to recognise and disclose. These are important areas for future research and investigation.

Key messages from this chapter

- Disabled children are at increased risk of violence, abuse and neglect compared to their non-disabled peers.
- Disclosure of abuse should be understood as a relational process whereby conditions are created that enable disclosure, promote active listening and result in child-centred responses.
- In order to address issues of intersectionality and multiple oppression, attention must be given to structural barriers to disclosure and children's rights.

Acknowledgements

We would like to acknowledge our co-authors of the two studies cited in this chapter as well as the members of the Study Advisory Groups. We would also like to thank all of the research participants who contributed to the studies, particularly the disabled people who had experienced abuse in childhood.

References

Akbas, S., Turiaa, A., Karabekirolgu, K., Pazvantoglu, O., Kekskin, T. and Boke, O. (2009) Characteristics of sexual abuse in a sample of Turkish children with and without mental retardation, referred for legal appraisal of the psychological repercussions. *Sexuality and Disability*, 27(4): 205–213.

Alaggia, R. (2004) Many ways of telling: Expanding conceptualizations of child sexual abuse disclosure. *Child Abuse & Neglect*, *28*(11): 1213–1227.

Alaggia, R. (2010) An ecological analysis of child sexual abuse disclosure: Considerations for child and adolescent mental health. *Journal of the Canadian Academy of Child and Adolescent Psychiatry*, *19*(1): 32.

Allnock, D. and Miller, P. (2013) *No one noticed, no one heard: a study of disclosures of childhood abuse*. London: NSPCC.

Blackburn C. M., Spencer, N. J. and Read, J. M. (2010) Prevalence of childhood disability and the characteristics and circumstances of disabled children in the UK: Secondary analysis of the Family Resources Survey. *BMC Pediatrics*, *10*(1): 21.

Briggs, F. (2006) Safety issues in the lives of children with learning disabilities. *Social Policy Journal of New Zealand*, *29*: 43–59.

Cossar, J., Brandon, M., Bailey, S., Belderson, P., Biggart, L. and Sharpe, D. (2013) *'It takes a lot to build trust'. Recognition and telling: Developing earlier routes to help for children and young people*. London: Office of the Children's Commissioner.

Franklin, A. and Smeaton, E. (2017) Listening to young people with learning disabilities who have experienced, or are at risk of, child sexual exploitation in the UK. *Children & Society*, *32*: 98–109.

Goodman-Brown, T., Edelstein, R., Goodman, G. and Gordon, D. (2003) Why children tell: A model of children's disclosure of sexual abuse. *Child Abuse & Neglect*, *27*(5): 525–540.

Hernon, J., Brandon, M., Cossar, J. and Shakespeare, T. (2015) Recognising and responding to the maltreatment of disabled children: A children's rights approach. *Social Work and Social Sciences Review*, *17*(3): 61–77.

Hershkowitz, I., Horowitz, D. and Lamb, M. (2005) Trends in children's disclosure of abuse in Israel: A national study. *Child Abuse & Neglect*, *29*(11): 1203–1214.

Hershkowitz, I., Lamb, M. E. and Horowitz, D. (2007) Victimization of children with disabilities. *American Journal of Orthopsychiarty*, *77*(4): 629–635.

Jensen, T. K., Gulbrandsen, W., Mossige, S., Reichelt, S. and Tjersland, O. A. (2005) Reporting possible sexual abuse: A qualitative study on children's perspectives and the context for disclosure. *Child Abuse & Neglect*, *29*(12): 1395–1413.

Jones, C., Stalker, K., Franklin, A., Fry, D., Cameron, A. and Taylor, J. (2017) Enablers of help-seeking and protection from abuse for deaf and disabled children: A qualitative study. *Child & Family Social Work*, *22*(2): 762–771.

Jones, L., Bellis, M. A., Wood, S., Hughes, K., McCoy, E., Eckley, L., Bates, G., Mikton, C., Shakespeare, T. and Officer, A. (2012) Prevalence and risk of violence against children with disabilities: A systematic review and meta-analysis of observational studies. *The Lancet*, *380*(9845): 899–907.

Lippert, T., Cross, T.P., Jones, L. and Walsh, W. (2010) Suspect confession of child sexual abuse to investigators. *Child maltreatment*, *15*(2): 161–170.

Kogan, S. (2004) Disclosing unwanted sexual experiences: Results from a national sample of adolescent women. *Child Abuse & Neglect*, *28*(2): 147–165.

Kvam, M. H. (2004) Sexual abuse of deaf children. A retrospective analysis of the prevalence and characteristics of childhood sexual abuse among deaf adults in Norway. *Child Abuse & Neglect*, *28*: 241–251.

Lippert, T., Cross, T. P., Jones, L. and Walsh, W. (2009) Telling interviewers about sexual abuse: Predictors of child disclosure at forensic interviews. *Child Maltreatment*, *14*(1): 100–113.

Marchant, R. (1991) Myths and facts about sexual abuse and children with disabilities. *Child Abuse Review*, *5*(2): 22–24.

McElvaney, R. (2015) Disclosure of child sexual abuse: Delays, non_disclosure and partial disclosure. What the research tells us and implications for practice. *Child Abuse Review*, *24*(3): 159–169.

McElvaney, R., Greene, S. and Hogan, D. (2012) Containing the secret of child sexual abuse. *Journal of Interpersonal Violence*, *27*(6): 1155–1175.

Murray, M. and Osborne, C. (2009) *Safeguarding disabled children: Practice guidance.* London: DCSF.

Ofsted. (2009) *Learning Lessons from Serious Case Reviews: Year 2.* London: Ofsted.

Reitsema, A. M. and Grietens, H. (2015) Is anybody listening? The literature on the dialogical process of child sexual abuse disclosure reviewed. *Trauma, Violence, & Abuse, 17*(3): 330.

Shah, S., Tsitsou, L. and Woodin, S. (2016) 'I can't forget': Experiences of violence and disclosure in the childhoods of disabled women. *Childhood, 23*(4): 521–536.

Sobsey, D. (1994) *Violence and abuse in the lives of people with disabilities: The end of silent acceptance?* Baltimore, MD: Paul H. Brookes.

Sobsey, D., Randall, W. and Parrila, R. K. (1997) Gender differences in abused children with and without disabilities. *Child Abuse & Neglect, 21*(8): 707–720.

Stalker, K., Taylor, J., Fry, D. and Stewart, A. (2015) A study of disabled children and child protection in Scotland – a hidden group? *Children and Youth Services Review, 56*: 126–134.

Sullivan, P. M. and Knutson, J. F. (2000) Maltreatment and disabilities: A population-based epidemiological study. *Child Abuse & Neglect, 24*(10): 1257–1273.

Taylor, J., Stalker, K., Fry, D. and Stewart, A. (2014) Disabled children and child protection in Scotland: An investigation into the relationship between professional practice, child protection and disability. Available at: www.scotland.gov.uk/Publications/2014/04/1108.

Taylor, J., Cameron, A., Jones, C., Franklin, A., Stalker, K. and Fry, D. (2015) Deaf and disabled children talking about child protection. NSPCC. Available at: www.nspcc.org.uk/services-and-resources/research-and-resources/2015/deaf-disabled-children-talking-about-child-protection/.

Taylor, J., Stalker, K. and Stewart, A. (2016) Disabled children's experiences of the child protection system. *Child Abuse Review, 25*(1): 60–73.

Thomas, C. (2004) How is disability understood? An examination of sociological approaches. *Disability & Society, 19*(6), 569–583.

Thomas, C. (2007) *Sociologies of disability and illness. Contested ideas in disability studies and medical sociology.* Basingstoke, UK: Palgrave Macmillan.

Union of the Physically Impaired Against Segregation (UPIAS) (1976) *Fundamental principles of disability.* London: UPIAS and The Disability Alliance.

United Nations. (1989) *Convention on the Rights of the Child.* New York: United Nations General Assembly. Available at: www.cirp.org/library/ethics/UN-convention/.

United Nations. (2006) *Convention on the Rights of People with Disabilities.* New York: United Nations.

Vincent, S. and Daniel, B. (2004) An analysis of children and young people's calls to ChildLine about abuse and neglect: A study for the Scottish Child Protection Review. *Child Abuse Review, 13*(2): 158–171.

Westcott, H. and Cross, M. (1996) *This Far and no Further: Tending the Abuse of Disabled Children*. Birmingham: Venture Press.

World Health Organization (WHO). (2011) World Report on Disability [online]. Available at: www.who.int/disabilities/world_report/2011/en/, accessed 5 July 2017.

World Health Organization (WHO) (2016). Child maltreatment [online]. Available at: www.who.int/mediacentre/factsheets/fs150/en/, accessed 6 July 2017.

Chapter 3

Forced marriage and Black Minority Ethnic survivors with learning difficulties in Scotland

Ashley Thompson and Mridul Wadhwa

Introduction

The Scottish Government defines forced marriage as:

> a marriage in which one or both parties do not (or, in the case of some adults with learning or physical disabilities, cannot) consent to the marriage and duress is involved.

In our experience, forced marriage is a process not an event. The risk of forced marriage cannot be identified by simply looking for evidence of a wedding that the victim cannot consent to, but rather by recognising the control and grooming behaviour that effectively restricts an individual from giving free and full consent.

We believe that to offer an effective and positive response to survivors and those at risk of forced marriage we must recognise it as a form of gender-based violence and not solely as a cultural issue that happens to people of colour and migrants. Presenting forced marriage as a cultural issue has generally allowed for the myths that exist among many who come into contact with victims, to make excuses for not engaging with this issue by saying they do not have familiarity with the cultural and religious background of the victim and perpetrators. Professionals are worried that they may come across as racist or culturally insensitive and frequently accept a particular format of arranging a marriage in a family as acceptable without appropriate probing, thus failing victims of forced marriage. The problem with seeing forced marriage as a cultural issue is that the experiences of women and girls with learning disabilities at risk of forced marriage are not visible or recognised as serious. While forced marriage often manifests itself within specific cultural contexts, we have seen women with learning difficulties at particular risk of forced marriage for purposes of financial or immigration gain and that is why forced marriage is not simply a matter of culture or old-fashioned tradition; it is about the position of women in society, which is essentially unequal. We must also recognise the role of the state in discriminating against immigrant women and girls, especially those with No Recourse to Public Funds, a United Kingdom (UK) restriction on new migrants most clearly defined in immigration law for people from outside of the European Union (EU).

Our experience has highlighted the importance of taking a long-term response for survivors that should include a bolder interpretation of legislation designed to protect victims from harm and the need to see those affected as individuals, rather than products of their culture and race. When considering forced marriage as a form of gender-based violence and how it impacts women from Black Minority Ethnic (BME) groups, it is important that we take a wider approach in identifying who the perpetrators are, because, for BME women generally, they are not only a partner or ex-partner but also members of the household, family and/or community.

Additionally, we also need to consider the role of popular politicians, the media (both social and traditional) and also government policy, all of which view forced marriage as a problem for the UK, including Scotland, that occurs solely as a result of migration and poorly integrated minority communities. These communities are collectively presented as extremely patriarchal and different from the white majority, thereby othering the experience of forced marriage. Forced marriage is limited to being spoken of in cultural and geographical terms and is therefore unhelpfully approached as a Pakistani, Iraqi, Indian and so forth issue rather than a problem for women and girls in Scotland. The reality is that forced marriage is a Scottish problem and has uniquely Scottish features. While we acknowledge that it is largely a minority ethnic issue, we recognise that in the case of women and girls, especially those with learning disabilities, the risk of forced marriage can extend to those who are outside Black Minority and Migrant communities.

What does forced marriage look like?

An *arranged marriage* is not the same as a *forced marriage*. What this process of arrangement looks like is different in different cultures, families and communities and is often unique for each individual. However, a good arranged marriage can be recognised by how the marriage is consented to. Consent is comprised of three layers.

1   The person getting married gives free and full consent to the idea of marriage i.e. they actually do want to get married.
2   The person agrees for their parents, extended family, friends or matchmakers to be a part of the process of arranging a marriage, i.e. they give permission for others to play a role in helping them finalise a potential spouse.
3   The person consents to marry the person they have chosen themselves.

The test of free consent in any arranged marriage is that a person is able to withdraw their consent, without consequence, at any time. In a forced marriage, the three layers of consent are either completely absent or compromised. The compromise can be to such an extent that even if the victim appears to give consent to a marriage, it is usually done under duress or deception from the perpetrators. It often involves grooming over a long period of time, frequently starting in early childhood.

Forced marriage is a negative manifestation of arranged marriage and is usually perpetrated in contexts where arranged marriage is a familial and cultural norm. The excuses listed by perpetrators for forced marriage are many. However, the one that is most common is that it is the family tradition, cultural and/or religious expectation. At face value, this is also the main reason why many individuals agree to an arranged marriage; because they have the mind-set for it. What is fundamentally different between the two types of marriage is that the process of an arranged marriage is constantly evolving and adapting to the attitude and choice of the individuals getting married. However, in a forced marriage, the process is rigid, restrictive and entirely led by the organisers of the marriage, i.e. the perpetrators, who are usually parents or extended family (living in Scotland or elsewhere), or sometimes the prospective spouse. The main objective is to achieve the status of marriage for a woman rather than focus on the arrangement of a wedding. It is about ensuring that she is no longer the responsibility of her parents and has gained respectability as a married woman.

So, what does forced marriage feel like for someone with a learning difficulty and how do they experience that duress? There are a host of motivators but one of the clearer motivations is that the perpetrators, usually parents, want to find someone who will care for her. This excuse is even more the case if the parents actually recognise that their daughter has a learning disability. In other cases, the disability might not even be acknowledged or recognised as a barrier to marriage. We believe that the extent to which family chooses to recognise their child's disability will determine how the family will approach the arranged marriage process i.e. will it be hidden away from the glare of professionals and extended family, or will it be public for everyone to see? We will explore the process and motivations in some depth later in the chapter.

Marriage is a universal human right and anyone over the age of 16 in Scotland has the right and fundamental freedom to marry with full consent. This includes women with learning difficulties. However, it is important to acknowledge that there may be specific access requirements that need to be put in place for someone with a learning difficulty to ensure they understand the concept and fundamentals of marriage. This is especially important if they are likely to choose a spouse through an arranged marriage process. For women and girls with learning difficulties who have been groomed into a forced marriage, understanding of choice and consent is complex and can be challenging to unpick. For many at risk of forced marriage, if they have grown up in a setting where they are surrounded by family and friends who have experienced arranged marriage it will often seem normal and even natural to go along with these expectations without questioning the motives or the process of arranging the marriage.

The desire to get a daughter with learning difficulties married often isn't fulfilled because her parents or family have malicious intent. An arranged marriage may be seen as a way of protecting their daughter, of ensuring that she is looked after when they are dead, or guaranteeing that she is accepted by the community. This is where the idea of 'protection' becomes harmful as perpetrators will assume full responsibility for establishing the marital relationship, excluding the woman to be married from the process, rather than empowering her to explore the desire and meaning of marriage for herself. Despite stated good intentions, it is the role of the professional to question and challenge motives, because if a family is truly acting out of positive concern and goodwill for their daughter, then they will change their process to empower their daughter rather than marginalise and disempower. If they don't, there is serious risk of forced marriage.

Citing cultural and religious motivations for forced marriage masquerading as arranged marriage is really just a smoke screen to throw off those to protect individuals at risk. A fair assessment of the risk and impact of forced marriage can only really occur if we take a gendered analysis of the motivations of perpetrators and the position of women and girls in the lives of the perpetrators, rather than looking at it as a cultural and/or religious issue. To do this it is essential that we explore the gendered nature of the concept of 'Honour'.

The universality of Honour and its relationship with migration and gender inequality

Forced marriage is classified in Scotland and the rest of the UK as Honour-Based Violence. We argue that, globally, experiences of Honour are gendered, and while there may be slightly different variations in different societies, there remain common themes that are easily defined as belonging to binary gender stereotypes. This is why we believe forced marriage is a form of gender-based violence. The experience of forced marriage is hugely based on binary gender stereotypes and is experienced as such by men and lesbian, gay, bisexual, trans-gender and intersex (LGBTI) victims as well. To ignore this reality is to limit your understanding of this issue and hinder your ability to risk assess and support those affected by forced marriage.

Universally, Honour is associated with female virginity, control of female sexual expression and the male's ability to protect women within his family. It is from these ideas we experience phenomena such as victim-blaming – where we move fault to women for dressing provocatively, being drunk, behaving in a sexualised manner or being out at night, rather than holding perpetrators accountable for their actions.

The gendered principle of Honour is that it is up to a woman to do everything she can do to keep her body safe from harm and violation and her reputation must not be tarred by even the slightest rumours about her character. A violation of any of these matters will bring negative consequences to her family, especially the men of the family for failing to perform their role as protector. In a culture dominated by concepts of Honour, women are not seen as autonomous beings and are passed from being a possession of the father to being a possession of the husband, looking to them for protection.

In some cultures, these ideas of womanhood are clearly visible to the outsider, such as in the case of cultures that have roots in South, Central and Middle Asia. In other cultures, they are less visible, for example in white Scottish culture, where women are shamed for having multiple sexual partners or for being raped while drunk.

The gendered concept of Honour expects a woman to be in perfect physical shape and for her to bring moral pride to her family and community. Anything less in a woman is seen as a problem; a problem that must be hidden away or removed.

So how, then, do disabled women fit into the discourse on Honour? How is their worth measured in this gendered context? We believe that for women with learning difficulties, the preferred modus operandi is to keep them isolated from their extended family or community or to explain away their learning disability as childlike innocence, clearly a virtue in an unmarried woman. However, while women and girls with learning difficulties might experience isolation within their community, it should by no means be accepted that they don't understand their responsibilities as 'honourable' women and girls.

The most effective way of teaching Honour in this gendered way is through the narrative of stories of virtuous and honourable women or through family or community examples of what happens if a woman breaks the rules. Usually referring to the negative fates that befall them for a misdemeanour of Honour or potential loss of Honour. An example of one such story is that of the twelfth-century Queen Padmini. As the story goes, Padmini was an exceptionally beautiful queen, so beautiful that poems of her beauty were spoken of far and wide. She lived with Ratan Sen, her husband in Chittor in Rajasthan, India, one of the most heavily guarded fortresses up in the hills. However, it was not long before the stories of Padmini's beauty reached the ear of the Sultan of Delhi. The Sultan raised his army that was far greater than that of Ratan Sen, and set off to capture Padmini for his own. The defences of the fort were breached and the fort was almost defeated. Ratan Sen knew that if Padmini was taken and defiled, that this would bring the ultimate dishonour to him in his present life and the next. So Jauhar[1] was declared by the King. Jauhar, simply explained, is a battle of no return where the men enter battle with the intention of killing and being killed and the women sacrifice themselves by jumping into a collective fire, thus ensuring that no shame is brought on the men for failing to protect the Honour of their women.

1   Jauhar was the South Asian custom of mass suicide by women to avoid capture, enslavement and rape by raiders, when their communities faced certain defeat in battle.

So why are we telling you this story? Padmini is still, to this day, hailed as being the ultimate woman, the woman that all other women should look up to and emulate. She gave the ultimate sacrifice, her life, so that the Honour of her husband and family was assured. There have been millions of Padminis who have committed suicide to protect their family Honour globally and in BME communities in the UK. The stories of many women killed in the UK because of perceived loss of Honour is a continuation of the story of Padmini but with less glorious outcomes; usually they become a tale of caution for other women and girls in the family and possibly community.

Despite the narrative presented here, Honour shouldn't be misunderstood as an exotic and alien concept, associated with migrant and minority communities in Scotland, that has no relevance whatsoever to indigenous White populations. Fundamentally, all societies and communities have a code of Honour. We might not recognise it as Honour but instead as the moral code of the society or community we live in. For many of us it is our sense of morality, often experienced as acting out rules from an unwritten rule book that represents our shared values and ethics with those we identify with as a group. Adhering to a given community's moral code is often described by survivors as offering a measure of predictability when guessing how people will respond in given situations. If you behave in a certain way, you will be accepted, you will belong. It is a way of being that you are groomed into from infancy, so that as you enter adulthood you are not even aware of it influencing your actions and decisions.

As families and individuals within these communities, we form our own relationships with the prevalent moral code prescribing, rejecting or changing our relationship with the code or changing the code itself to suit our individual needs and values. In many ways, we have found that subscribing to a prevalent moral or Honour code instils a sense of belonging and reinforces identity especially for migrant communities in Scotland.

Our work with survivors from migrant communities in the UK has shown us that those from a migrant background tend to cling more strongly to the values and traditions with which they, or their families, have migrated. We find that migrant communities rely heavily on those few who understand their way of being and tend to band together in a manner that they might not have in their home culture, often blurring the lines between family and community. In Scotland, we have found that, over the decades, South Asian migrants have been slower to reject/change traditions and values with which they have they migrated. They often continue to practise their cultures and its associated morals in what many from their home cultures might today consider archaic, old fashioned or even unacceptable. It is not unusual, in our line of work to come across women from certain communities in Scotland with origins in South Asia who are more likely to be married earlier, and have limited access to further education and employment than women from their cultural and faith backgrounds in South Asia who have access to similar economic, material resources as the women living in Scotland.

We believe that this is a direct impact of migration into a hostile society, where the majority community in subtle and obvious ways constantly reminds BME individuals and their communities that they are different, unwelcome and will always belong elsewhere no matter if they have lived in Scotland for generations. The consistent marginalisation due to racism along with sexism has empowered the patriarchal control of women within BME communities especially of disabled women and girls. This environment has provided little incentive for women's unequal position within BME communities to change at the same rate as it has for women in the majority community. We have found that old-fashioned views of Honour continue to thrive in BME communities as any attempts from the state to challenge their gendered nature of oppression usually only occurs at times of crisis, such as when someone is facing an imminent risk of forced marriage.

In the cases that we have dealt with, we have found that those who seek to control women and girls' lives are driven not just by concepts of Honour that exist within BME communities, but also by the prejudice, unconscious bias and overt racism that is perpetrated towards the community. They succeed by justifying their behaviours as necessary because they need to protect women and girls from the negatives of being a minority and, in the case of disabled women and girls, by casting them as individuals who need additional protection. It is often believed that disabled women are unable to take care of themselves due to their impairment and are given limited opportunity or support to develop their life skills. It is assumed that because they are unable to do things in the same way as the majority, they are unable to do it at all. Therefore, problem solving for alternative strategies doesn't occur for life skills such as time keeping, reading and writing or independent travel etc. The one exception to this will often be in relation to the traditional female roles related to cooking and housekeeping that are seen as being desirable for ensuring marriageability. Commonly we see women and girls being isolated from peers within their community and the disabled community, often by controlling or limiting access to specialist services.

As we move on to look at perpetrator motivations in more detail, it is important to remember that culture is fluid and constantly changing. Even within one community group there will be many interpretations of that community's wider Honour code. Taking a gendered approach helps us reflect on the interactions of factors such as Honour, migration, cultural norms, faith and tradition on the lives of disabled women and girls.

Motivations of perpetrators and victims

In our experience of working with women and girls, we find that they speak positively about the idea of marriage. However, this is really a surface response and requires probing irrespective of whether they have capacity to give consent or not. Frequently, women and girls tell us of their delight at the idea of being a married woman and conforming to a cultural norm, as they believe this might afford them a higher status. They are aware that they are considered not equal to or the same as the other woman in the family because of their learning difficulty and see marriage as allowing them to be 'normal' and like everyone else. Additionally, being married promises a pathway to achieving greater independence and autonomy over their lives. Therefore, with the positive promise of marriage it can become difficult to explore its more challenging aspects, let alone the harmful experiences of forced marriage. So, it shouldn't be surprising to the professional if they are met with hostility, denial, accusations of not understanding the culture or religion by the person at risk, when questioning the process and motivations of an impending marriage. This makes confidential discussion and risk assessment with the women/girl at risk on issues such as consent for marriage and sex, emotional and physical duress and other marriage-related matters quite challenging.

Perpetrators in cases of forced marriage of women and girls with learning disabilities are often identified as the parents, but can also include siblings, grandparents, uncles, aunts and, occasionally, non-familial members of the community. The main actors are usually clearly visible and are often those with caring responsibilities of the victim. Their main motivations for arranging a marriage, as they often are willing to state without fear of repercussion, is to ensure their daughter will have a permanent carer. This 'permanent carer' is invariably a fully able man. In some cases, at the point of intervention, this man is known and identified but mostly there isn't a specified person but a search is on for him. However, we must ask what are the motivations of an able man wishing to marry a woman/girl with a learning difficulty? If we have observed behaviour towards the person at risk that suggests that she is seen as a clear liability in her family and possibly her community, then how do we know that a potential groom doesn't see her as one too?

How does a parent who is intent on getting their daughter married find the ideal spouse for their child? In our experience, it is mostly through deception and/or bribery. The deception being that the learning disability is hidden from the prospective groom or the bribe is financial gain, e.g. a share in the family business, a property, or the promise of gaining a favourable immigration status. It is important to highlight here that within the UK immigration system, people who are in receipt of Disability Living Allowance have to meet a lower financial threshold to sponsor a spouse from overseas. This can also put women with learning difficulties, who may not be from BME backgrounds, at risk of forced marriage by those looking to regularise their immigration status as spouses of British Nationals (if the woman is British), or possibly as the spouse of an EU citizen exposing the links between forced marriage and human trafficking.

It is, therefore, important to understand that, as practitioners, we have a particular challenge in dealing with forced marriage when it comes to BME women and girls with learning disabilities. We find that both victims and perpetrators are likely to talk about marriage as being a positive experience and outcome for themselves. The professional involved in this situation needs to develop a clear understanding of the following:

(a)   The woman has capacity to consent. Specifically, capacity to consent to the process of an arranged marriage.
(b)   The woman always has the opportunity to refuse the marriage without negative consequences.
(c)   The woman and the professional are aware of what an arranged marriage looks like within that family's context.
(d)   The motivations of the parents and others involved in arranging the marriage, and the extent to which the process gives the woman full autonomy to make the crucial decisions involved in being part of an arranged marriage.
(e)   What the woman herself understands about marriage, especially her rights as a spouse, and the nature of marriage, i.e. beyond the sexual context of marriage.

The significance of knowing the answers to these questions becomes clearer when we discuss the law later.

Professional confidence in investigating and responding to forced marriage

The forced marriage narrative that grabs headlines and public attention is one of extreme violence and death. However, the 'force' in forced marriage is much more subtle and can't always be seen clearly, which is why risk in many cases is not identified until crisis stage. Forced marriage is a process of grooming that for many begins in early childhood with the pressure building up closer to the time that the perpetrator feels that a marriage must take place.

Behaviours related to such force include: denial of access to further education, restrictions in attending group activities, being told how or how not to dress, gatekeeping access to social care and care workers, perpetrators citing culture or gender reasons for not engaging with professionals or accessing services. More information about indicators of forced marriage is to be found in Scottish Government Guidance on Forced Marriage. However, what we have found is that often professionals involved in safeguarding base their decisions of risk of forced marriage by looking for evidence of a wedding such as a date, a groom, location etc., rather than assessing perpetrator behaviour and control of the girl as an indicator of risk of forced marriage.

To be clear, a wedding is not a marriage. The spouse and wedding date are replaceable. The intention is to get a woman married and sometimes it might mean waiting until the scrutiny of professionals dissipates. Our aim, as practitioners, should be to protect and prevent a girl from finding herself in a relationship she doesn't want or can't consent to, rather than avoiding a wedding.

We have found that seeking out facts around wedding plans rather than questioning behaviours of potential perpetrators leads to situations in which professionals have to respond to a crisis such as sudden trips overseas, abrupt ending of educational or withdrawal from services by those with parental/ guardian responsibilities. Forced marriage responses in crisis stage often lead to short term responses leaving little opportunity to work collaboratively with the individual at risk.

The recognition of subtle controlling behaviours as indicators of risk, such as isolation from peer group, strict curfews and dress codes, or being inflexible about who provides support and how (which are often justified under the garb of cultural/religious norms and traditions), might allow a professional to take an early intervention approach with the person at risk. For an early intervention approach to work effectively, stakeholders should reframe forced marriage in their minds as a violation of human rights rather than a culture specific practice. A view of forced marriage as a cultural issue provides excuses to avoid early intervention as professionals get bogged down with concerns of being per-ceived as racist, not understanding cultural norms and/or of jeopardising their relationship with the race/cultural community that the person at risk comes from.

There are other challenges too that professionals need to navigate, such as engaging with the family while planning an intervention for a female at risk. We must give thought to accepted guidance that mediation is not an option in forced marriage cases, i.e. attempts to reconcile or manage family attitudes around forced marriage. Prior to intervention, direct enquiries about a potential marriage with the family could increase the risk for the victim as they might bring forward such a marriage, restrict and withhold information, mislead till such a date that professionals lose interest or are under the impression that the risk has been averted. Therefore, professionals will need to rely on those already involved with the family, third-party voluntary agencies such as the one where we (the authors), have gained our experience and most importantly the individual herself.

It is important to watch out for defences from the family, which are likely to include that their child, i.e. the person with a learning disability, has mis-understood, cannot be trusted or is simply lying. They can do this with great ferociousness and with the support of more than the visible perpetrators, i.e. extended family, community members and sometimes misinformed com-munity organisations. They may also reference the very gender- and disability-related inequalities discussed earlier in the chapter as reasons why it is impossible for their daughter to get married and attempt to convince professionals that their concerns are misguided.

Forced marriage legislation

Currently, two separate pieces of civil and criminal legislation cover forced marriage in Scotland. A specific criminal offence of forcing someone to marry in Scotland was created under section 122 of the Anti-Social Behaviour, Crime and Policing Act 2014. The civil legislation is the Forced Marriage etc. (Protection and Jurisdiction) (Scotland) Act 2011. This law introduced civil orders called forced marriage protection orders (FMPO). These are mainly preventive in nature and the burden of proof is the balance of probability, i.e. how likely is it that X is going to be forced into marriage to Y by Z or others. The law clarifies that for its purposes the marriage doesn't have to be a legal marriage; it is sufficient for the law that the parties involved believe that a marriage has taken place or is going to take place.

This acceptance of marriage under this legislation as not necessarily being a legal marriage is significant, particularly for those with learning difficulties. As this creates opportunity for them to give valid evidence of their risk even where they may not be able to speak about their wedding or marriage in clear terms and may not be able to recall or even be aware of details of a planned/completed wedding ceremony. From our experience, it is not unusual for marriages to have taken place online via webcam, via phone, or even by proxy, which can be accepted as legitimate by families from certain Asian, Middle Eastern and African cultures. There may also be a religious legitimacy to such marriages in certain faith communities and also within some non-UK jurisdiction legal systems. Additionally, perpetrators, i.e. family members, will be talking about the intention to get their son/daughter married but may not have ever spoken of a clear identifiable spouse and wedding event or date.

Using the law

As it currently stands, the 2011 legislation states that the local authority is the only authorised third party that can apply for an FMPO. We will reflect on our experience of two cases in which we were involved where interim FMPOs were granted. The orders were applied for by local authority social workers with responsibility for adult protection. In one case we were involved in an advisory capacity and in the other we pursued the case of a woman to the local authority identifying her as at risk of forced marriage.

The discussion on preventing forced marriage arose when the women themselves articulated to various professionals about possible marriages being planned for them. In both cases it was clear that the risk of forced marriage was evident many years before formal discussions on applying for FMPOs took place. There was evidence of domestic abuse towards the mother of the women from the father; higher levels of control of the movements and social participation of the women within their own communities and also of accessing services, especially group activities designed for people with learning difficulties. The families' excuse for creating these barriers to accessing service providers was cultural and religious difference. Professionals were however able to work individually with the woman but in full sight of the family and within the parameters set by the family.

In our view, the concerns for the safety of the women should have been raised much earlier; however, attempts to be culturally sensitive and working within the sensibilities of the family were given greater priority. These cases were very different from each other and the women had different levels of ability. One of the women had been deemed to have capacity to consent in a previous assessment and the other hadn't had a capacity assessment prior to discussions on risks of forced marriage. We are very keen to stress here that any capacity assessments that take place must consider the capacity to consent to the process of an arranged marriage and not simply the capacity to consent to a marriage or even sex. It is also worthwhile to point out that in one case the woman was deemed to have capacity to consent to marriage but not to consent to a sexual relationship.

The other issue of discussion was identifying who the perpetrators were and what the safety factors were in the home. Our biggest challenge was to convey to social workers that there are unlikely to be any safe people in the home. Given that there was domestic abuse towards the mother in the home, it was unlikely that any single person could be seen as being able to ensure safety of the woman. There was no evidence to suggest that the non-abusive parent, who was also the main carer, had any intention of leaving or ending the abusive relationship or if they did leave that relationship the mother would be willing or able to prevent a forced marriage. Therefore, if care plans are formed around the idea of the mother ending the abusive relationship and moving out to safeguard her daughter we suggest extreme caution. In the long term our experience suggests that this does little to reduce the risk, and is more likely to increase the danger to the mother and her daughter from perpetrators in the extended family and wider community, as they desperately seek to establish the status quo. Discussion on post-legal interventions consequently need to explore a range of possibilities.

Professionals need to consider whether alternative care arrangements can be made, such as independent living or adult foster care. If it is felt that existing carers can continue offering support despite being subject to an FMPO, then professionals must consider what will be the safety and quality of this care and support and how effectively can it be monitored? The answer to this question is fundamental to any use of legal intervention and follow-up support plans. It is important to remember that FMPO legislation is not intended to be used solely in isolation, and can be used alongside a variety of other legal measures. It may also be decided that legal remedies other than the FMPO are more suitable. It has been our experience that frequently after the FMPO has been applied for more invasive orders, such as guardianship orders have been necessary.

The course of action taken depends greatly on the views of the protected person, their willingness/ability to engage with the safety plan professionals wish to implement, and the professional's ability to listen to the complexity of culture, race and religion that forms the narrative of their view. If individuals have given an opinion, you need to carefully consider how their view can be protected and hidden from the perpetrators. Or if they do not want you to intervene, then what next?

As explained earlier, there is a need to be mindful that these decisions need to be made without speaking to the family. Therefore, effective discussion between stakeholders such as the police, social work, voluntary agencies and health professionals about risks and plans is vital. However, getting a clear intervention strategy is only part of the challenge. We found that the challenge has been in convincing legal teams that there is enough evidence of a forced marriage; because the feeling is that the risk only arises when certainties are identified such as a clear plan of a wedding. We believe that it is the warning signs that serve as the evidence. The signs that suggest that someone is being groomed for a marriage are in fact reasons to intervene. In both cases we have highlighted, the local authorities were successful in getting interim (emergency) orders based on these warning signs.

We are aware that not all legal jurisdictions will have civil legislation specifically for forced marriage and the only recourse if any available might be through the criminal courts. Forced marriage prevention and criminalisation of perpetrators is a recent development in the Scottish context, although we, as practitioners in women's support services, have been responding to forced marriage for much longer.

Conclusions

Irrespective of what legal approach is used to safeguard a woman or girl from harm, we must consider long-term rehabilitation and independence for those at risk of forced marriage. This is significant where a woman/girl has been removed from the family home or she has chosen to live independently. We are strong advocates for foster-type placements for women/girls with learning difficulties. Our experience has shown that BME women and girls, irrespective of ability, are more likely to find the strength to stay away from family when they are supported in a family context. However, this doesn't mean that the placement should necessarily be with someone from a BME context. We feel that a placement should be made within situations where women/girls are most able to experience gender equality and independence. We don't mean that she must be removed from her culture, as we believe cultural identity is crucial to thriving outside of the abusive context. Therefore, the professional on the case should work with the woman/girl to find safe ways to explore and engage with their cultural and/or religious identity.

We must also recognise that the family can wait a long time for attention to shift from the individual at risk to implement their plans. Compliance with legal or professional requirements for contact and engagement with the person at risk doesn't automatically equate to a change in attitude or things being safer. Professionals must therefore look for evidence of motive of the family's ongoing engagement with professionals and the woman/girl. This is why addressing forced marriage as an abuse of power and gender-based violence is crucial. It is the only way that a robust risk assessment and ongoing support plan can be implemented. Understanding the gendered experience of Honour and shame will support professionals to ask the appropriate questions and understand the victims' wider cultural context. It is important to remember that, as professionals, we are preventing an individual from a marriage not a wedding and therefore our focus should always be to empower a woman/girl and provide all the support she needs to make free and independent choices for herself. She must have all the resources she needs to deal with the onslaught of family, community, culture, faith, migration and tradition that will be used against her by perpetrators to undermine her safety and independence.

Finally, it is vital that professionals understand that forced marriage cannot be dealt with by one single individual agency or organisation. It requires a multi-agency response with partners from the public sector such as police, health, education and social work and the voluntary/third sector women's organisations. For the response to work there should be recognition that the partners are equal and have a shared ethos and approach to tackling gender-based violence.

Key messages from this chapter

- Forced marriage is a violation of human rights and is an accumulation of a grooming process that, for many, begins in early childhood with the pressure building up closer to the time of the marriage. Therefore, an early intervention approach that focuses on the subtle indicators of control (i.e. isolation from peer group, strict curfews and dress codes) instead of the wedding plans, is crucial.
- When assessing for risk, professionals need to use a gendered understanding of Honour, focusing on the long-term support needs of BME women that address ongoing risk of harm from perpetrators and address the isolation they are likely to experience from being separated from their culture and community.
- Professionals should design specialist services that account for the particular vulnerabilities that BME women with disabilities face, while acting from an understanding that mediation is never an option.

References

Adults with Incapacity (Scotland) Act 2000.
Adult Support and Protection (Scotland) Act 2007.
Anti-Social Behaviour, Crime and Policing Act 2014.
Forced Marriage Unit (2010) Forced Marriage and Learning Disabilities – Multi-Agency Guidelines.

Mental Health (Care and Treatment) (Scotland) Act 2003.

Scottish Government (2009) Safer Lives, Changed Lives: A Shared Approach to Tackling Violence against Women in Scotland.

Scottish Government (2010) A Partnership Approach to Tackling Violence Against Women in Scotland: Guidance for Multi-Agency Partnerships.

Scottish Government (2014) Forced Marriage Practitioner Guidance.

Scottish Government (2014) Forced Marriage Statutory Guidance Revised Edition.

The Forced Marriage etc. (Protection and Jurisdiction) (Scotland) Act 2011.

Part 2

Adulthood

Chapter 4

Creating safer spaces for the empowerment of self-identified disabled women

Reflecting on a study from Iceland

Freyja Haraldsdóttir

Introduction

Through the last decade, by practising activism, I have gained increased interest in internalised oppression and the psycho-emotional effects of multiple discriminations for disabled women. I have been confronted by the emotional labour caused by having to fight for basic human rights, tackling ableism, sexism and other oppression in everyday life and needing to resist personally and politically. Over and over again, I have come across disabled women exhausted by this situation; scared, angry and hurt. What often seems to add to this situation is shame, being either desexualised or hyper-sexualised, and experiencing constant dehumanisation. For us as disabled women, to admit that we are in pain is extremely difficult, for fear that we will then be stereotyped as victims leading tragic lives.

In this chapter I explore the dynamics of direct and indirect violence against disabled women and effects for their everyday lives. I look into the psycho-emotional consequences and how oppression and violence, both sexist and ableist, can be internalised. I will also reflect on my experience of building up and working at Tabú, a feminist disability movement in Iceland, and the way we seek to shape an intersectional feminist space, where our difference is our strength and a place for unity. A space where we don't have to separate our disability from our gender; where we can be vulnerable and strong together; and where we can practice self-care and resistance and work through our internalised oppression. It is a space also where we can feel more safe and free from judgement, stigma, hate and other forms of violence. Furthermore, I will shed light on the main findings from a research project that explores the psycho-emotional effects of multiple oppression for disabled women and how it is possible to heal, become empowered, take up space and claim control of our bodies and lives.

Discussion

Disabled women across the globe have a history of being exposed to multiple systems of oppression, for example on the grounds of disability and gender and other factors such as race, class and religion (Barrett *et al.*, 2009). As Vernon (1998) stated, 'often a combination of two or more stigmatised identities can exacerbate the experience of oppression' (Nixon, 2009, 85).

Despite the lack of research available, data suggests that disabled women are at higher risk than non-disabled women and disabled men of being abused and experiencing violence in their lifetime (Attard and Price-Kelly, 2010; World Health Organization (WHO), 2011). In the United Kingdom 50 per cent of disabled women experience violence at some point in their lives (Shah, Tsitsou and Woodin, 2016) and the same goes for Australia (Attard and Price-Kelly, 2010). Existing research also reveals that women with learning disabilities are at an even greater risk of being survivors of violence. For example, findings show that 68 per cent of Australian girls with learning disabilities will experience sexual abuse and adult women with the same label are four times more likely to experience sexual abuse or assault compared to non-disabled women (Pestka and Wendt, 2014).

Direct and indirect violence

As for many oppressed groups, disabled women can experience violence in different ways and spaces than non-disabled women. The violence is not always direct, or as Johan Galtung (2007, 151), a theorist in peace studies, would define as 'harming others with intentions'. Exploring disabled women's experiences of violence from the standpoint of peace studies theories can be helpful to understand the complexities. The discrimination and oppression that disabled women encounter are not always seen as violence because they are not always a particular act of a particular person/group. Galtung (2007) suggests that indirect violence can be defined as both *cultural and structural*. Cultural violence makes oppression and other forms of violence, for example, sexism and ableism, look normal and acceptable, at least so it is not seen as wrong. The violence becomes a mundane part of the structure of society. Both those who go through the violence and those who are perpetrators, directly and indirectly, often do not see this culture as violent. The power imbalance is seen as something that has always existed and is inevitable, for example, forced sterilisations of disabled women, and public discourse through the media and other representations of disabled women as desexualised and dependent victims (Galtung, 2007; Haraldsdóttir, 2017).

Cultural violence, therefore, is in a way what keeps structural violence going. Structural violence can cause power imbalance where, e.g. disabled women are in little or no control over their situations or actions and are put in a position of powerlessness (Haraldsdóttir, 2017). It is when political, economic and cultural structures, slowly but surely, cause massive suffering for societies and/ or socially devalued groups. The harm comes with time (sometimes referred to as slow death) from unjust structures of society, being deprived of freedom of choice and access to personal and public decision making on one's own issues. It is when socio-political structures and decisions hinder people's access to 'basic needs necessary for fulfilling one's own potentials in life' (Galtung, 2007, 151). As Galtung (2007) points out, structural violence is deeply rooted in harmful masculine attitudes, which write off the seriousness of violence and normalise violent structures by demanding that oppressed people do not complain. At the same time, oppressors are pushed towards not giving in to change and sticking to the status quo. The violence is subtle and invisible (Haraldsdóttir, 2017). Lydia Brown (2016) an autistic, disability queer activist of colour, explains ableist violence, direct and indirect:

> We know hate and we know violence, because it is written on our bodies and our souls. We bear it, heavy, wherever we go. Ableism is the violence in the clinic, in the waiting room, in the social welfare lines, in the class-room, in the recess yard, in the bedroom, in the prisons, in the streets. Ableism is the violence (and threat of violence) we live with each day.
>
> (Brown, 2016)

In my research on the psycho-emotional effects of multiple oppression for disabled women with various impairments, the participants experienced multiple forms of oppression in different areas and times in their lives. The oppression represented itself through direct violence, e.g. physical abuse, sexual abuse and verbal abuse. Also, the representation was through more subtle and indirect ways like structural and cultural violence and micro-aggressions. All the women encountered experiencing oppression in multiple spaces and there were not many places they could be sure to be safe or feel comfortable. The spaces they mentioned feeling unsafe and uneasy on regular basis were in family settings, among friends, in the school and health care system, with social services, in disability and feminist movements, through the media, on the internet and out on the streets (Haraldsdóttir, 2017).

This echoes other research that shows that disabled women often lack resources, appropriate services and access, and are exposed to a great amount of stigma, for example, concerning their bodies, independence, sexuality and humanity, which put them in a position of powerlessness. That easily deprives them of opportunities to control their lives, participate in society, work or study and be mobile. This can lead to being stuck in abusive situations and institutionalisation, and therefore experiencing less safety (Hague, Mullender and Thaira, 2011).

Internalised ableism and sexism

Experiencing oppression over a lifetime can lead to internalised oppression for disabled women, where we start to take in the messages of being inferior and abnormal or belonging to a group that is stigmatised similarly. Internalised oppression can operate on a group and individual level, with the aim of keeping people oppressed and at the same time maintaining the power and privileges of the oppressors. At an individual level, self-loathing or self-hatred can lead to addiction, anger and sometimes violence (Sue, 2010). In addition, research suggests that even though indirect violence seems harmless and innocent, it can be just as harmful, or perhaps even more so, for example in hate crimes. Oppressed groups often find it easier to deal with straightforward attacks because 'no guesswork is involved in discerning the motives of the perpetrators' (Sue, 2010, 23).

Internalised sexism is a subtle but almost inevitable part of girls' and women's lives, and it can intersect with other forms of internalised oppression, for example, racial, ableist and ageist oppression. It is when women believe they are inferior and do not deserve equal treatment to men. Just like intimate partner violence, rape and other forms of direct violence can be harmful and traumatising for women. Differently manifested discrimination, like not getting equal pay or being devalued in educational settings, can also be harmful, cause pain and add to daily stress factors.

According to several US studies disabled women who have experienced violence have greater health difficulties and depend more on health services than disabled women who have not been subjected to violence and the non-disabled women who have experienced violence. Disabled women are often dependent upon the people who are violent for assistance with daily living and professional support. They have a history of being disbelieved by the people around them when they share with them incidents of violence. Also, traditional definitions of violence do not in all aspects capture the abusive situations disabled women experience, so it is very difficult for them to leave situations of violence without jeopardising their lives (Hague, Mullender and Thiara, 2011).

Based on my research on the psycho-emotional effects of oppression for disabled women, the emotional consequences varied but, despite different age and impairment, the participants' experience was in many ways similar. Many of the women in the research encountered that they were tired or exhausted from needing to fight for their rights and go through the system to find appropriate help on daily basis, doing activism, needing to constantly educate others, prove themselves in different spaces or keep up an image to resist stereotypes or stigma. In the worst cases, they experienced burnout and stopped seeking the support they needed. Stress, anxiety and fear took a toll on many of the participants and seemed to be a matter of fact in their life. Often they did not disclose that to anyone. Their anxiety mostly revolved around social situations in public spaces, lack of information, inappropriate services and difficulty in communicating with sign language interpreters or personal assistants (Haraldsdóttir, 2017).

Some of the women regularly felt frustrated and angry. They found it difficult to deal with such emotions and some felt bad for being irritated with people around them. These instances were usually related to lack of access, paternalistic behaviours of professionals and support workers, micro-aggression in public spaces and bullying. Anger seemed to be a very troubling emotion for them, because it does not sit well with preconceived ideas about disability and femininity. As disabled people we are supposed to be thankful and resilient, and as women we are supposed to behave ourselves and be polite. Overall, shame concerning multiple emotions was apparent, because almost all the women felt they should not show anger, express anger or feel anger – even in extremely violent and frustrating circumstances, e.g. where you are being bullied or cannot access important settings. The majority of the women felt like they were not entitled to feel, and like they experienced pressure to stay happy and not complain. Complaining was often dismissed or belittled by others, so in a way they did not see the point of mentioning discomfort or unhappiness. Also, their experience of victimisation made them uneasy when they admitted they were not always happy, or sometimes resented their impairment or related oppression. They also discussed that they felt uncomfortable talking about what they were going through personally, in fear of being a burden. This closely interconnected with the feeling of being dependent on family, friends and service systems. Also, the system's reaction to their requirements or disclosure of discomfort, made them feel like they were a financial burden. The women also felt that politicians sometimes made them feel like a burden by their discourse and emphasis (Haraldsdóttir, 2017).

Some of the women had experienced partial or extensive trauma through their lives and often because of ableist structures, violence and prejudice. Some had suicidal thoughts or had attempted suicide and two developed unhealthy relationships with alcohol and sex, to numb the pain they were going through (Haraldsdóttir, 2017). The feeling of being dehumanised and desexualised, as an effect of discrimination and oppression, in their everyday lives, was apparent. When dehumanisation intersects with desexualisation, an attack on women's identity occurs in multiple ways. The women shared feelings of disgust towards their bodies, movement and speech and found that sexist micro-aggression often takes away their confidence in a split second. It is of concern that the women used terms like 'a piece of trash' in reference to themselves and found themselves in a position where they have to 'become' real women by ticking some gender boxes that an ableist and sexist society has made (Haraldsdóttir, 2017).

Healing and empowerment

Research shows that people experiencing internalised oppression often do not seek help (Sue, 2010). Also, depression has been shown to decrease when internalised oppression is a central focus of therapy (Watermayer and Görgans, 2014). From personal experience of activism, offering counselling and research work, I have come to realise that many disabled girls and women have had bad encounters when seeking counselling from psychiatrists, social workers and doctors or do not access services for fear that they will be stigmatised. This is a serious matter and a violation of the UN convention on the rights of disabled people. It emphasises that disabled women and girls are often at greater risk of being victims of violence and experience multiple discrimination. It is thereby stated in Article 6 of the convention that:

> States Parties shall take all appropriate measures to ensure the full development, advancement and empowerment of women, for the purpose of guaranteeing them the exercise and enjoyment of the human rights and fundamental freedoms set out in the present Convention.
>
> (United Nations, 2006)

Article 16 states that victims of violence should be secured the right to 'physical, cognitive and psychological recovery, rehabilitation and social reintegration' (United Nations, 2006). It also states that:

> Such recovery and reintegration shall take place in an environment that fosters the health, welfare, self-respect, dignity and autonomy of the person and takes into account gender- and age-specific needs.
>
> (United Nations, 2006)

In addition, in Article 26, peer support is stated to be optional for disabled people:

> States Parties shall take effective and appropriate measures, including through peer support, to enable persons with disabilities to attain and maintain maximum independence, full physical, mental, social and vocational ability, and full inclusion and participation in all aspects of life.
>
> (United Nations, 2006)

Donna Reeve (2010) argues that counsellors often hold the same views and stereotypes of disabled people as the rest of society and therefore ongoing oppression can take place in the counselling room (Reeve, 2010). This relates closely to the discourse of critical psychology that criticises mainstream psychology for institutionalising 'a narrow view of the field's ethical mandate to promote human welfare' (Austin, Fox and Prilleltensky, 2009, 3). Albee (1990) pointed out that defining a problem that confronts thousands and even millions of people as 'individual' was absurd and would decrease advocacy for social change (Austin, Fox and Prilleltensky, 2009). Most critical psychologists, despite political diversity, believe that something is fundamentally wrong when a discipline fails to challenge unjust societal practices and instead reinforces them, sometimes for their own good.

In relation to disability, Reeve (2010) argues, in this sense, that counsellors are often not aware of their disableist attitudes, which can lead to oppressive situations for disabled clients (Reeve, 2010). Disabled people seek counselling for various reasons, just like non-disabled people, but additionally may need therapy or counselling because of hard experiences of structural barriers, from the medical system and other oppression. Reeve suggests that 'disability counselling' could enable disabled people to 'deal with the relationship between the experience of individual impairment and the experience of a disabling society' (Reeve, 2010, 671) where people could choose whether the counsellor was disabled or not and where the social model of disability would ground the practice.

Although it is possible to agree with Reeve, it is necessary to acknowledge more directly what Lorde and Smith phrased well: 'there is no such thing as a single-issue struggle because we don't live single-issue lives' (Lorde and Smith, 1985, 57). Disabled women are likely to be subjected to oppression on the grounds of gender and disability, as well as possibly other factors, likes race, class and age. Therefore, I would argue that it is important for disabled women to have access to counselling and therapy that is aware of disability oppression and gender dynamics. In that case, feminist therapy is an approach that listens to and privileges the voices and experiences of women and other persons who have been perceived as 'the other'. It is practiced in a way where people are seen as 'responsive to the problems of their lives, capable of solving those problems, and desirous of change' (Brown, 2010, 113). Also, it is important that the psychotherapy process is brought into the social and political contexts, which take into account the constructions of gender, power and powerlessness. The therapy evolves, not only on the therapy itself, but the everyday life of the person seeking counselling and the politics of power and privilege in our social structure and culture. Unlike in traditional psychotherapies, feminist therapy as a model does not have particular treatment goals, but the treatment outcome is determined and assessed in collaboration with the client. Therefore, the power to define outcome is in the client's hand (Brown, 2010).

Finally, it is interesting, in relation to critiquing the issue of therapy, to consider peer counselling and disability, with roots in the Independent Living Movement. Again, the problem is positioned outside the person and the aim is to reflect on what, in the person's environment, has to be changed for them to have a better life. In peer counselling the counsellor is a disabled person as well, so that a client can have the opportunity to model someone who has similar experience and understands the politics of disablism and ableism. Peer counselling comes in many forms, is available both on an individual level and in groups, as well as being practiced in therapeutic and activism work (Sisco, 1992).

Looking back on my research on psycho-emotional effects of oppression for disabled women in Iceland, it is important to stress, before focusing on how the women in the research practiced healing and resistance, that, in their view, these psycho-emotional effects are first and foremost a consequence of ableist and sexist imbalanced power structures and oppressive systems and cultures. But while we strive for social change and, in some ways, heal and resist in that striving, we cannot escape our personal lives. When living in a world that stigmatises and defines disability and illness as tragic and something to 'cure' or make disappear, claiming power over self-identification is a radical act of resistance and healing according to some of the women in the research. Disabled women are so used to being the objects of definition and representation of others that they have little control over the discourse around their identity. Most of them have complicated relationships with the term disability because it has been in the hands of non-disabled people who define it as something that has gone wrong, is broken, a burden and disruptive for society. Some of the women still shy away from the term, not because having an impairment is negative in itself, but because they do not want to undergo the negative and dominant discourse of disability. Others have reclaimed the power of the definition and embraced being disabled as more of a sign of diversity, belonging to disability culture and benefitting from seeing the world from a different and meaningful perspective (Haraldsdóttir, 2017).

The women in the research tried various ways to push back oppressive attitudes, micro-aggression and other forms of cultural and structural violence. For some, they just had to take the battle where they were standing/sitting but others experienced some kind of momentum, where they had enough and started to work towards change. With that in mind, the women also talked about the importance of gaining knowledge on intersectionality, and that they could also be experiencing sexism though it tends to 'hide behind ableism'. It was interesting that, despite struggling with seeing their disabled bodies as feminine, they saw femininity as a form of strength, independence, speaking up for themselves and setting boundaries, even though it also involved more traditional views of wearing dresses and putting lipstick on. In relation to the latter, it is important to realise that, for a disabled woman, it can be a strong form of resistance to sexism intersected with ableism to act on traditional gender roles, because, in a way, we are reconstructing definitions of both femininity and disability. The women all discussed the importance of the support of their family and friends and having an opportunity to seek encouragement and empathy from people around them as well as the importance of feeling their experience was taken seriously and the ways they were feeling were accepted (Haraldsdóttir, 2017).

The women explained that having access to peer support in the disability community was vital, as was meeting others who were going through the same experience. Two young women stressed the importance of participating in disability youth groups and others to have access to safe spaces for disabled women. A woman with mental health difficulties discussed that it was important for her to be a part of a group of women and to have a friend with similar experiences. In that sense, most women believed in the importance of breaking the silence for self-healing and the healing of others in similar situations. They also believed that the power of disabled women's stories is important. A woman without sight said that solidarity among disabled women is vital. She explained that a cross-disability approach was important because, if women with specific impairments only worked together, the groups would be to small, confidentiality would become a problem and it would more likely develop into a group of friends then an activist group:

> By working across borders of disability we learn to break down walls of prejudice inside the disability community. I learned so much by taking the workshop at Tabú because the group was so diverse.

She added:

> The most important thing would be to become collective, that disabled women would get to know each other like we did in the workshop, tighten our group and build a community. They would be united. They would get people's attention and make others pay attention to what they stand for – together.
>
> (Haraldsdóttir, 2017)

Creating safer spaces and resisting violence

In this part of the chapter I will shed light on intersectionality and how disabled women often fall between the cracks of different movements. Also, I will share my experience of building up Tabú and working for the empowerment of disabled women.

Being at the intersections: disability and gender

Intersectionality is a definition used to describe the experiences of people who face oppression on the grounds of multiple factors. It acknowledges that systems of gender, ability, race, age and social class are mutually constructed features of organisation (Collins, 2002). Intersectionality rejects categorisations of identities and challenges 'the essential views of groups, single-axis analyses and additive models of identity' (Artiles, 2013, 336).

Intersectionality acknowledges that within marginalised groups there are people with different identities. Not only because they may belong to other marginalised groups, but also because they can have different experience and backgrounds. When denied, it can contribute to tension within groups and marginalise members even further (Crenshaw, 1994). As Audre Lorde (2007, Kindle location 1884), stated: 'I find I am constantly being encouraged to pluck out some one aspect of myself and present this as the meaningful whole, eclipsing or denying the other parts of self.' Ágústsdóttir (2015), a queer feminist disabled activist, points out a similar viewpoint:

In my case, and probably most, it is impossible to break to pieces the discrimination I encounter. I can't be disabled on Mondays, a woman on Tuesdays and a lesbian on Wednesdays to fit better into social movements' agenda's each time.

(Ágústsdóttir, 2015, 69)

Disabled women experience being marginalised inside disability justice spaces and feminist spaces, both where activism takes place and in the academia. As women our voice is not heard where disability is up for discussion and as disabled we are not heard where gender issues are in the forefront. In relation to violence, Nixon (2009) points out that feminist, non-disabled women have often been hesitant to change definitions of violence and broaden the gender-based approach because of the fear that it will affect the safeguarding of women. Furthermore, disabled people organisations have been hesitant to realise that gender is a factor for the fear of losing a holistic approach in disabled people's rights activism (Nixon, 2009). Sometimes, intersections of other identities, for example, race or sexual orientation, also comes in the way of the agenda of different organisations or developing theories. There is a tendency to believe that each group should take care of itself. This can lead to ignorance and even competition between groups.

As a disabled feminist activist, former politician and scholar myself, I can relate to this dilemma. When working for The Independent Living Movement in Iceland in a leading role as a director I found that disabled and non-disabled men dismissed me and belittled my efforts. I was accused of being too sensitive or 'caught up' in the personal matters of the disabled people I was working with and for. I was supposed to be *political* and focused on *disability*. As a feminist I felt excluded by access barriers and ableist micro-aggressions in the feminist movements in Iceland and found that when I, and other disabled women and comrades, brought up disability issues or pointed out that we were being excluded, we were, as Sara Ahemed would call it, *killjoys* (Ahmed, 2010). We were spoiling the mood and disrupting solidarity among women (and disabled people). There was a great divide in the understanding that disabled and non-disabled women were facing similar and different issues that were based on sexism. There came a point where we had enough and started our own feminist disability movement: Tabú.

Tabú: a feminist disability movement

In 2014, my colleague, friend and comrade, Embla Guðrúnar Ágústsdóttir, and I, decided to leave our former jobs at the Independent Living Movement and follow our instincts, forming a feminist disability movement. We packed our bags and went out in the country for a weekend and shaped the foundation for Tabú. We wanted to make a safer space for disabled women, cross-disability, to come together and share our stories with each other and society.

We wanted to be uncomfortable for the mainstream and discuss issues that disabled women are often prohibited to talk about: sexuality, motherhood, sex with others, masturbation, different forms of violence, body shame and more. First and foremost, we wanted it to be a place for disabled women to become empowered, through learning about the collective struggle of other disabled women, with the hope that they could personally and politically, eventually, take a stand one way or the other against violence and towards social change. We wanted it to be platform, not an organisation, and we did not want hierarchies, but a community that could be responsive and quick in its reactions when the need came and when we felt like it. It started with a blog and a Facebook page. We were conscious that it would take a long time for things to get moving. Now, 3 years later, we are a group of 30 disabled women who have published over 100 articles, organised protests and workshops, participated in intersectional activism with other minority groups, influenced policies, regulations, law reforms and practice and become very well recognised in Iceland.

Workshops: the personal in the political

Tabú has developed in multiple ways in working with disabled women and one of them is through workshops. They have developed through time but the aim is always to offer disabled women a space to learn, share and claim power over their stories, bodies and lives. The workshops have been from 4–10 weeks where we meet for 3 hours at a time with breaks included. For the last workshop we, for the first time, met up with all the participants beforehand, heard of their expectations and concerns, and answered questions they had. That was important for those who led the workshops because, with the knowledge we gained from meeting them, we were better equipped to respond to the women's needs and expectations and shape the themes of the workshops.

We start each workshop by defining, as a group, how the space can be safe. This leads to important discussions about different experiences and needs and makes the group aware of how we can better support each other. As disabled women, we are not often used to thinking about what makes a space safe, even though we often feel very unsafe. For us, the process of creating a space that is safe brings the women closer together; they share what makes them feel unsafe, realise that they are not alone being afraid in oppressive public and personal spaces, and learn to understand each other better. Even though the definitions of safer spaces can vary between groups, there are certain themes that come up each time:

- confidentiality;
- accessibility;
- respecting different opinions and experiences;
- free from ableist and sexist language;

- respect for different ways of communication and expression;
- no fear of accepting and refusing help;
- an opportunity to enjoy feeling both happy and sad together, and everything in between;
- room for being ourselves.

(Ágústsdóttir and Haraldsdóttir, 2016)

Following this, on each day of the workshop we have a certain theme to discuss. We explore what disability means to us, as well as talking about sexism, ableism, violence and body image. Embla and I deliver short presentations and then we have group discussions. Throughout the workshop we have assignments where participants write diaries about what is going through their minds (not mandatory). Also, we encourage the women to write themselves a letter, to their younger selves and, if they wish, to share it with the group. This has been a very successful tool to help the group connect, share and empathise with each other.

In writing this chapter I have sought knowledge and experience from my sisters in Tabú. What they stress is the meaning of having a space where they can come together, in their feelings of joy, sadness, anger and hope, where they are a part of a community and their feelings, humanity and gender, is validated. María Hreiðarsdóttir, a woman with learning disabilities and an activist in Tabú, explained that:

A safe space to me is to be at a place where people understand what I say and who are in similar situations. And who respect me. Also, I have gained better consciousness on equality and human rights.

(Hreiðarsdóttir, M, personal communication,
15 March 2017)

Sigríður Jónsdóttir, a woman with a physical impairment and an activist in Tabú adds:

To me it means intimacy that involves shared understanding through shared experience, which still is diverse. Safe space leads to self-identification and empathy. We are far from being alone in our experience. In a safe space you find power. In a safe space you gain the power to develop the discourse and define your experience. In a safe space there are no 'victims'. In a safe space our stories are important and valid.

(Jónsdóttir, S, personal communication, 16 March 2017)

Þorbera Fjölnisdóttir, another woman with a physical impairment and an activist in Tabú said:

I care about our safe space, precisely because it is ours. We made it and defined it by ourselves. Our shared experience, as disabled women, ties us together. We don't need to explain ourselves or justify anything because we understand. The workshops shaped the ground for the safe space. There we always got some specific topics for thought and to discuss. It was informative and sometimes painful but to laugh and cry together made us so close and for that I'm grateful.

(Fjölnisdóttir, personal communication,
15 March 2017)

Speaking out: the political in the personal

In working closely and intimately with each other we have built up courage and strength to step forward and use our personal empowerment for social change. Tabú's webpage has become an important tool to share articles by disabled women and interviews. We have also, collectively, written critical statements about matters that are close to our heart, for example, disabled women refugees, discrimination against disabled children and institutional violence. Presenting these different voices of disabled women has made the activism against violence, ableism and sexism more accountable and powerful in the past 3 years we have gained a lot of attention through the public media. We have achieved this by breaking silence about discrimination on the labour market, sexual freedom of disabled women, violence and how it can manifest differently in disabled women's lives. We are challenging traditional discourses and practices, through mechanisms such as writing statements and testimonies about parliamentary bills, regulations drafts and policies, and sometimes receiving more seats at the table where big decisions are being made (though, not often enough). We are also breaking barriers between disabled women and seeing more diverse groups of disabled women cooperating successfully, e.g. women with hidden impairments.

As a way of healing and empowerment we have participated in public events like the *Slut Walk of Reykjavík* where we have come together as a group of disabled women and taken up space and claimed power by defining our identities and struggles. It has not only been empowering and change making for the women in Tabú to march down the streets of Reykjavík screaming 'Stop rape' or 'I'm a slut', but also to take part in the preparation. Discussing what themes we want to have, designing protest signs and finding creative ways to remove barriers to attending an event like this can be deeply meaningful. It can also be part of a healing process from the harm of life-long oppression and violence.

What has also been a part of our empowerment and healing is the collective work we engage in across the margins, for example, within the queer movement, anti-racism activist spaces and weight-stigma organisations. Together with Samtökin '78, the Queer Movement of Iceland and Trans Ísland, the trans organisation of Iceland, we planned a 2-day conference and a grassroot festival, titled *Disturbing Existence*, where different marginalised groups came together, shared experience and explored the difference and sameness in our struggles, looking at how we can all be more inclusive and work better together for social change (Truflandi tilvist, 2017).

Conclusions

Violence and oppression on the grounds of disability and gender are neither individual problems nor disabled women's responsibility to solve. It is a consequence of a patriarchal system and power imbalance which we need to fight against with better laws, justice systems, social services and health care, access, political participation and inclusive social movements and activism. On the other hand, while we keep fighting for social change and pushing for revolutions, we need to take care of ourselves and have access to emotional support and mental health care that respects our whole selves, not just bits and pieces. It is our human right.

Creating feminist safer spaces like Tabú can be extremely beneficial for disabled women so they can take control and power over their self-identification and life stories – sharing them with other women whom they identify with and trust, and even engage politically and publicly. Also, I find it important that disabled women can access mental health care where there is knowledge, not only about impairments, but disability as an identity and a social location. In addition, intersectional approaches, acknowledging and celebrating difference, are necessary so gender, racial and classist dynamics are recognised within therapy. Finally, I would suggest that collaboration between activist spaces, peer support groups, and the mental health care system, could benefit everyone and offer disabled women holistic ways in working through their internalised oppression and violence related trauma. The political and the personal must go hand in hand for the empowerment and healing for disabled women.

Key messages from this chapter

- When tackling violence in disabled women's lives it is highly important to acknowledge the harm that both direct and subtle violence can do. This needs to be addressed without victimising them or approaching their lives as not worth living.
- When tackling violence in disabled women's lives intersectionality is key. We need to think of gender and disability, as well as sexuality, race, class etc.
- When tackling violence in disabled women's lives we need to accept that it is both political and personal. It is a consequence of a patriarchal system and power imbalance. This can be addressed with reforms to legal and justice systems, social and health care services; through political participation and activism of disabled women; and by creating feminist safer spaces for disabled women and girls to take control over their self-identification,

bodies and life stories. The work that goes on in political spaces and personal spaces needs to go hand in hand.

References

Ágústsdóttir, E. G. (2015). Fötluð á mánudögum, kona á þriðjudögum og samkynhneigð á miðvikudögum? 19 June, 68-70.

Ágústsdóttir, E. G. and Haraldsdóttir, F. (2016, July). The Power of Dealing with the Personal to Become Political: Disabled Women's Feminist Activism in Iceland. Paper presented at Theorising Normalcy and the Mundane: (Re)claiming the Human: In Times of Crisis, Manchester Metropolitan University.

Ahmed, S. (2010). *The Promise of Happiness*. Durham and London: Duke University Press.

Artiles, A. J. (2013). Untangling the Racialization of Disabilities: An Intersectionality Critique Across Disability Models. *Du Bois Review*, 10(2), 329–347.

Attard, M. and Price-Kelly, S. (ed.). (2010). *Accommodating Violence. The Experience of Domestic Violence and People with Disability Living in Licenced Boarding Houses*. Sydney: People with Disability Australia.

Austin, S., Fox, D. and Prilleltensky, I. (2009). Critical Psychology for Social Justice: Concerns and Dilemmas. In Fox, D., Prilleltensky, I. and Austin, S. (eds) *Critical Psychology: An Introduction* (2nd ed.). London: SAGE, pp. 3–19.

Barrett, K. A., Carlson, B. L., O'Day, B. and Roche, A. (2009). Intimate Partner Violence, Health Status, And Health Care Access Among Women with Disabilities. *Women's Health Issues*, 19, 94–100.

Brown, L. S. (2010). *Feminist Therapy*. Washington, DC: American Psychology Association.

Brown, L. X. Z. (2016). Ableism is Not 'Bad Words.' It's Violence. Retrieved 25 July 2016: www.autistichoya.com/2016/07/ableism-is-not-bad-words-its-violence.html.

Collins, P. H. (2002). *Black Feminist Thought: Knowledge, Consciousness, and the Politics of Empowerment*. (2nd ed.). London: Routledge.

Crenshaw, K. (1994). Mapping the Margins: Intersectionality, Identity Politics, and Violence Against Women of Color. In Albertson Fineman, M. and Mykitiuk, R. (eds) *The Public Nature of Private Violence*. New York: Routledge, 93–118.

Galtung, J. (2007). Introduction: Peace by Peaceful Conflict Transformation – the TRANSCEND Approach. In Galtung, Í. J. and Webel, C. (eds). *Handbook of Peace and Conflict Studies*. New York: Routledge, pp. 14–34.

Hague, G., Mullender, A. and Thiara, R. K. (2011). Losing Out on Both Counts: Disabled Women and Domestic Violence. *Disability and Society*, 26(6), 757–771.

Haraldsdóttir, F. (2017). 'I Am Discriminated against Because I Exist': Psycho-emotional Effects of Multiple Oppressions for Disabled Women in Iceland (Master Thesis). The University of Iceland, Reykjavík.

Lorde, A. (1982). *Zami: A New Spelling of My Name*. New York: Crown.

Lorde, A. (2007). *Sister Outsider: Essays and Speeches*. New York: Crown.

Lorde, A. and Smith, C. (1985). *The Cancer Journals*. San Francisco, CA: Sheba Feminist Press.

Nixon, J. (2009). Domestic Violence and Women with Disabilities: Locating the Issue on the Periphery of Social Movements. *Disability and Society*, 24(1), 77–89.

Prilleltensky, O. (2009). Critical Psychology and Disability Studies: Critiquing the Mainstream, Critiquing the Critique. In Fox, D., Prilleltensky, I. and Austin, S. (eds). *Critical Psychology: An Introduction* (2nd ed.). London: SAGE, pp. 250–266.

Reeve, D. (2010). Oppression Within the Counselling Room. *Disability and Society*, 15(4), 669–682.

Shah, S., Tsitsou, L. and Woodin, S. (eds). (2014). Access to Specialised Victim Support Services for Women with Disabilities Who Have Experienced Violence. Retrieved 16 August 2016: http://women-disabilities-violence.humanrights.at/resources/national-report-united-kingdom-empirical-report.

Shah, S., Tsitsou, L. and Woodin, S. (2016). Hidden Voices: Disabled Women's Experiences of Violence and Support over the Life Course. *Violence against Women*, 22(10), 1189–1210.

Sisco, P. (1992). *Peer Counselling and Overview*. Retrieved 7 May.

Sue, D. W. (2010). Microaggressions, Marginality, and Oppression. In Sue, D. W. (ed.) *Microaggressions and Marginality: Manifestation, Dynamics, and Impact*. New Jersey: John Wiley, Kindle location pp. 236–660.

Tabú. (2014). Um Tabú. Retrieved 3 December 2016: http://tabu.is/tabu/um-tabu/.

United Nations. (2006). Convention on the Rights of Persons with Disabilities. Retrieved 25 August 2016: www.un.org/disabilities/default.asp?id=259.

Watermeyer, B. and Görgens, T. (2014) Disability and Internalized Oppression. In David, E. J. R. (ed.) *Internalized Oppression: The Psychology of Marginalized Groups*. New York: Springer, pp. 253–281.

World Health Organization. (2011). *World Report on Disability*. Geneva: World Health Organization.

Chapter 5

Malaysian disabled women's experiences of healthcare settings

A qualitative study

Aizan Sofia Amin

Introduction

As a post-colonial country, Malaysia has undergone significant improvements and transformations in disability welfare since the period of imperialism. Currently the primary welfare provider is the Department of Social Welfare (DSW) under the Ministry of Women, Family and Community Development (MWFCD). Other ministries such as the Ministry of Health (MOH), Ministry of Education (MOE) and Ministry of Human Resource (MOHR) are also responsible for supporting disabled people in matters pertaining to healthcare, education and employment. The DSW defines a disabled person as:

> Any person who is unable to obtain for himself/herself, fully or partially, the normal requirements of an individual and/or is unable to participate fully in the community due to shortcomings either physically or mentally and whether it occurred since birth or later in life.
>
> (Department of Social Welfare, 2009)

It has been argued that the definition used by the DSW is based on the medical approach (Kuno, 2007), which focuses on impairments rather than environmental restrictions (Sinnasamy, 2006). However, the Persons with Disabilities Act 2008 (Act 685) or PWDA 2008 defines disabled people differently:

> Persons with disabilities include those with long term physical, mental, intellectual or sensory impairments which in interaction with multiple barriers may hinder their full and effective participation in society.
>
> (Persons with Disabilities Act, 2008: 8)

The PWDA 2008 definition integrates the medical model and the social model of disability in contrast to the DSW definition that is solely focused on impairment. However, both definitions are used concurrently in the Malaysian practice. In the post-independence era Malaysian women have gradually enjoyed equal opportunities in their access to basic social needs and services. They have gained significant life improvements and play important roles at the family, organisation and societal level in contributing to the national agenda, together with men (MWFCD, 2007). As a member of the United Nation Human Rights Council (UNHRC), Malaysia has signed the Convention on the Elimination of All Forms of Discrimination against Women (CEDAW) in 1980, and acceded to the Convention in 1995 with some reservations[1] (UN Women Regional Office for Asia and the Pacific, 2013). In January 2001, the Ministry of Women's Affairs was established and later it was expanded and renamed as the Ministry of Women and Family Development in February 2001. In March 2004, the roles and functions of the Ministry were further broadened and subsequently the Ministry was restructured and renamed as the Ministry of Women, Family and Community Development (MWFCD), which is also responsible for looking after disabled people (MWFCD, 2013).

Discussion

Gender norms

Disability is argued to have some relation to gender (Thomas, 1999) and culture (Riddell and Watson, 2003). Women's identities are acquired through their reference to gender norms that make up their social worlds (Thomas, 1999). Gender is not the biological difference between male and female, rather the socio-cultural distinction between men and women (Oakley, 1972). Gender norms are therefore:

> Socially-constructed ideals, scripts, expectations for how to be a woman or a man; [. . .] they determine who does what, to whom, when, and how.
> (Wallace and Wilchins, 2013: 1)

Gender norms play significant roles in how women are perceived within a society and thus disabled women may be perceived differently across cultures. This section will explore how cultural conceptions of the traditional gender roles, and societal stereotypes of what constitutes 'femininity', may influence disabled women's lives.

In any given society, especially in traditional societies, men and women are expected to perform different gender roles (Thomas and Thomas, 1998).

---

1   Malaysia ratified the CEDAW with some reservations on Article 5 (a), 7 (b), article 9, paragraph 2, article 16.1 (a) and paragraph 2. 'The Government of Malaysia declares that Malaysia's accession is subject to the understanding that the provisions of the Convention do not conflict with the provisions of the Islamic Sharia' law and the Federal Constitution of Malaysia' (UN Women, 2009).

Gender roles are determined by historical, ideological, ethnic, religious, economic and cultural factors. Malaysia, for example, still maintains strong traditional gender roles within its society. Although recently women in Malaysia have been given opportunities to play significant roles outside the family, they are still bound to the traditional socio-cultural values of Malaysian society. Traditionally, the role of women in Malaysia is associated with engaging with the family, marriage and children (Yun, 1984). The traditional role of women is to take responsibility for all domestic chores and to undergo the basic duties of a wife and mother, such as cooking, cleaning and caring for the household (NGO Shadow Report Group, 2005). Moreover, women in the family-building stage tend not to work, as the primary focus is given to the family (Chattopadhyay, 1997).

Disability can therefore have a profound impact on disabled women's ability to carry out traditionally expected gender roles because disabled women are stereotyped as 'incomplete' (Mehrotra, 2008: 40) and perceived as unqualified to perform such roles. Disabled women in rural areas of South Sulawesi Indonesia for example were viewed as incapable of carrying out domestic activities within the family (Schuller *et al.*, 2010). Disabled women in Arab countries are also subjected to gender-based prejudice and many disabled women suffer from 'double discrimination' due to prejudiced perceptions and discrimination against them (Nagata, 2003). Some studies have also suggested that disabled women may be less likely to get married than disabled men and non-disabled women (Nagata, 2003) due to the societal perception that their disability will prevent them from fulfilling the traditional gender roles within a family (Begum, 1992). As Thomas and Thomas argue:

> Many people carry the misconception that because of her physical disability, a woman may not be competent in any sphere, and that a physically disabled woman is also unable to think, learn or work.
>
> (Thomas and Thomas, 1998: 61)

In addition, disabled women are also subjected to societal stereotypes of what constitutes 'femininity'. For example, physical appearance has something to do with the cultural norms of how society determines the ideal concept of physical image. Disabled women may be most 'disadvantaged' in the cultural conception of what constitutes an acceptable physical appearance within society. Lonsdale argues:

> Physical appearance has long been recognised as something which has particular relevance to women. Women in Western society are required to conform to an image which is based on certain sexual, physical and behavioural stereotypes (which also often imply certain cultural and material lifestyles).
>
> (Lonsdale, 1990: 3)

The societal conception of a woman's stereotyped image may have negative consequences for women with physical impairments who may not conform to the physical attributes traditionally embedded within society. Morris (1989), for instance, analysed disabled women's experience of paralysis and found that their feelings about their physical appearance were altered in societies which placed great emphasis on the 'beauty' of women's bodies: 'The myth of the beautiful body that society and the maker has created, define the impaired female body as unfeminine and unacceptable' (Ghai, 2009: 288). Consequently, disabled women with physical impairments may be subjected to psycho-emotional consequences and identity conflicts.

In the Malaysian context for instance, the mass media reinforces a stereo-typical image of women as young, slim and fair (All Women's Action Society (AWAM), 2003). Many advertisements also use non-disabled beautiful women to portray Malaysian women. Moreover, women on television are portrayed as weak or dependent on male characters so the locally produced women's programmes reinforced the stereotypical and traditional role of women as dependent on men (Azman and Juliana, 2005). At the same time, images of disabled women have rarely been represented on local screens. Therefore, the physical appearance of disabled women in the mass media is almost invisible and, as such, Malaysian society may not be aware of how disabled women look. In conclusion, the gender norms that are strongly embedded within society may influence disabled women's lives at the personal, familial and societal level.

Access to healthcare

Disabled women are not only subjected to the strong traditional gender roles and stereotypes within society but they also have less access to healthcare and rehabilitation services (Thomas and Thomas, 1998; The World Bank Group, 2013). This is more profound in developing countries like Malaysia with a diverse geographical population. Although the accessibility of healthcare to the general population is relatively adequate, rural populations, especially in the largest states like Sarawak, Sabah and Pahang, have limited access to the local health facilities (NGO Shadow Report Group, 2005). Hospitals or local clinics are usually located in highly populous areas, and as such, people who are living far from the heart of medical facilities may have limited access to proper medical treatment and information. This is especially so for those with mobility impairments. The MWFCD, in its Report to the United Nations Committee on CEDAW (First and Second Report), reported,

> Indirect and qualitative evidence to suggest that some groups of women (e.g. disabled/ migrant/ aboriginal or indigenous women) and those who are living or working in estates and plantations are marginalised in terms of access to health services and facilities.
>
> (NGO Shadow Report Group, 2005: 74)

Moreover, evidence suggests that the government does not have gender disaggregated data and analysis on healthcare issues although women are more likely to develop impairment at a later age due to their longer life expectancy than men in Malaysia (Noran *et al.*, 2010; Department of Statistics Malaysia, 2011). The NGO Shadow Report Group (2005) argues that there is a critical need to have gender disaggregated data and analysis for the Malaysian population. The health data collected for the country has not been subjected to gender analysis. Gender analysis is important to the population's health to identify the prevalence of diseases significant to males and females and the intervention and treatment necessary at the national level. For example, the incidence of hypertension, psychiatric morbidity and cancers (all sites) were found to be more common among females than males in the National Health and Morbidity Survey II (Ministry of Health, 1997). Therefore, without gender disaggregated data and analysis, Malaysian women may be at greater risk of acquiring disability at later age due to not having the correct intervention and treatment plan at the national level.

In addition, disabled women in Malaysia may experience socio-cultural barriers to proper healthcare treatment and rehabilitation. Some women may be unable to leave the house without their husband's permission and have no access to alternative childcare and a lack of education (NGO Shadow Report Group, 2005). Likewise, many women in a traditional society such as India, especially those who live in a village, do not go out of their houses to seek healthcare assistance if the care-provider is a male (Thomas and Thomas, 1998). Thus, the cultural attitudes towards gender, coupled with a lack of women practicing in rehabilitation professions, may dissuade disabled women from receiving adequate assistive devices and treatments (Thomas and Thomas, 1998; The World Bank Group, 2013).

Violence and abuse

In the previous sections, it has been shown how disabled women in Malaysia and elsewhere experienced significant challenges in their lives. This section develops some of these ideas to explore issues around violence and abuse towards women in Malaysia that may suggest:

> Women with a disability continue to experience social oppression and domestic violence as a consequence of gender and disability dimensions. Current explanations of domestic violence and disability inadequately explain several features that lead women who have a disability to experience violent situations.
>
> (Mays, 2006: 147)

For example, in India there is ample evidence that disabled women experience domestic and sexual abuse although it is not officially documented. A report in Orissa, India, found that 100 per cent of disabled women in the study sample were beaten at home and a quarter of women with mental health problems had been raped (Ghai, 2002). According to the 1995 United Nations Development Programme (UNDP) Human Development Report, disabled women are twice as prone to divorce, separation and violence as non-disabled women (UNDP, 1995). The United Nation panel discussion on preventing and ending violence against women with disabilities also found that:

> Women with disabilities experience higher rates of gender-based violence, sexual abuse, neglect, maltreatment and exploitation than women without disabilities. Violence may be experienced in the home and in other settings, including institutions, and may be perpetrated by care givers, family members or strangers, among others. Violence against women with disabilities can also take the form of forced medical treatment or procedures, including forced sterilisation, the incidence of which has been documented in many countries and regions.
>
> (United Nations Enable, 2012: 1)

In the context of Malaysia, women in general are more likely to be exposed to violence by their husbands or family members and also by their colleagues. A national survey conducted by Women's Aids Organisation (WAO) in 1990 to 1992 estimated that approximately 1.8 million women or 39 per cent of women above the age of 15 years were physically beaten by husbands or boyfriends (Rashidah et al., 1995). Also, 2,555 cases of domestic violence were reported to the police, 165 cases reported to the MWFCD and 636 cases were recorded by the DSW. For these reasons, Malaysia enforced the Domestic Violence Act in 1994, to allow women to acquire protection against their abusers (MWFC, 2007). However, many victims did not report their case, possibly because they were afraid of the abusers – often their own partners or family members – or felt circumscribed by the social stigma of being divorced and the concomitant impact on their children. Despite significant efforts over two decades by social activists attempting to address this issue, violence against women continues to rise and has proved difficult to eradicate (Ng et al., 2006). This may be attributed to the traditional gender stereotyping in Malaysia that places women under men's responsibility. Men thus appear to have more power over women, and violence against women is more likely to occur at home. Women who have children and are financially dependent on their husbands are also vulnerable and at risk of becoming victims of domestic violence (Aminah, 1998). WAO reported that most of the women who ran away from home and sought protection with the organisation were the victims of domestic violence (NGO Shadow Report Group, 2005). As for disabled women, their impairment can increase their vulnerability to violence and exploitation because they are arguably more likely to be in a state of physical, social and economic dependency (Driedger, 1996). For instance, it is argued that disabled women, either with physical or mental disabilities, are even more vulnerable to rape due to their inability to fight off the rapist (NGO Shadow Report Group, 2005). This suggests that disabled women in Malaysia may have a greater risk of experiencing violence and abuse in their lives than non-disabled women.

Study design and context

The empirical findings reported in this chapter are based on a PhD research conducted by the author to examine the experience of Malaysian disabled women in terms of their access to healthcare in Malaysia. This qualitative study was conducted in three states of Peninsular Malaysia: Kuala Lumpur, Selangor and Negeri Sembilan. However, the majority of informants formerly lived in other states in Malaysia; all over the country including states in Borneo. The data was collected via in-depth interviews with 33 Malaysian women with physical (mobility) impairments. The author is herself a Malaysian woman with mobility impairment and a registered counsellor, so she had an insider perspective of the issue under investigation and a professional ability to listen.

Study findings

Access to modern medicine

Access to modern (western) healthcare was difficult for many of the participants. There were many causes for this, including finance, geography and poor transport. For example, Jiaying[2] described how her family's low-income condition prevented her from getting modern medical treatment:

> From what I learned from my mother, I got Polio because of a high fever. I was about 1 year old at that time. My mother had very little money because she was only a rubber tapper. My father was a carpenter. Our life was so hard at that time because I had many brothers and sisters. I have 14 siblings [. . .]. So, when they knew that I fell sick, they took me to see a Buddhist monk. They never took me to see doctors but they always took me to pray.

Finance was not the only barrier to accessing modern healthcare among the participants; geography was another factor, as described by Farah who lived in a village and had limited transportation:

> *Researcher.* So, this means you never went to hospital? Is it that X [her village area] is a rural area that is far from a hospital?

2   All the participants' names were referred to using pseudonyms to protect their identity and to ensure anonymity.

Farah: It's quite far. My mother is poor. We were using a bicycle to travel from one place to another. That's why we never thought to go to the hospital; never going for any treatment. I went to see a doctor at the vocational centre for disabled people while I was studying there.

In the early years after independence, the Malaysian healthcare system was predominantly focused on catering for the needs of people in urban areas rather than those in rural communities. 'Rural health services were largely non-existent and, if available, were based in health centres located in small country towns' (Kamil and Teng, 2002: 99). Therefore, people in rural areas had limited access to the healthcare services provided by the state. This was confirmed by many of the women interviewed who lived far from the city.

The absence of healthcare services in rural areas and the high incidence of poverty meant that many women were brought by their families to receive traditional treatments from local traditional healers. As Ika described:

Ika: When I was 2 years old, my bone was not bending – it was normal. Then when I was in standard 1 [7 years old], it started to bend.
Researcher: When it started bending, did you see a doctor?
Ika: No, never. I just went to traditional massage – my mother took me to have a normal massage.
Researcher: Oh, so that means you have never been into a hospital?
Ika: No.

Consequently, many of the rurally located women interviewed obtained traditional rather than modern medical treatments, due to the difficulties of accessing modern healthcare. Therefore, the remedies available to them tended to be the ones offered by the local traditional healers, shamans or religious persons. It would, however, be wrong to claim that participants only turned to traditional medicine because they could not access western medicine. The use of traditional medicine was widespread among all the participants and it was clear that the majority of them, regardless of age, ethnicity, class or location, had obtained some form of traditional treatment at least once in their lifetime, often by choice. This suggests a pervasive cultural influence in their healthcare experience, which this chapter will now turn to.

The role of traditional medicine

The section above highlighted how although participants' choice of pursuing traditional medical treatments was primarily driven by participants' economic background (poverty) and their location (rurality), the majority of them had voluntarily sought traditional treatments at least once. This suggests a greater cultural influence than that of just economics and geography. For example, a Malay woman Yasmin, who came from a rural area, mentioned that her family brought her to seek various traditional treatments instead of modern medical medicine because they had little faith in the hospital:

> When I was in my hometown, my family took me to seek traditional treatments from many traditional healers. You know, villagers don't really have faith in the hospital. They thought my condition had resulted from evil spirits.

Many families believed that their daughters' impairment resulted from demonic possession or evil spirits as described by the two women below, on Hindu and the other Muslim:

> I have tried many traditional treatments since I was small. I think the last time was 10 years ago. That Hindu monk said that I was possessed by an evil spirit, so he asked me to stay in his place for two weeks.
>
> (Prema, Hindu)

> I went to see a religious person. He said it had something to do with an evil spirit. So, he used Quranic verses to treat me. He asked me to recite some verses frequently.
>
> (Nora, Muslim)

These common cultural beliefs and a tendency to seek help from the traditional healers or religious persons were evident across different ethnic groups (religions) and socio-locations. It therefore indicated that there were significant cultural and religious influences in meeting the need for a cure among the participants. As Kamil and Teng argue:

> Despite the wide availability of modern scientific healthcare services that are accessible to Malaysia's rural and remote populations, traditional healthcare services are still used by Malaysian communities for a variety of health and psychosocial problems.
>
> (Kamil and Teng, 2002: 102)

For example, Cuifen (Chinese), who lived in a city and acquired her impairment at age seven, talked about the role of traditional medicine in her life:

> No matter whether it was Indian, Malay or Chinese, we went to them all. Whenever my father heard about any good traditional healer, he took me there. He wanted me to be cured. But, it didn't work.

The actions of Cuifen's family, with their strong reliance on traditional medicine, were driven by the quest for cure. People were not interested in the type of healthcare or in its origin; all they wanted was a cure. This cultural representation of healing is complex and should be understood from different ontological levels: biomedical and psychological intervention (see Shakespeare, 2006: 112–117). Disability in Malaysian culture, as in most other cultures, is generally seen as a negative attribute that people do not want to be associated with. Many women and their families were culturally informed that having an impairment was defective and actions should be taken to eliminate it.

However, modern medicine 'failed' to cure these women and consequently they turned to traditional remedies. This life course effect caused significant psycho-emotional damage to these women as they grew up, reminding them that they were seen as 'not perfect' and 'different'. Moreover, they were influenced by their cultural and religious beliefs that created a self-perception that their impairment might be linked to demonic possessions or evil spirits and must be treated. 'Among Malaysians, and especially the Malays, the traditional belief that spiritual forces play a great role over physical and mental health is dominant' (Haque and Masuan, 2002: 277). Thus, we can see the intersectionality between disablement, economic, geography and cultural belief.

Sexual abuse in traditional settings

The strong cultural belief and traditional practice not only had a psycho-emotional impact on the women interviewed, but they were also subjected to sexual abuse by the traditional healers. For example, Ainul described how she was traumatised when her private parts were touched by her traditional healer without her consent:

> *Researcher:* So, it means he massaged your private parts? Where, your vagina or your breasts?
> *Ainul:* The vagina. When he touched it I felt scared. Then I tried to avoid him whenever he came to my parents' house. When I thought about the incident, I felt scared. I had a spinal injury and I don't feel anything from the waist to the bottom of my body. I was scared of not realising that people were taking advantage on me.

Ainul felt all the more under pressure because of her parents' belief in the traditional healer – a respected man in her village and a family friend. Therefore, she was reluctant to inform her parents of the incidents as she felt that they would not believe her and this could create tension over their relationship with that man. As a result, she kept it to herself and this caused intense emotional impact over her bodily experience.

The close relationship between the traditional healers and the families of disabled women had prevented them from exposing such incidents to their family and seeking justice. This was reinforced by the collective nature of Asian society that values religious figures and those in higher authority. Yasmin, for instance, confided that she had nearly been raped by a well-known shaman in her village:

> I was nearly raped by a shaman in my hometown. I was given a medicine and fell asleep. Then the man asked my father to wait outside the room. When we were alone in the room, he switched off the light. Fortunately, my father secretly watched through the holes of the room. When he saw the man try to rape me, he rushed into the room and saved me.

Despite the seriousness of this incident and her father's awareness of it, they did not report the sexual assault to the police. This was because the sexual perpetrator was her family's friend and therefore the incident remained secret. She has remained traumatised by the incident and has never received justice for herself. Indeed, of the 33 women interviewed, five of them confirmed they had experienced sexual assaults from their traditional healers and none of them reported it to the local authority. This can be regarded as a cultural constraint where the Malaysian culture was embedded in these women to such a degree that they were unable to challenge the respect given to religious figures and those in higher authority within their local area. As a result, this cultural influence led to significant life course impact to their physical and psychological wellbeing. Many of the women interviewed were not only subjected to sexual exploitation in traditional treatments but also in modern medical treatments; as will be described next.

Sexual abuse in modern healthcare settings

The previous section described how some of the participants were subjected to sexual exploitation by their traditional healers. Such mistreatment not only occurred in the traditional settings but also in western biomedical settings. Discussion here explores the sexual abuse in modern healthcare settings. Two women described how they were sexually abused by their healthcare professionals. Eryna, for example, told of how she was traumatised by the sexual abuse experienced in her early years:

> Then it happened in the hospital. It was my first time going to the X Hospital. Before I was referred to a specialist, I was checked by a medical doctor. He took off my clothes, everything including my underwear. I don't know what he was trying to check by doing that. But it shouldn't be [like that] as it has nothing to do with my leg. He took advantage as I was only 14 years old at that time. Why did he want to take off my underwear right? It wasn't right. It happened once before when I went to see a specialist. I didn't tell my family, I just kept it to myself.

As mentioned in the previous section, regarding the traditional settings, Eryna was also prevented from expressing her concerns over her physician's misconduct towards her as she felt that he was superior to her. By contrast Wei Yin strongly objected to what she perceived as inappropriate treatment undertaken by her physician:

> *Wei Yin*: When I was in standard 1 or 2 [7 years old], my father brought me to see a doctor in the X Hospital. During our second or third meeting, the doctor asked me to take off all my clothes. I am a girl right and I felt embarrassed. I refused but my father convinced me to follow the doctor's will
>
> *Researcher*: Although he did not do anything in front of your father, you felt . . .
>
> *Wei Yin*: Oppressed! At that time, I felt humiliated you know. It was just like my dignity as a human being was gone. Although my father protected me, he could not object to his order at that time. Why did my father follow his will? Is that because he was a doctor? Because he was highly educated? I felt it was unfair to me! This is unfair to me I said!

Although Wei Yin had exercised her agency by expressing her objections, she remained helpless because she was overshadowed by a significant male figure in her life – her father. Such an unforgettable incident created tension for her and it made her feel oppressed and vulnerable, even 40 years later. Since that incident, she refused to continue her medical treatment and never wanted to go to the hospital again.

Understanding the findings

The study is consistent with the previous findings elsewhere that found disabled women with physical impairments are subjected to physical and sexual abuse by their healthcare providers (Young *et al.*, 1997; McFarlane *et al.*, 2001). This universal characteristic of the female disabled experience that observes an explicit lack of power exhibited by these women towards their healers/physicians had profound impact on their life course. It not only tainted their psychological wellbeing but also prevented them from getting adequate healthcare assistance. This can be intensified by cultural attitudes which witness that many women in a traditional society such as India, particularly villagers, do not seek healthcare assistance from male practitioners (Thomas and Thomas, 1998). It thus implies that disabled women may be reluctant in seeking assistance from male care-providers (Thomas and Thomas, 1998). Therefore, it is important to ensure that healthcare settings have an adequate number of female practitioners. This alarming phenomenon is consistent with the findings across the globe (Ghai,

2003; Mays, 2006; United Nations Enable, 2012). This effect could be greater for Malaysian disabled women as a result of both their gender and disability (NGO Shadow Report Group, 2005). The United Nations Convention of Persons Disabilities (UNCRPD) addresses about freedom from exploitation, violence and abuse against disabled people in the Article 16 (United Nations Enable, 2014). Therefore, in agreement with the Article 16 of the UNCRPD (United Nations Enable, 2014), this issue should be addressed effectively to ensure that Malaysian disabled women are protected against any forms of exploitation, violence or abuse in various life settings.

The sexual abuse experienced by these women in healthcare settings, both in traditional or modern medical healthcare, significantly impacted upon them over time and violated their dignity as women. It did not only 'bruise' their physical and psychological persona but it prevented them from getting appropriate healthcare services too.

It is important to point out that these are not uncommon experiences for disabled women in other countries. As McFarlane *et al.* (2001) have argued, disabled women with physical impairments in Scotland 'are more likely to experience physical or sexual abuse by attendants and healthcare providers'. Young *et al.* (1997: 43) likewise found that 'women with physical disabilities also were more likely to be abused by their attendants and by healthcare providers'. This lack of power appears to be an almost universal characteristic for disabled women and a unifying feature of the female disabled experience.

The examples provided in this chapter highlight the imbalance of power between the research participants and their physicians. Again, evidence confirms this is not uncommon in other parts of the world, as Lundgren *et al.* (2001) have demonstrated, 'it is the power–imbalance between professional and patient that allows healthcare professionals to exploit or abuse as well as to heal'. Such types of exploitation made the women in this study develop negative attitudes towards medical practice. Consequently, it prevented them from getting adequate medical advice and services, resulting in an intensification of their impairment and disablement experiences. In brief, getting access to adequate healthcare was not a simple issue for many of the women interviewed. It involved a complex interaction between economic, geography, traditional/cultural beliefs, sexual abuse in the healthcare settings and gender issues that hindered their opportunities to access adequate healthcare.

Implications for practice

The key recommendations from the study are outlined at the end of this chapter. First and foremost, sexual abuse in healthcare settings must be addressed – in both the traditional and the modern healthcare practice. This study has documented that significant numbers of women were subjected to sexual exploitation either by their traditional healers or physicians. The state should strongly address this issue by instructing the MOH to protect disabled women from being sexually exploited by their physicians or attendants. The state should take all appropriate measures to educate disabled children and women, as well as their families, about different scenarios that may occur during physical examinations and what may be considered as unethical practice in modern medicine. For instance, sexual health education should be introduced for to disabled young people. The imbalance of power between healthcare providers and patients should also be reduced and at the same time disabled children and women should be empowered to report any malpractice by their healthcare providers. In so doing disabled children and women could hopefully be protected from such disturbing occurrences that may act to impede their wellbeing.

Equally important is that this issue should also be addressed in the context of traditional medicine. While traditional medicine is culturally acceptable among many Malaysians, and across different ethnic groups and religions, parents of disabled children should be made aware of potential dangers to protect their children from being sexually exploited. For example, disabled children and women should not be allowed to attend appointments with traditional healers alone and they should be accompanied by at least one family member or friend at all times. They should also be encouraged to report such experiences to the state or local authorities even if it involves someone known to their family or a respected figure in their hometown.

Conclusions

This chapter has reported on part of an empirical study that explored Malaysian disabled women's experiences in healthcare settings. The results of the study found that there was strong intersectionality between the effect of rurality-poverty, cultural belief, disability and gender in Malaysian healthcare settings. In expressing their healthcare experiences, the women observed that rurality and poverty increased the risks of acquiring impairment because modern medical healthcare was inaccessible to many of them. Lack of healthcare services in rural areas often made them dependent on the traditional treatments offered by local shaman or religious persons. This encouraged a strong cultural belief in the effectiveness of traditional remedies rather than modern medical treatments. Due to a strong dependence on traditional medicines some women were exposed to sexual abuse by the traditional healers. However, these incidents were never revealed to the authorities as the perpetrator was usually known to the family of these women.

Key messages from this chapter

- Put measures in place to prevent the occurrence of sexual abuse occur in both the traditional and the modern healthcare practices towards disabled women and girls.

- The state should take all appropriate measures to educate disabled children and women, as well as their families, about different scenarios that may occur during physical examinations and what may be considered as unethical practice in modern medicine. Introduce sexual education to disabled young people.
- Educate parents of disabled children about the possibility of sexual abuse occurring in traditional medicine. Children and women should not be allowed to attend appointments with traditional healers alone and they should be accompanied by at least one family member or friend at all times. They should also be encouraged to report such experiences to the state or local authorities even if it involves someone known to their family or a respected figure in their hometown.

References

All Women's Action Society (AWAM). 2003. *Media Monitoring Research, Preliminary Findings: Gender sensitive and Gender-biased Advertisements*. [Online]. [Accessed 22 May 2011]. Available from: www.iwraw-ap.org/resources/pdf/Malaysia_SR.pdf.

Aminah, A. 1998. *Country Briefing Paper on Women in Malaysia*. [Online]. [Accessed 20 October 2010]. Available from: www.adb.org.

Azman, A.A. and Juliana, A.W. 2005. *Power and Patriarchy: Women's Programmes on Malaysian Television*. The 14th AMIC Annual Conference Media and Society in Asia – Transformation and Transition, Beijing.

Begum, N. 1992. Disabled Women and the Feminist Agenda. *Feminist Review*. 40, pp. 70–84.

Chattopadhyay, A. 1997. Family Migration and the Economic Status of Women in Malaysia. *International Migration Review*. 31(2), pp. 338–352.

Department of Social Welfare. 2009. *Social Welfare Department*. [Online]. [Accessed 20 January 2011]. Available from: www.jkm.gov.my.

Department of Statistics Malaysia. 2011. *Population Distribution and Basic Demographic Characteristic Report 2010*. [Online]. [Accessed 10 February 2013]. Available from: www.statistics.gov.my/portal/index.php?option=com_content&id=1215.

Driedger, D. 1996. Emerging from the Shadows: Women with Disabilities Organise. In: Driedger, D. et al. eds. *Across Borders: Women with Disabilities Working Together*. Canada: Gynergy Books.

Ghai, A. 2002. Disabled women: an excluded agenda of Indian feminism. *Hypatia*. 17(3), pp. 49–66. [Online]. [Accessed 15 May 2013]. Available from: http://muse.jhu.edu.ezproxy.lib.gla.ac.uk/journals/hypatia/v017/17.3ghai.pdf.

Ghai, A. 2009. Disability and the Millennium Development Goals: A Missing Link. *Journal of Health Management*. 11(2), pp.279–295.

Haque, A. and Masuan, K. A. 2002. Perspective: Religious Psychology in Malaysia. *International Journal for the Psychology of Religion*. 12(4), pp. 277–289. [Online]. [Accessed 18 April 2013]. Available from: http://dx.doi.org/10.1207/S15327582 IJPR1204_05.

Kamil, M.A. and Teng, C.L. 2002. Rural Health Care in Malaysia. *Australian Journal of Rural Health*. 10(2), pp. 99–103.

Kuno, K. 2007. *Does Community Based Rehabilitation Really Work? Community Based Rehabilitation (CBR) and Participation of Disabled People.* ISM Research Monograph Series No. 5. Kuala Lumpur: Social Institute Malaysia.

Lonsdale, S. 1990. *Women and Disability: The Experience of Physical Disability among Women.* New York: St. Martin's Press.

Lundgren, K.S., Needleman, W.S. and Wohlberg, J.W. 2001. Above All, Do No Harm: Abuse of Power by Health Care Professionals. *Therapy Exploitation Link Line.* [Online]. [Accessed 12 March 2012]. Available from: www.therapyabuse.org/p2-abuse-of-power.htm.

Mays, J. 2006. Feminist Disability Theory: Domestic Violence against Women with a Disability. *Disability & Society.* 21(2), pp. 147–158.

McFarlane J., Hughes R. B., Nosek M. A., Groff J. Y., Swedlend N., and Mullen P. D. 2001. Abuse Assessment Screen-Disability (AAS-D): Measuring Frequency, Type, and Perpetrator of Abuse toward Women with Physical Disabilities. *Journal of Women's Health & Gender-Based Medicine.* 10(9), pp. 861–866.

Mehrotra, N. 2008. Women and Disability Management in Rural Haryana, India. *Asia Pacific Disability Rehabilitation Journal.* 9(1), pp. 38–49.

Ministry of Health (MOH). 1997. *Report of the Second National Health and Morbidity Survey Conference.* 20–22 November, Kuala Lumpur Hospital.

Ministry of Women, Family and Community Development (MWFCD). 2007. *Measuring and Monitoring Gender Equality – Malaysia's Gender Gap Index.* [Online]. [Accessed 15 November 2010]. Available from: www.undp.org/content/malaysia/en/home/library/womens_empowerment/MGGI/.

Ministry of Women Family and Community Development (MWFCD). 2013. *Background behind the Establishment of the Ministry Of Women, Family and Community Development.* [Online]. [Accessed 22 July 2013]. Available from: www.kpwkm.gov.my/latar-belakang.

Morris, J. 1989. *Able Lives: Women's Experience of Paralysis.* London: The Women's Press.

Nagata K.K. 2003. Gender and Disability in the Arab Region: The Challenges in the New Millennium. *Asia Pacific Disability Rehabilitation Journal.* 14(1), pp. 10–17.

Ng, C., Mohamad, M. and Tan, B.H. 2006. *Feminism and the Women's Movement in Malaysia: An Unsung (R)evolution.* London: Routledge.

NGO Shadow Report Group. 2005. *NGO Shadow Report on the Initial and Second Periodic Report of the Government of Malaysia: Reviewing the Government's Implementation of the Convention on the Elimination of All Forms of Discrimination against Women (CEDAW).* [Online]. Kuala Lumpur: NCWO and WAO. [Accessed 2 April 2011]. Available from: www.iwraw-ap.org/resources/pdf/Malaysia_SR.pdf.

Noran, N.H., Bulgiba, A., Cumming, R. G., Naganathan, V. and Mudla, I. 2010. Prevalence and Correlates of Physical Disability and Functional Limitation among Community Dwelling Older People in Rural Malaysia, a Middle Income Country. *BMC Public Health.* 10(492), pp. 1–13.

Oakley, A. 1972. *Sex, Gender and Society.* London: Gower.

Persons with Disabilities Act 2008. 2008. *Persons with Disabilities Act 2008 (Act 685). Law of Malaysia.* Percetakan Nasional Malaysia Berhad: Kuala Lumpur.

Rashidah, A., Raj-Hashim, R. and Schmitt, G. 1995. *Battered Women in Malaysia, Prevalence, Problems and Public Attitudes.* [Online]. Women's Aid Organisation. [Accessed 12 July 2011]. Available from: www.wao.org.my/Domestic+Violence_37_5_1.htm.

Riddell, S. and Watson, N. 2003. Disability, Culture and Identity: Introduction. In: Riddell, S. and Watson, N. *Disability, Culture and Identity*. London: Pearson Prentice Hall, pp. 1–18.

Schuller, I. 2010. The Way Women Experience Disabilities and Especially Disabilities Related to Leprosy in Rural Areas in South Sulawesi, Indonesia. *Asia Pacific Disability Rehabilitation Journal*. 21(1), pp. 60–70.

Shakespeare, T. 2006. *Disability Rights and Wrongs*. London: Routledge.

Sinnasamy, M. 2006. *Human Resource Development on Social Work: A Study in Malaysia*. Working Paper Series WP-2006–01-E, [Online]. [Accessed 1 December 2010]. Available from: www.nihonfukushi U p/coe/report/pdf/wp-kuno.

Tarmiji, M., Usman, Y., Norizawati, M.A. and Aimi, S.M. 2012. Population and Spatial Distribution of Urbanisation in Peninsular Malaysia 1957 – 2000. *Geografia: Malaysian Journal of Society and Space*. 8(2), pp. 20–29.

The World Bank Group. 2013. *Malaysia Overview*. [Online]. [Accessed 12 July 2013]. Available from: www.worldbank.org/en/country/malaysia/overview.

Thomas, C. 1999. *Female Forms: Experiencing and Understanding Disability*. Buckingham, UK: Open University Press.

Thomas, M. and Thomas, M.J. 1998. Status of Women with Disabilities in South Asia. *Asia Pacific Disability Rehabilitation Journal*. 9(2), pp. 60–64.

UNDP. 1995. Human development report 1995. [Online]. New York: Oxford University Press. [Accessed 3 June 2011]. Available from: http://hdr.undp.org/sites/default/files/reports/256/hdr_1995_en_complete_nostats.pdf.

United Nations Enable. 2012. *Panel Discussion on Preventing and Ending Violence against Women with Disabilities*. [Online]. [Accessed 13 February 2014]. Available from: www.un.org/disabilities/default.asp?navid=46&pid=1602.

United Nations Enable. 2014. *Article 16 – Freedom from exploitation, violence and abuse*. [Online]. [Accessed 20 March 2014]. Available from: www.un.org/disabilities/default.asp?id=276.

UN Women. 2009. *Declarations, Reservations, and Objections to CEDAW*. [Online]. [Accessed 14 July 2011]. Available from: www.un.org/womenwatch/daw/cedaw/reservations-country.htm.

UN Women Regional Office for Asia and the Pacific. 2013. *CEDAW implementation*. [Online]. [Accessed 10 February 2014]. Available from: http://cedaw-seasia.org/malaysia_cedaw_implementation.html.

Wallace, S. and Wilchins, R. 2013. *Gender Norms: A Key to Improving Health & Wellness among Black Women & Girls*. [Online]. [Accessed 20 April 2013]. Available from: www.truechild.org/Images/Interior/findtools/heinz%20report.pdf.

Young, C.R., Weiss, E.L., Bowers, M.B. Jr. and Mazure, C.M. 1997. The Differential Diagnosis of Multiple Sclerosis and Bipolar Disorder. *Journal of Clinical Psychiatry*. 58(3), p. 123.

Yun, H.A. 1984. Women and Work in West Malaysia. In: Yun, H.A. *et al*. eds. *Women in Malaysia*. Kuala Lampur: Pedanduk.

Chapter 6

Negotiating violence in contexts of poverty in South Africa

An empirical study of disabled women's stories

Theresa Lorenzo and Harsha Kathard

Introduction

For the women who took part in the study, two themes are presented in this chapter that reveal disability as an added burden of family deprivations within their homes and communities. In contrast, disability was presented as a gain, inciting roles of provider and active contributor in their families. The women's stories illuminate their experiences of different forms of structural violence, where poverty and disability are seen as deprivations of fundamental human needs and not just material deprivation (Max-Neef, 1991).

The women who shared their experiences had moved from rural communities to an urban sprawl of informal settlements on the outskirts of Cape Metropole in search of work and better health and social services. Some women had moved before their impairment for similar reasons. These reasons for migration were common to other women in South Africa (Meer, 1998; Taylor and Conradie, 1997). Many women had family members who remained in the rural communities of Eastern Cape, a distance of 1,000 km travel by car, leading to a loss of family support and subsequent human poverty of affection and protection. The women experienced a breakdown of family structure with the frequent migrations. In South Africa, migrancy has been associated with a sense of dislocation, as migrants have to re-establish support while often trying to meet the human need for subsistence, a primary human need (Ramphele, 2002). Barberton (1998) classified obstacles of location related to where poor people live as a determinant of participation.

Living in informal settlements of the Cape Town Metropole reflected how women's social and economic rights – the right to adequate housing, welfare, education, health care and a clean environment – were sorely under-provided for. Such deprivations reflect the oppressive nature of both poverty and disability. The potential to achieve these rights are mitigated by social realities such as violence, poverty and political power (Ramphele, 2002). In researching South Africa's transitional historical context, Henkeman *et al.* (2016) differentiate between invisible violence that is cultural, structural and psychological, and visible violence that is physical. Cultural violence refers to the feelings of inferiority or superiority reflected in the unequal relationships between people. Structural violence is seen as the growing inequalities between different groups of people as a result of the social arrangements that put individuals and populations in harm's way (Farmer, 2006 in Henkeman et al., 2016). Historical and economic forces constrain individual agency. They recognise that nested inequalities are seen in poverty and unemployment.

The fragmentation and disempowerment that women, whether disabled or not, experience as a result of violence and trauma is characteristic of impoverished communities in South Africa (Buchanan and Hilton-Smith, 2004). Fragility related to their impairments and family networks exacerbates their vulnerability to the vicious cycle of poverty, especially physical and emotional ill health (Duncan, 2004; Swartz, 2004). Meer and Combrink (2015) highlighted the vulnerability to gender-based violence that women with intellectual disability face, due to the complexity of stigma and the limited understanding of intellectual disability by the public at large. Fourie et al. (2004) found that women living in poverty in previously disadvantaged communities in the Cape Metropole spent most of their time occupied by the struggle to meet the survival needs, such as food. They do not have enough space for 'time-out', which was similar to other women in South Africa (Taylor and Conradie, 1997; Watson and Lagerdien, 2004). Nosek et al.'s (2003) findings of a study in America found an interconnection between women's losses and their self-esteem, which is associated with greater functional limitation. She claimed that losing the ability to perform activities of daily living could threaten one's sense of self.

Women's ability to exercise agency in the face of adversity, related to human poverties, provides hope that meaningful social change towards an inclusive society is possible. The stories, cited in this chapter, cast light on the ordinary, everyday occupations of disabled women – in the home and informal trading, and their experiences of balancing and juggling responsibilities while getting little respite from the daily grind and struggle against poverty. They describe the barriers to human development at an individual and family level, and the strategies woman adopt in meeting needs.

Both the literature and the stories in this chapter show the commonality of experiences between the women and non-disabled women regarding employment. Fourie et al. (2004) and more recently Moodley and Graham (2015) found that poverty and disability were the greater factors affecting most black women in South Africa. Their analysis of the National Income Dynamics study in South Africa revealed that 'disability intersects with gender as well as age and race to result in negative outcomes in education, employment and income for all people with disabilities, but particularly black women with disabilities' (Moodley and Graham, 2015:15). Gender bias was also found to be significant in Uganda (Mpagi, 2002). Vernon and Swain (2002) reviewed studies in Britain which found that black disabled people experience high unemployment rates as well as concentration in low-paid and low-skilled jobs. Barberton (1998) and Taylor and Conradie (1997) found that black women were mostly self-employed in the informal sector or in low-paid work such as childcare in crèches or domestic work in both rural and urban communities in South Africa. Other significant occupations were vegetable gardening and selling in the informal sector, similar initiatives to the women in the study, which hardly enables a subsistence existence. The small profit that was generated contributed to school fees and buying children's clothes. For the women, these obstacles would include having too many children from the extended family as a responsibility, a tension that Ramphele (2002) uncovered among many families generally in some of the same communities of this study.

Methods

A Participatory Action Research (Reason, 1994) was used to encourage the participation of disabled women to produce new knowledge and conscious-ness-raising related to the barriers faced and strategies used for their economic development. The research partners were a Primary Health Care Non Governmental Organisation (PHC NGO) and the Disabled Women's Development Project of Disabled People South Africa. We used the snowballing technique to select disabled women as participants. Data generation methods included storytelling, narrative action reflection (NAR) workshops and reflective journaling. NAR workshops (Lorenzo, 2010) involve creative activities with participants to generate data of disability experiences collectively rather than on a one-to-one basis. The method enables cycles of storytelling and action learning by marginalised groups in impoverished contexts to mobilise collectively for social inclusion and equal opportunities in human development.

In the study with disabled women, we used Max-Neef's (1991) Human Scale Development framework, which maintains that development is driven by people and human needs are resources in themselves. There are nine fundamental human needs, which are the same across all cultures and historical times. Subsistence is seen as the priority human need, while the other eight needs are interrelated and not hierarchical. Deprivations occur when human needs are not satisfied, which leads to human poverties. Conversely, a potentiality indicates that human needs are satisfied. The dynamic interconnectedness between these two concepts could break the vicious cycle of poverty and disability. The two themes related to disability as a burden and a gain will now be explored.

Disability as an added burden of family deprivations

The disruption to family systems due to rural-urban migrations in search of work and health care resulted in fragile networks for many women. Their stories painted the same bleak picture of the various factors that contributed to disability as a burden, which included the death of parents following illness, and carrying the responsibility of caring for younger siblings. These stressors left many women feeling more vulnerable. Philiswa's story demonstrated the benefits of the migration for access to health care were short-lived as her visual impairment was exacerbated by domestic violence, resulting in unemployment:

> I have drawn a house here with a candle. The candle symbolises me as a spark at home before I got disabled. I used to light this candle when I pray to God for strength. Then I got an eye problem . . . at that time I was in the Transkei. But when I grew older I came to Cape Town as the eye problem became worse . . . I had an eye operation at Tygerberg and it became better . . .

Domestic violence and abuse created an additional load for the women, who had to negotiate the functional implications of their impairment, together with the emotional and physical consequences of enduring conflict. Unemployment and substance abuse in the family contributed to fragile networks for support.

> But 2 months ago, I was beaten up and injured by my husband in the same eye; I couldn't see anything with it. It is still blind even now. As the result of this I stopped working. My elder daughter was arrested for theft, and I am now looking after her daughter. Now the things that I live on are things that I am given by my neighbours. I am totally depending on them for food.
>
> (Philiswa)

Their stories revealed the women's inability to complete everyday tasks and activities that were familiar roles of ordinary life for them before sustaining an impairment. Their low self-esteem and sense of helplessness revealed their own attitudes and fears.

There seemed to be little recourse to justice or protection from physical harm that occurred when their partners were violent and under the influence of alcohol and/or drugs. Women reported repeated incidents of violence and abuse to community and neighbourhood structures such as street committees. But these structures seemed to be ineffectual, which caused the women to be publicly marginalised.

> My husband is still getting drunk and beating me up. I reported this matter to the street committee but they referred me back to my family [who] didn't come because it is too far away.
>
> (Philiswa)

Another woman shared a similar story:

> I have also got another problem: the father of my children is a drunk and drug addict. He beats me now and every time I reported him to the police in the street committees but he doesn't stop.
>
> (Ncebakazi)

Emotional exploitation also occurred when family members controlled or determined how the young women spent their disability grant. Even though Nonkosi received a disability grant, she experienced severe depression as a consequence of feeling helpless and trapped in a cycle of repeated abuse from her husband. A further gap in resources for protection occurred when she could not escape to the safety of neighbours either:

> I am a disabled mother who is getting a disability grant. I would be saying I do not have any problems if it was not for my husband. I cry on a daily basis. Whether he is working or not that is the same, he beats me day and night. I cannot ask for help from my neighbours because he will follow me and beat me in front of them.

The frequency of physical violence and abuse left women vulnerable to emotional trauma. The women drew on their own emotional resources, often to the detriment of their mental well-being. Together with the loss of power, the different forms of exploitation left them feeling at risk to further psychosocial impairment:

> I stay with my children and I don't have a husband. There are so many things happening in my life. One child was stabbed and the other one was burnt with hot water by his girlfriend. My soul doesn't rest. I wish I could stay alone and not meet with other people because I'm not happy.
>
> (Ncebakazi)

One woman with a stroke told of how her husband had beaten her because of her inability to complete the expected domestic chores. It is very likely that her impairment may have been caused by the beatings:

> My husband used to leave me alone maybe for a week and I didn't know where he was. And when he comes back he'd ask for food and when I didn't have food he would beat me up.
>
> (Nolitha)

It was heartening to observe how the older women provided support to the younger women, by visiting their families to speak to them about disability, as culturally, older women occupy different positions to younger women. One young woman, after being quiet and reserved in previous workshops, shared her distress as she felt there was little room to refuse to do household tasks that included the domestic chores for visitors:

> I identify myself with an animal with loads (crying). I do everything; I wash the clothes. They don't help me after school. I don't get the chance to go to church. A guy staying in our back yard wants me to do his washing

as well. My mother and my sisters overwork me and my mother takes my disability grant.

(Mavis)

The women's stories also revealed a more subtle form of abuse than physical violence, as they experienced emotional exploitation and a sense of rejection in the denial of their needs. Arriving from rural areas of Eastern Cape, which is 1,000 km from Cape Town by road, proved to be a mixed emotional experience for the women as they were faced ridicule from their families. The women were on the receiving end of mockery, contempt, scorn and disrespect between siblings, which lead to the risk of social isolation:

When I think about our load as disabled people, sometimes even if you were disabled long time ago, there are days when you feel you need support from the family. You need strength. If the family is throwing rude words at you, you can't succeed because you can't even think properly and your thinking is always about the bad treatment you are getting at home.

(Sikelalwa)

The other thing is that of not being accepted in our families because we are disabled. They are wrong even by the things they are saying. They say 'I am not the reason why you are disabled'. You are then forced to go and live by yourself.

(Sikelalwa)

Women who were also mothers of disabled children felt that they carried a double load as they experienced further rejection and ridicule after they acquired their impairment:

We want to do as much as we can . . . because we have our disabled children who are dependent on us. You find that in your family, this child is not liked . . . so you get problems since you are also disabled, you are no longer like the old mother.

(Anna)

The women also experienced financial exploitation. They carried a burdensome load in their struggle to generate meagre profits from self-employment initiatives, in an environment of dire social disintegration and violence. They found that it was a struggle to succeed because family members were largely dependent on them as a source of income. The load of responsibility to meet family needs became a burden. Nonzaliseko who had sustained fractures of her leg in a road traffic accident, struggled to make a profit in her small business, as her family did not pay attention to her pleas:

> Most of [my family members] are drunkards so I look after their children.
> I also buy and sell meat but they eat the meat I am supposed to be selling
> . . . My relatives are the ones that are abusing me financially. I have tried
> to talk to them but to no avail.

Material poverty often meant that the women put the needs of family members before their own, especially where matters of health and well-being were concerned. Many women spoke about the load they carried as they felt responsible for paying the debts incurred by their children, adding to the sense of financial exploitation:

> You have to pay those loans when you get your money. They take clothes
> on account and they say 'mama I will help you pay it'. And they only pay
> once and you have to pay it on your own. If the person sees someone
> who is selling the clothes they ask them to come to me. The person will
> beg me to take something for him. They want jackets that cost R300.
> When you get home with your disability grant, the child tells you that
> she wants to go to the doctor, to pay his accounts . . . You are forced to
> give this money. This morning my son said, 'I'm going to the doctor, give
> me the money'. I also need the doctor but I haven't been able to go because
> I can't afford.
>
> (Siphokazi)

A typical story that showed the complexity of family involvement illustrated another dimension of financial exploitation by unsupportive families. Nomonde had not been to school as she became disabled at a very young age. She sustained a mobility impairment in the rural area of Eastern Cape where she stayed. Later, she decided to come to her sister in Cape Town. Her experience illustrates the barriers created from illiteracy and subsequent dependency on others for information:

> I then came to Cape Town to my sister and her husband. She is working
> as a domestic worker. I have not got a DG [Disability Grant] and I don't
> know why because she is responsible for everything. She does not tell me
> why social services are not responding to my DG application.

A pervasive sense of powerlessness was the result of resourced-based obstacles to participation identified by Barberton (1998). These obstacles are related to poor people's economic circumstances as a consequence of low levels of schooling and high rates of illiteracy. The consequences are evident in the inability to access information about processes to access childcare grants and disability grants, adult education classes and further skills development. Women lost opportunities for employment due to their impairment, with subsequent loss of income and food security. Such losses resulted in deprivations in the human needs of subsistence, understanding and creation, which may then affect other human needs as well.

Disability as loss of cultural rituals and traditional values

A picture that emerged from the narratives of women was how impairment and ill health resulted in a sense of powerlessness and hopelessness at an individual level because of the nature of losses that were experienced. These losses had a ripple effect at a family level, together with the loss of cultural rituals because of their impairments. Their perception appeared to be reinforced by gendered roles imposed at a societal level.

Many women felt personally marginalised as a result of imposed boundaries related to a desire for an ordinary family life. In African culture, the value of children is deeply acknowledged. A few of the women spoke of the burden of not having children. Although infertility is a common problem with non-disabled women as well, the stories illustrated how the women were primarily emotionally connected to their cultural roots first. They aspired to having children despite their impairment. It may also reflect the pressure they felt related to gender roles and cultural expectations that all women would bear children (Meer, 1998). It was not surprising that one of the women felt more vulnerable, as she had not been able to have children:

> I am the woman who said she doesn't get children. That's why I'm saying my disability is bothering me.
>
> (Edith)

Traditionally, in African culture, male family members were the breadwinners and financial providers for family needs if the husband left or died (Meer, 1998). Ironically, the traditions were often reversed in situations where brothers and children were dependent on the women who became the providers, carers and nurturers. The loss of traditional values where the male members of the family usually provided the support was evident in the stories. If their husbands had left them, the women had anticipated assistance from their male siblings, who are deemed responsible (culturally) for providing for the needs of their disabled sisters. But this help seldom materialised. The words of one woman expressed their intention not to burden the family members with the load of their impairment:

> My load at home is heavy . . . because I'm the head of the family. As a head of the family, my brothers and my child are all dependent on me . . . the family doesn't like you, but likes your money.
>
> (Nobom)

Family responsibilities

Some women carried the burden of motherhood that added to already strained relationships in the family. They felt responsible for preparing their children to have the emotional strength to face the world. The young disabled women in the group gave another perspective on the strained relationships with their non-disabled mothers, as they expected their mothers to provide for their financial needs, which was not forthcoming because of the burden of poverty:

> As disabled youth, government is not providing anything for us. Even at home our mothers are dependent on the small businesses, which are not good because people don't have money. Our mothers and us are not on good terms. Even when we want things as youth, if you want to buy that, the parent tells you 'the food that I'm buying in the house is from my money and I'm supporting you'. So, you end up not having any support. So, the solution, I wish there could be something that I can do to start up a small business.
>
> (Small group)

Many women still felt responsible for the schooling not only of their own children, but also the children from the extended families. The needs of their children were found to be a powerful motivator for the women to succeed, as they realised their power and ability to shape their children's future. The women recognised their responsibility as mothers to give children appropriate social skills and teach respect:

> Your child has a right to ask for things from you but you need to teach them to talk nicely when they are asking for something. They mustn't go and ask for something from other people because they think you can't do things since you are disabled.
>
> (Gloria)

The women felt pressure to do better than non-disabled mothers despite their impairment. There was a pervasive sense of powerlessness related to the struggle to have enough money for the children they felt responsible for. Such imposed pressure sometimes meant that they contributed to the well-being of their neighbours' children, even if it meant that they incurred a debt, creating vulnerability to stress from deeper material deprivation:

> [I] buy clothes for other people's children and even when they are sick, you have to borrow money for their children. Sometimes you borrow this money from outside.
>
> (Bulelwa)

In contrast to the burden of disability in the family experienced by some disabled women, other disabled women gained from disability as they became the provider and active contributor in their families.

Disability as a gain by being a provider and active contributor

Some women expressed that there was an expectation that the women would provide for family needs as they received income from their disability grants. They had assumed the additional responsibilities of being providers as well as carers and nurturers. They worried that there was little chance of success because of this dependency on them:

> I can't even bank some money because there is family. It's like all the time you didn't have this family and as soon as you get your [disability grant], you find that all your family is there. When you have problems, they stay away from you and you keep saying 'I have a brother and he will never come and he is the one who was supposed to be helping me'. When he's working, he's not helping you.
>
> (Nobomvu)

There was a sense of pride that the women experienced in facing and overcoming the struggle to succeed, even though they felt that they are 'left with nothing' after meeting different obligations within the family. It was clear from the stories and experiences that the women took on responsibilities of mothering as providers and nurturers. Their stories showed that such pride was often coupled with the tension of bearing the responsibility of being the only source of income in the family, which changed the perception of the women being passive and dependent. They struggled to make their business ventures a success, as revealed in Thandiswa's story:

> I wish I could have a business because R500 is little as all my siblings are dependent on me as our parents left us (died). So, I need more money because I have to send some money to the homelands to give those who are here and I'm left with nothing. So I wish I could have a better business that will make me develop and be a better person among people.

Some women had met cultural expectations such as having children, building up a home and marrying, showing their desire for an ordinary family life, which was an integral part of fostering a healthy and balanced life:

> [Non-disabled women] get married and we also get married, they get children and we also get children and we also go to work just like them.
>
> (Nt's Small group)

Our neighbours have houses and we also have them. Even when they buy furniture, we can buy furniture.

(B's Small group)

Despite these desperate family circumstances, the women maintained an honest sense of their reality. In her story, Vuyo describes her authentic concern for her mother's well-being and her desire to change the family circumstances by being a source of income and support for their households:

I'm disabled. I have one arm working. My young brother is a taxi driver and my young sister is a drunkard. When she is drunk she abuses my mother who lives in [another township]. I get worried and I feel like if both my arms were working, I would stop her. I have my disability grant and I sell niknaks. I see myself straight like this line [basketball field] . . . until I die. I want to be straight to my mother and even with other people.

They found ways of extending boundaries, through strategies to participate in economic development. They had a determination and vision that prevented them from giving up. These stories revealed disability as a gain, as Bulelwa shared:

With the grant that I get, I am able to provide for my family and support them. I can handle my load. We know that in our families we are bread-winners even though we are disabled. All the loads are ours. We feed our families . . . we are even able to buy clothes for ourselves and we can carry that kind of load. You buy chips and sell and buy beef stock and put in your food and eat nicely.

The women's resourcefulness was seen in the many stories of optimising their disability grants, which gave them a role of provider in their family again as it enabled them to meet basic family needs for survival. Disability grants were instrumental in enabling women to take the first steps towards economic empowerment and social re-integration. The grant quickly became seed money for small business initiatives. From the many stories told in focus groups, it was clear that disability grants were not mere hand-outs that fostered dependency, but a vital means to self-empowerment.

We are disabled [but] we can do business and handwork. We don't just sit, like myself at home I'm making dolls using the small pieces of material. If it's big material I make duvets and pillows. I don't just sit. My grant gets stopped sometime, but I tell myself I must try so that I can get something to eat. Like now I don't have anything to eat and I don't know what I'll do. But I do make those dolls and go and sell them I can go and buy something to eat.

(Edith)

Voicing their needs was a strategy that reinforced self-reliance as the women actively sought advice and assistance in accessing development opportunities. The women voiced their vulnerability related to policy changes that necessitated annual re-evaluation of their disability grants. Such a measure would mean that their one source of income was not guaranteed. Some women asked for assistance to investigate why they did not get disability grants. In many families, the control of the disability grants was in the hands of family members who accessed the grants. The women were left with little recourse to justice, as they did not have adequate understanding of how to access the public social services system. The women appreciated any feedback on the progress and outcome of their disability grant applications.

I have four children and I do not know what to do and where to get help . . . Is it possible that they will build houses for the disabled only? I cannot see a future and success with the person I am staying with. Please can I talk with you after the meeting?

(Nonkosi)

The stories suggest that the women actively sought advice on how to access resources to ensure success in their self-employment initiatives and entrepreneurial development:

Fortunately, one of my brothers was in Cape Town. I also got my disability grant so I could buy and sell meat. I have tried to talk to family members who are eating the meat but to no avail. I would like to speak to you after this meeting to find if there is anything that I can do to relieve me from financial exploitation by family members who eat the meat I want to sell.

(Siphokazi)

The struggle to survive was evident in the fact that the women mentioned very little about how they meet their human need of rest. They seemed to have little time and energy left for any personal interests and had limited choices or alternatives to meeting family needs. Going to church was a significant and meaningful occupation for many women in these communities. They also attended women's prayer afternoons once a week, in addition to attending funerals or weddings over the weekend. The fragile networks reflected the abuse and exploitation they experienced would have to change dramatically for them to experiences of physical and emotional well-being. The stories echoed the words of Coleridge (1993) about life lived on the edge of survival.

Discussion

The process of storytelling, taking actions and later reflecting on actions collectively offered hope, as the women gained from the positive self-images and strong role models within the group. The process helped the women to understand their own situation and find solutions or ways to resolve it themselves. The image of a donkey carrying a load to depict the situation in their families illustrated the two sides of the experience: some women found the family responsibilities burdensome, while others found them an achievement and source of pride.

Other studies on South African experiences confirmed our findings that women were often single parents, who carried the load of responsibility to meet extended family needs, using income from their disability grants or profit of small businesses (Haricharan and Rendall-Mkosi, 2002; Ramphele, 2002; Lorenzo and Cloete, 2004). The women experienced emotional drain in their everyday struggle to succeed in their small business initiatives. Their capacity to problem-solve was compromised by stressful and physically and emotionally abusive family dynamics.

Both Thomas (2004) and Reeves (2004) have identified that these feelings may relate more to the psycho-emotional responses to impairment than the physical impairment itself. Thomas (2004) concurs that the psycho-emotional effects of impairment would be a hindering factor to social and economic development. The women's loss of confidence and low self-esteem following their impairment revealed human poverties of identity, affection, protection and understanding. These human poverties had ripple effects on the other human needs, such as subsistence, participation, freedom and creation. Women were disconnected and isolated from sources of support systems and intimacy, employment opportunities and limited opportunities to establish satisfying relationships because of imposed boundaries caused by feeling personally and publically marginalised from opportunities for social and economic participation. These human poverties are often the consequence of powerlessness and oppression. The interconnections between these personal losses and self-imposed boundaries perpetuated spirals of violence at the individual, family and community levels.

The women's losses also illustrated the experience of disability as a complex interaction between race, gender and poverty as forms of oppression. Vernon and Swain (2002) found that black, disabled women in the UK who experienced multiple oppressions were not able to identify a single source as the root of discrimination. Nosek et al. (2003) found that social isolation was the most common secondary condition associated with any primary impairment, and emotional, physical and sexual abuse.

The narratives raised awareness about the complexity of disability in impoverished contexts by signalling the deprivations (identified as barriers that may be imposed boundaries to participation) and the potentialities (identified

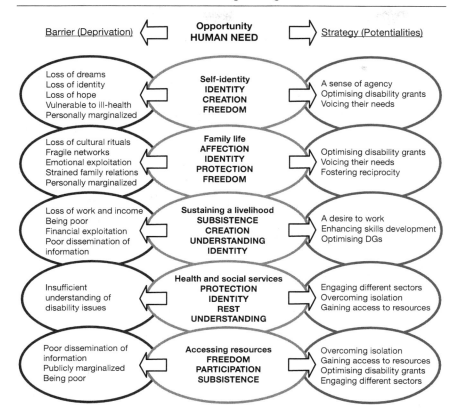

Figure 6.1 The push-pull tension in addressing fundamental human needs of disabled
women to equalise opportunities for their social and economic development

as strategies that extend boundaries of participation) of the women's fundamental human needs. Congruence emerged between the fundamental human
needs and the opportunities for participation in development (United Nations
(UN), 2006). The dynamic interplay between opportunities to participate in
activities that would contribute to their social and economic development is
illustrated in Figure 6.1. The overlapping circles depict the movement that
occurs laterally, as well as upwardly and downwardly, between the different
opportunities for inclusive development that would meet personal fundamental
human needs.

Giddens (2001:698) comments that self-identity is 'the ongoing process of
self-development and definition of our personal identity through which we
formulate a unique sense of ourselves and our relationship to the world around
us'. The potential of the women's empowerment for development was revealed
in their sense of agency that extended to their desire to work and to foster

reciprocal relationships. Pivotal in the process of social change is that the women feel good and sure of their own value. A positive self-identity advances the sense of agency and the ability to effect change in one's live. Coleridge (1993) has argued that a healthy self-esteem gives the power to begin changing circumstances through a combination of practical action and advocacy. Self-identity was a positive synergistic satisfier in situations where women were able to generate change through their sense of agency and desire to work. They were able to optimise their disability grants and voice their needs, which helped to foster reciprocity so that a space was created to nurture their sense of self, well-being and wholeness. Their stories demonstrated that human needs become the resource for action, as individuals choose to act collectively to change the root causes of their problems (Bauman and Tester, 2001) and Max-Neef (1991).

Skills development for self-employment and finding a place to work were identified as synergistic satisfiers of human needs to equalise opportunities, as the human need of identity were meet in resuming the provider role; the human need of affection in situations where there was respect and reciprocity in the family and community; the human need of protection in being able to access health and social services; and the human needs of understanding and creation through learning new skills leading to satisfaction of the human need of subsistence from income generated to provide for family needs.

The stories reflected how the women accepted the responsibility for protecting, maintaining and promoting health and well-being within the household, as they juggled the different roles of sibling, daughter, mother and partner, similar to the experiences of non-disabled women (Doyal, 2003). Read (2000) also found that children's needs and wants were powerful in shaping and structuring a collaborative relationship with the mother. As their children grew older, their personal, educational and social needs changed, which was not so different from their other siblings.

The women's narratives provide evidence that they were able to act on the world as opposed to being merely acted upon. They were active, contributing citizens who coped under very demanding situations, similar to the creativity and a dogged determination in seeking solutions to problems. Such agency could be explained by Max-Neef's (1991) claim that human needs become a resource and motivation that mobilise people to find strategies to overcome the pressure to provide for family needs.

It is evident that the complexities of disability created tensions for the women as they experienced the transitions from one state of being to another. The importance of nurturing emotional resourcefulness at an individual level was evident in their stories. The struggle to survive the different forms of deprivation and the potential to succeed appeared strongly related to and involved with individual, family and community dynamics. Such actions could contribute to breaking the vicious cycles of deprivation as a consequence of poverty, physical weakness, isolation, vulnerability and powerlessness. Stone (2001) adapted Chamber's deprivation trap (1983) to include impairment and disability. For these women, the experience of impairment led to a sense of self-pity and self-imposed isolation and personal marginalisation, which exacerbated the vicious cycle of poverty. The women recognised that they undermined themselves and were undermined by others. Often, they felt isolated, as they did not know any other disabled people nor did they identify with disabled people, leading to experiences of depression and anxiety related to poverty, violence and other forms of victimisation and chronic health problems.

The women showed resilience in overcoming their struggles, probably due to the belief that the family holds such importance in this culture (Broodryk, 2002; Tutu, 2004). Tutu (2004) argues that it is in the family that children learn about the nature of the world, power and justices, peace and compassion. The family is where oppressive or liberatory behaviours are first experienced and learned. It is in the 'humdrum, ordinary, unexpected and unlikely places and people' that change occurs (Tutu, 2004:95). The stories suggested that the caring role may be enhanced if the person gets a disability grant because it enables them to take on a provider role. The women continued to play the primary provider and nurturer role, especially for children in the family. So, paradoxically, the provider role of the women effectively dispelled the myths of 'laziness' associated with inability and dependency. It challenged the myth of women being dependent passive victims, supported by Priestley (1999) and Thomas (1998) who both indicated that disabled people are active agents. The women experienced some vulnerability and valued support at the same time, although vulnerability did not necessarily mean a low self-esteem. Experiencing vulnerability as strength seemed to depend on the nature of support systems and access to resources that made the difference between fragility and resilience.

> When we accept our own vulnerability just as we accept the vulnerability of others, we can be compassionate with ourselves and with our fears and frailties.
>
> (Tutu, 2004:88)

Intergenerational experiences of younger and older women exposed the constant need to change and adapt. Other women also felt the pressure to challenge stereotypes and prejudice about their disabilities. The need to understand and appreciate the consequences of the loss of family and cultural traditions in the equalising of opportunities for development is supported by Mazwai (1999:419) who claimed:

> Our customs and other indigenous knowledge systems [will be] the instrument of socio-economic development, freedom is the right to self-determination and the right to a better life.

In order to equalise opportunities in social and economic development, women need an effective judicial system through street committees, police and courts. These measures are called for in the Social and Empowerment Components of the Community-Based Rehabilitation (CBR) Guidelines (World Health Organization, 2010). Strengthening networks for collective action between Disabled People Organisations (DPOs) and NGOs as organs of civil society in equalising opportunities through creating access to justice need to be explored.

Conclusions

The subtlety and complexity of living with impairments in a disabling society has been uncovered in the women's narratives related to their human deprivations (barriers of imposed boundaries and marginalisation) caused by structural violence associated with poverty and disability, and their human potentialities (strategies for extending boundaries) for changing their circumstances through individual and collective action. The women have shown that the vicious cycles of poverty and disability caused by structural violence can be broken by the concerted efforts of all stakeholders.

The women's strength and resilience were rooted in their spirituality, which was vibrantly evident during the NAR workshops, in the women's skills in songs, dance and other cultural traditions, which need to be fostered (Lorenzo, 2003). Their religious beliefs infused all the workshops through their singing and rituals of prayers. Their symbolism in the creative activities should be explored to reveal the meanings and role of their spirituality in equalising opportunities.

The women's narratives reflect how it is possible to reduce the human poverties caused by impairments and environmental factors that influence participation, through individual and collective action that contributes to equalising opportunities for social and economic development, and vice-versa. Strategies to equalise opportunities become synergistic satisfiers of human needs (Max Neef, 1991) so that the vicious cycle of poverty and disability is broken and replaced by a benevolent cycle of humanity and generosity, reflected in the African values of Ubuntu.

Key messages from this chapter

*   Inclusive development is a complex interaction of individual abilities and contextual factors, involving relationships at family and community level that determines how one's fundamental human needs are met or can lead to human poverties.
*   The process of storytelling, taking actions and later reflecting on actions collectively is empowering for disabled women. The collective is stronger than the individual; the individual strengthens the collective.

- In order to equalise opportunities in social and economic development, women need an effective judicial system through street committees, police and courts.

References

Barberton, C. (1998) Obstacles to effective participation by poor people. In *Creating action space: The challenge poverty and democracy in South Africa* (edited by C. Barberton, M. Blake, and H. Kotze). Cape Town, South Africa: David Philip. 244–271.

Bauman, Z. and Tester, K. (2001) *Conversations with Zygmunt Bauman*. Cambridge: Polity.

Broodryk, J. (2002) *Ubuntu: Life lessons from Africa*. Pretoria, South Africa: Ubuntu School of Philosophy.

Buchanan, H. and Higson-Smith, C. (2004) Trauma, violence and occupation. In *Transformation through occupation* (edited by R. Watson and L. Swartz). London: Whurr. 219–232.

Chambers, R. (1983) *Rural development: putting the last first*. London: Longman Scientific and Technical.

Coleridge, P. (1993) *Disability, liberation and development*. Oxford: Oxfam.

Doyal, L. (2003) Sex and gender: The challenges for epidemiologists. *International Journal of Health Services*. 33 (3) 569–579.

Duncan, M. (2004) Promoting mental health through occupation. In *Transformation through occupation* (edited by R. Watson and L. Swartz). London: Whurr. 198–218.

Fourie, M., Galvaan, R. and Beeton, H. (2004) The impact of poverty: the potential lost. In *Transformation through occupation* (edited by R. Watson and L. Swartz). London and Philadelphia: Whurr Publishers. 69–84.

Giddens, A. (2001) *Sociology*. Cambridge: Polity.

Haricharan, S. and Rendall-Mkosi, K. (2002) 'The Joint Primary Health Care Programme, Final Evaluation Report'. December. Annexure 8. Zanempilo Health Project, Cape Town.

Henkeman et al. (2016). Open guide to a deeper, wider and longer analysis of violence. Transdisciplinary project for social justice. Social Law Project, University of Western Cape and Centre of Criminology, University of Cape Town.

Lorenzo, T. (2003) No African renaissance without disabled women: A new way of looking at social and economic development of disabled women in South Africa. *Disability and Society*. 18 (6) 759–778. October.

Lorenzo, T. (2010) Listening spaces: Connecting diverse voices for social action and change. In *New approaches for qualitative research: wisdom and uncertainty* (edited by M. Savin-Baden and C. Howell Major). London: Routledge. 131–144.

Lorenzo, T. and Cloete, L. (2004) Promoting occupations in rural communities. In *Transformation through occupation* (edited by R. Watson and L. Swartz). London: Whurr. 268–286.

Max-Neef, M.A. (1991) *Human Scale Development*. London: The Apex Press.

Mazwai, T. (1999) Epilogue: Bricks and mortar for the African Renaissance. In *African Renaissance* (edited by M.W. Makgoba). Sandton, South Africa: Mafube; Cape Town, South Africa: Tafelberg. 417–428.

Meer, S. (ed.) (1998) *Women speak: Reflections on our struggles 1982–1997*. Cape Town, South Africa: Kwela Book.

Meer, T. and Combrinck, H. (2015) Invisible intersections: Understanding the complex stigmatisation of women with intellectual disabilities in their vulnerability to gender-based violence. *Agenda.* 29 (2) 14–23.

Mohamed, K. and Shefer, T. (2015) Gendering disability and disabling gender: Critical reflections on intersections of gender and disability. *Agenda.* 29 (2) 2–13.

Moodley, J. and Graham, L. (2015) The importance of intersectionality in disability and gender studies. *Agenda.* 29 (2) 29–33.

Mpagi, J.S. (2002) Government's role in CBR. In *CBR: A participatory strategy in Africa* (edited by S. Hartley). London: University College London, Centre for International Child Health. 86–96.

Nosek, M.A., Hughes, R.B., Swedlund, N., Taylor, H.B. and Swank P. (2003) Self-esteem and women with disabilities. *Social Science and Medicine.* 56 (8) 1737–1747.

Priestley, M. (1999) *Disability politics and community care.* Philadelphia, PA: Jessica Kingsley; London: Regional Studies Association.

Ramphele, M. (2002) *Steering the stars: Being young in South Africa.* Cape Town, South Africa: Tafelberg.

Read, J. (2000) *Disability, the family and society: Listening to mothers.* Buckingham, UK, and Philadelphia, PA: Open University Press.

Reason, P. (1998) Three approaches to participative inquiry. In *Strategies of qualitative inquiry* (edited by N.K. Denzin and Y.S. Lincoln). Thousand Oaks, CA, London and New Delhi: Sage. 261–291.

Reeve, D. (2004) Psycho-emotional dimensions of disability and the social model. In *Implementing the social model of disability: Theory and research* (edited by C. Barnes and G. Mercer). Leeds: The Disability Press. 83–100.

Stone, E. (2001) A complicated struggle: Disability, survival and social change in the majority world. In *Disability and the life course: Global perspectives* (edited by M. Priestley). Cambridge: Cambridge University Press. 50–66.

Swartz, L. (2004) Rethinking professional ethics. In *Transformation through occupation* (edited by R. Watson and L. Swartz), London: Whurr. 289–300.

Taylor, V. and Conradie, I. (1997) *'We have been taught by life itself': Empowering women as leaders: the role of development education.* Pretoria, South Africa: Human Sciences Research Council.

Thomas, C. (2004) *Female forms: experiencing and understanding disability.* Buckingham, UK, and Philadelphia, PA: Open University Press.

Tutu, D. (2004) *God has a dream: A vision of hope for our time.* South Africa: Random House.

United Nations (UN) (2006) Convention on Rights of Persons with Disabilities. New York: United Nations.

Vernon, A. and Swain, J. (2002) Theorising divisions and hierarchies: Towards a commonality or diversity. In *Disability studies today* (edited by C. Barnes, M. Oliver and L. Barton). Cambridge, UK: Polity Press. 77–97.

Watson, R. and Lagerdien, K. (2004) Women empowered through occupation: From deprivation to realized potential. In *Transformation through occupation* (edited by R. Watson and L. Swartz). London: Whurr. 268–286.

World Health Organization (2010) *Community Based Rehabilitation Guidelines.* WHO: Geneva

Chapter 7

Fear at home
Surviving a quiet black British sexual abuse

Lois Llewellyn

Introduction

When I was first interviewed for the project that I will talk about in this chapter, I had come out of a space with regular access to counselling and I was used to talking. But it's been a few years since then and I've lost that skill. To write this chapter I sat down at my desk and made myself remember. I just wrote it all down. For 4 hours solid. Normally I don't remember much of my childhood. Vague incidents here and there, created memories through anecdotes, but my genuine memories are mostly gone.

> It is normal to remember back to ages three or four. When someone tells me that they cannot remember anything before the age of 13, for example, it is invariably a sign of some type of major childhood trauma.
>
> (Kendall-Tackett, 2001, p. 12)

Generally, that is my experience. The timelines are fuzzy when I speak about my childhood, because I don't have many reference points. My survivor memories live in a separate space in my head. They don't really merge with 'my life', and 'what I lived' until I reach 15. For most of the time, it's like it didn't happen to me.

As I go through my journey to recovery, I've dealt with the post-traumatic stress disorder (PTSD), the triggers and even now, the resurfacing of some forgotten incidents of abuse. Where the right support doesn't happen at the critical point of disclosure, and 'where the children do not receive adequate help and support following a disclosure, the damage and negative effects can be lifelong' (Goodyear-Brown, 2012). It is only recently that I have been able to look in a mirror without being reminded of my abuser. When I compare myself to her, I now have the tools to separate them and face my biggest fear of becoming like her.

As I travel through this chapter, I will take a life course approach. This examines changes: biological, social, psychological, developmental, historical and geographical, and identifying, which impacts the 'arc of change' (Hendricks,

2012). I analyse the bit of my life I have available and look for answers to a question that has been plaguing me of late: *What happened, Lois?*

Background

In the UK, one million grandparents take up a caring role because their children cannot afford childcare (Smethers, 2015). My family was no different. I'd often stay at a grandparent's house with my siblings and while growing up two of my cousins lived there too. School holidays, days worked late, Sundays after church we'd be there. And so would she. My cousin. My nemesis. A woman who changed my life. I normally refer to her using expletives, but let's call her ZC. This was the routine of my life and one that could not be changed. As a family, we were just about managing. I had no other options than to be in this place.

Our family was part of an Assemblies of God Church, part of a Pentecostal movement with children's, youth and young adult ministries as well as teaching, training and community ministries (Assemblies of God Incorporated, 2017). At one point, I was spending about 4 or 5 days of the week at church. Pentecostalism is a large part of our identity and to be anywhere else, I needed a good reason. I had my tutoring here, my music lessons, my social life, my leadership training. It was here where I met my first rapist, we'll call him Erin. In most black churches, 'women outnumber men by more than two to one; yet in positions of authority and responsibility the ratio is reversed' (Harris, 1990); there is a longstanding patriarchal culture, despite many women being around. Safeguarding policies in churches were lax back then – the exposure of some of my story led change. How do you tell people what's going on in a place you must be for most of your life? The places I was supposed to feel safe were both soured and true security was just out of reach.

Growing up vulnerable: the earliest abuse and gender

It would be easier to talk about if it followed a simple route through my life. It didn't start sexual. It was just quiet bullying. As a child, I apparently fed her Barbie doll to the dog, so she fed it my soft toy. It started with the sleepovers. I never instigated them, ZC would ask my parents. They'd accept, not having any idea not to. I hated it. At the sleepovers, I didn't have an enjoyable time. The first incident that sticks out in my mind was the time they made me stay up. I was six, seven. I was shattered. My bedtime was 8pm. This older cousin made me keep my eyes open till at least 11pm. I don't remember the exact words but:

> You're here to keep me company so you have to stay awake, you can't go to sleep or I'll tell my mom and you'll be in trouble.

I'd get pinched hard if I closed my eyes. Each coercive action used the threat of an adult's anger to underpin it. I learned compliance early on because my choices were few. I would get in trouble, not be taken seriously, or people would be angry with me. Eventually I would be alone with ZC again. ZC was clever enough to only hurt me when we were unsupervised, and just old enough to be able to convince me of anything. ZC always made sure that she wasn't the only thing I feared. She invented bigger threats to keep me quiet. My experience was in line with the conclusions of Kendall-Tackett (2001); female perpetration being seen as 'the most secretive and closeted of all types of sexual abuse'.

I feel obliged to note this behaviour wasn't every occasion. They were isolated incidents spread far apart that I wouldn't react negatively upon seeing her, but close enough that I would remember what ZC could do. ZC's abuse was devastating because of who she was. Thinking of her identity, it is the 'vexed dynamics of difference vs the solidarity of sameness' (Cho et al., 2013), which mean she gained the access necessary to abuse me. We were both young, black girls – her being perhaps 5 or 7 years older than me. This 'sameness' implied a protection – someone to look up to, whose experience I could learn from and who would, in turn, look out for me. She was supposed to be a safe choice and a good influence. I was preyed upon because of the exclusive access gender gave to her; I was not her only victim, but her only female one. Within the politically liberal yet complex matriarchal (Reynolds, 2004) power structures of a black British family, built on conservative Caribbean values, I was younger and weaker.

Beatings as punishment were not uncommon (UNICEF Jamaica, 2006). A cousin of mine got whipped with a curtain wire for lying, once had an iron thrown at his head, and growing up, my father was made to go find his own switches from the trees in the garden with which to be beaten. These were the funny anecdotes I grew up on, the level of violence that was acceptable as punishment[1]. It was harder to talk about ZC doing things like pinching me because she'd only be 'troublin' me',[2] not doing harm.

I was left alone with ZC so often because *she* requested it. As an only child, my parents would comply – presuming I'd be safe. ZC permanently violated the safety of the family space. Reverse her gender, include the age gap and it isn't 'proper' to let children spend too much time alone; she wouldn't have been able to abuse me so easily. Gender identities are taught from a young age (El-Bushara and Sahl, 2005, p. 93) and ZC deviated from the 'nurturing female' role our family expected. She used the power of these heteronormative gender roles to gain access to a young victim. Her sameness worked in her favour for a presumed innocence. The international media focus on the rapes of

---

1   Although my parents were much milder and we only ever got so much as a shoe on the hand, my parents turned their back on beatings as a disciplinary tool. My younger siblings have never been hit.
2   Caribbean equivalent of just bothering someone, being annoying.

women (Sivakumaran, 2010) and the subsequent narrative that it sells creates a normative understanding of what abuse is and how it is framed. The hetero-normative lens feeds into the assumption that men harm women and women harm men. When there is a lack of attention on male victims, scrutiny of their perpetrators is also forgotten. Her sameness worked in her favour. Why would you harm what you are? If 'identity based politics are a source of strength' (Crenshaw, 1991), then ZC didn't uplift me as a fellow woman, she did not take me under her wing but she tore me down. If she saw the sameness in me that I see in her, then she hated me because she hated herself.

Tainting a developing sexuality and repeating rituals

As time goes on, the impact of ZC's early abuse is becoming clearer. Once she made me masturbate her with a pearl shaped light bulb. I was disgusted. I was too small to know what female body parts were like intimately; I was under the age of ten. I hadn't even discovered myself yet. I cannot understand the mind of an abuser. She made me masturbate myself, encouraging me to put my little finger in my holes. It was too small and it hurt, but she made it seem like the most normal thing to do and just said that I 'wasn't developed enough yet'. When I was old enough for sexual education in schools, we'd be told to go home and have a look at ourselves using a mirror. I have never been able to look at my own genitals, because they look like hers. I can't watch porn with black women in because black sexuality is tainted for me.

There are traits in ZC that I have struggled to separate from myself. Her damage was impactful and enduring. I fight against the reflections of her character in me but perhaps the part of me she distorted most was my approach to sex and sexuality. I believed my consent didn't matter; I had learned it would be disrespected anyway. Instead I sought out protection and comfort from the boys around me because I couldn't fully trust girls. My trust issues started early. Having trust betrayed by perpetrators is cited as a contributor to lasting difficulties in the area of interpersonal trust among adult survivors (DiLillo, 2001). I started remembering what I had forgotten (Williams, 1995) through this life course approach exercise and questioned my longstanding assumptions. The aspect I've probably minimised most is my rape. Rapes. As I entered puberty, my differences became more obvious to myself and those around me. I had weird feet and as I was once so kindly told, my legs looked like 'chicken legs'. My hands were odd, I couldn't run around and play like I used to. I couldn't keep up. I got tired quickly, I was learning what pain was but most essentially, I wasn't like everyone else. It's what painted me as a target to this boy. Vulnerability to abuse may increase with the severity of one's disability (Platt et al., 2017), and school-age children are less likely to file a report or notify authorities of sexual violence (Alriksson-Schmid et al., 2010). He offered himself as a boyfriend (Pemberton, 2016) and (Dagon, 2012), Erin.

He'd take me behind buildings and kiss me. He asked things I wasn't ready for. I didn't want to but, 'My uncle has just died and you won't even do this one thing for me?' Just like a lollipop, he said. He'd make me or tell everyone that I was a slut, starting rumours about me so I complied. Soon, I was told to get on all fours in an alleyway. He pushed into me. I had no choice. I stayed quiet pretending I enjoyed it. He wasn't rough, he didn't need to be. I thought about running away but I knew that I couldn't get far. I wore bandages on both knees to reduce my pain. Looking back on it with my buckled glasses, double bandages and insecurity, I was an easy target. It doesn't have to be brutal for it to be a rape. It doesn't have to be television pretty, I didn't need to wait until dark bruises formed. I said no. I knew I couldn't escape. I couldn't run and knew that if you crossed him he wouldn't just hurt you. Even then he had been expelled a few times and was friendly with the police. He kept me quiet by threatening to tell my parents what I'd done, what he made me do. As my father later said, the tragedy is, had he told, I would have gotten help.

Would I have experienced this if I were a boy? Unlikely. Our culture is historically homophobic (West and Cowell, 2015). Would I have been raped by this straight man if I weren't female or disabled? No.[3] In this case, I would have been safer. I wasn't equipped to understand what had happened to me, so I remember whispering to a friend as if seeming happy about the loss of virginity it would make it okay. The feelings of shame and guilt that come from the abuse can reduce the likelihood of that child making a disclosure (Allnock, 2010). Years later I heard a rumour he'd been jailed for sexual assault. I've since tried to find out what happened to him, but I've not heard a word about him, not since the arrogant son of a bitch contacted me to threaten doing it all over again. He could easily find me because of our church ties (Krause and Wulff, 2009). Erin will always know how to find someone who knows how to find me so I am never safe.[4]

I became overtly sexual as a way of taking control and ensuring it would fall into the background narrative and just be part of who I was. I met Brad while I was walking to an afterschool club. He was at least 10 years older than me, and he knew it. I had been wearing my school uniform at the time. He was a white man and conscious of being seen with me, always wondering what people might think. Race riots had happened in living memory. He cared about my race, not my age. I was about 15, turning 16. He was in his mid-twenties and

---

3   Female high school students who reported a physical disability or long-term health problem were more likely to report having been physically forced to have sexual intercourse than those who did not (Alriksson-Schmid et al., 2010)

4   I dealt with this threat by getting blackout drunk and being returned to my halls of residence by an irate taxi driver in front of most of the residents on their way for a night out. While an effective method for me, I'd recommend anyone else being threatened by a former abuser seek counselling and approach the police for help.

convinced me to sleep with him in an alleyway not far from Erin's. By this point I had learned. If a man asks, you do. People who are stronger than you can and will hurt you, so you do what they want and when they want.[5]

I was a vulnerable child that had been twisted into having sex, taught to stay quiet and unable to escape. I know now he was a paedophile. He attempted to isolate me further, asked me to move in with him, wouldn't leave me alone. I was never showered with gifts by any of these men. Not groomed in that way. These men reinforced the idea that I was worth nothing and I repeated that behaviour. The side effect from ZC, Erin and Brad was that the freeze response became my only response. Around this time every man who asked for sex got it. Later in life, at university, I instigated sex often. Better to give them what they want first so they won't take it.

Two years later, I was raped by my boyfriend Jake. We'd already been active but on this occasion for whatever reason I had said no, quietly. He carried on. It took a lot of effort to object because I deeply believed I was supposed to just accept whatever happened to me. He was on top of me, I tried to push him off but my arm was weak; I couldn't. I didn't try too hard to push because I was worried about hurting myself. I was very fragile and nearing wheelchair use. I wore bandages from ankle to above the knee and covered them with socks. I couldn't push him off me, I couldn't keep saying 'no', so I gave in. Lying there barely moving and tears falling down the side of my face, I moved a little, because I had to convince him I was enjoying it and couldn't think of what might happen if he realised he'd raped me. Eventually he climbed off. All he said was, 'Sorry'. Then he left the room. I thought this was okay. I thought Jake my last chance to create an understanding of healthy relationships. After this, I expected men to do damage and I accepted it.[6]

Family intersection and the beginnings of self-advocacy

I had mostly 'moved on' by the time I'd started university and I drank how I thought strong people should; whiskey not white wines. Like a man, I thought. Somewhere along the line I'd learned to hate my gender or the traits of femininity that I thought equated to weakness. I preferred men as friends because I believed having men on side was safer than not. One morning, I received a call from a close friend. We had Erin in common. She wanted to speak with me but 'didn't want to ruin my day'. I brushed off her concerns. I learned that she'd told her story to her parents and told them I was a survivor.

---

5   Obviously, this is a stupid, terrible conclusion to come to and in the time since I have learned better. Please do not follow this ridiculous advice.

6   My favourite quote at the time was *Hamlet* Act 2 Scene 1. Polonius says this of Hamlet while talking to Ophelia: 'This is the very ecstasy of love; whose violent property fordoes itself and leads the will to desperate undertakings'. I saw their actions as a kind of affection, or I used this kind of logic to forgive the men who hurt me.

Because of who the perpetrator was and the location, it was discussed at board level as a safeguarding issue. My father sat on that board.

To my knowledge this was the first time that my survivor status was disclosed without my consent. I had no say in who found out what happened to me, or the terms. I had no control over the rapes and abuse. Telling people was the only part I had a legitimate choice in. That choice was gone, yet I did not feel some great relief to know that my parents now knew, or that my friend had unburdened herself. I felt numbness. A friend had betrayed my confidence and my abuse was no longer a secret: it felt like everyone knew. I was starting my journey to PTSD and this was the trauma.

The dynamics in black families are often marred by mainstream media representations. My grandmother fits media representations of a predetermined role for black women of a certain age. You can see it most clearly in black films (Reid, 1993) the head of a family, either alone or accompanied by an irrelevant husband. The ultimate strong black woman, who has lived through oppression and battles yet come through it all more powerful. The strong black woman stereotype means that we are expected to live through all sorts of terrible things without acknowledgement or care.[7]

In *How to Get Away with Murder* (Rhimes *et al.*, 2014, S1 Ep13), the lead character Annalise Keating confronts her now geriatric mother about the childhood abuse she experienced and the audience are invited to celebrate the mother finally opening up about how she knew and let the house burn with the abuser inside. We are not invited to question choices about the lack of physical or emotional support offered to Viola, because we see both elements of the black woman stereotype at play. The matriarch, powerful enough to commit immense acts of violence alone in unquestioned circumstances and without challenge. We have accepted the institutional racism at play, one that prevents black women accessing police justice on the same level as their counterparts (Henerey, 2017). It is a narrative that adds legitimacy to the vigilante approach to dealing with abuse. The impact of this stereotype is Annalise. Abused at an early age, offered no support in the family, no one to speak with and the damage done to her is just accepted, as if she should brush it off. Black women are expected to be strong and therefore must accept more damage and violence before help is offered. Their bodies and personhood are not valued to the same extent. While the black matriarch is powerful in her brand of vigilante justice, the black community's preference to favour silence means that she offers no care and causes an equal amount of damage.

---

7   In the television show *The Vampire Diaries*, the father of African-American character Bonnie is publicly and brutally murdered and there is no significant impact on the storyline; nor is there any real response from her white friends, especially in comparison to the reaction of those friends to more trivial events to other white characters in the group. For example, there is a similar non-reaction to the deaths of Bonnie's mother and grandmother, leaving her effectively orphaned, yet the death of the mother of a white character spanned a season and impacted nearly everyone. The trauma of black women is regularly minimised.

On some occasions, I could approach my grandmother for an immediate, powerful respected reaction. On others, this powerful reaction was wielded as a threat against me by ZC, who knew that the anger of an adult could put the fear of God into a child – especially the anger of a Caribbean woman. There are instances where I was coerced into participation; she turned my grandmother not into a safe figure but one to both fear and respect. Respect formed a significant part of our family dynamics. I do not lie to my parents and I do not disrespect them. There is a tone of voice that parents have and when they use it, you comply. When my father requested videoconferencing to discuss Erin it was not a request. I couldn't get out of this without being disrespectful and I was not ready to destroy the status quo. The videocall was sound only, he could not see my face. I told my father about Erin and he asked me if anything else had happened. A wise person would have stopped there or lied. I told him in brief of the childhood abuse inflicted by ZC. I had established a relatively good relationship with ZC. If you ever wonder how people can forgive or forget after those closest to them do horrific injustices, for me it was because it was easier than addressing it. I had one important request. *Don't do anything.* I had been getting along relatively okay with ZC, and I knew this would make it worse. During this hell happening to me, all I wanted was for no action, so I could get back to normal.

When I arrived home my parents brought me into the sitting room. Erin took up very little attention and ZC took centre stage. This was the last time Erin was ever brought up, the experience minimised so completely I don't know if I was over it or if I was so drastically retraumatised by current events it didn't get a chance to feature. I hadn't ever spoken about ZC and what she did by choice, so in these circumstances it was even more difficult, and instead I wrote. I only remember that I left the piece of paper in the room. I should have burned it. The next day I was taken by my father to visit ZC, ZC's parents and the parent of someone else I'd mentioned in the note. I'd said that I'd been forced to act out something, and another incident that I think has led to my discomfort with seeing black female genitals. Somehow, I got dragged in a room in front of all of these people and was interrogated. They asked me for dates and times of incidents that happened when I was 6 years old, they asked me to describe if the room was locked, and other trivial details, trying to somehow prove what I was saying was false.

These were unreasonable questions given that the events in question happened more than a decade before and my age. I was the youngest person in the room so I was mobbed by people who should have known better.

During this victim-blaming parade ZC was given the opportunity to confront me. She asked why I didn't bring it up with her sooner and personally. She used it against me as if it was my responsibility to advocate against her wrongs, because she *couldn't accept who she is* and believed her own lies. I now know that what she did was textbook gaslighting, 'child abusers may also attack a victim's very basic sense that she can trust her own senses, her own perception of reality' (Mertz and Lonsway, 1998, p. 1424). It sickens me to acknowledge but this situation probably shocked and terrified her and as done in the past, she had to come out on top.

My rational mind knows I could have left, I could have gotten up and walked out but I felt trapped because I had been driven to this venue. As recently as the previous year I started using two crutches and was heavily dependent on my parents for transport. I couldn't afford a taxi, I couldn't get far away enough to get to the buses and all people present were able-bodied and would have been able to stop me. This is the kind of vulnerability that disabled people face; I was the weakest one in that room. I was trapped. I'd been driven. My legs. This incident happened with my consent – I agreed to attend because I blamed myself, I felt like I was in trouble so I behaved like a chastised child and did what I was told. As I recall the nature of what went on, the more surreal it feels.

The next thing I can remember is mid-afternoon the next day. I had been in a fine mood, happy as anything and just doing what I was doing. My father asked me if I was okay – he seemed concerned and I was confused. Very confused. Until I vaguely remembered what had happened the day before. I used to be known for my strong memory; my mind immediately protected me from that day but I can promise you – I haven't been the same since.

Years later, I had the opportunity to ask why it had happened. My father had been privy to another family where something similar had happened and was not addressed, so he felt this must be addressed, to avoid similar damage to the family. Not to me, to the family. I no longer see that half of my extended family. I asked why I had been ignored, why my one request had been comprehensively stomped on. They 'couldn't remember' and they sincerely apologised for the impact of their actions. A culture of victim-blaming underpinned their actions. I should never have been questioned – ZC should. I have many examples of bearing the brunt of this. As a Christian, I was pressured to forgive (Redmond, 1989). I broke the dynamic when tensions arose over me not sharing my address. To be told 'not to worry' because ZC wasn't mad with me told me that not only did my family fail to understand and support me at the time, the years had changed nothing.

I wasn't viewed as a survivor, I was a problem. I had gone through this entire experience as a passenger, with my wants ignored and betrayed through forced interactions with the family over the years. There are certain obligations that one must fulfil to be considered a good or bad member of the family or role model (Reynolds, 2006). In mine, showing up is one of them. Not rocking the boat is another. It was difficult to escape without being branded as a bad family member; I had seen it happen to others. When my tolerance left, I introduced a level of disrespectful open commentary that meant I was finally heard. I regained some of the autonomy that had been stripped away. I had been silenced by our family culture (Reid *et al.*, 2014) as much as I had been silenced by ZC.

Very recently, I've accessed a specialist counsellor and spoke about this. I was told that parents find disclosure of sexual abuse traumatic because they have failed to protect their children (Manion *et al.*, 1996). Here is where they failed me. They should have known to go to the police or get me help but instead I have had nearly a decade of trauma to deal with because my request was ignored. I asked for fundamentally so little, and didn't even receive that. With time, I have forgiven them because parents are human, not fortune tellers. Even in this situation, I wasn't treated as the victim. I wasn't important and what I wanted did not matter. ZC received more sympathy than I did, and her feelings mattered more than mine. Where I should matter, I did not.

True adulthood and medical agency

I tried to return to university like nothing had happened. I failed. My symptoms were interfering with daily life; I had counsellors and therapists but was oblivious to the formal diagnosis of mental health. I had approached them for my depression and naturally began talking about this in sessions. I was distressed, in pain, couldn't remember anything and due to have one of the biggest operations of my life because of my disability.

I ended up with PTSD. The counsellors and therapists knew and were not equipped to help me. I was an odd mix of historical abuse, family trauma, anxiety and depression. The former meant that I wasn't eligible for talking therapies in my local NHS Trust. Nearly every professional I came into contact with turned me away. Too complex for them to help. Their 12-week maximum sessions were nowhere near what I needed, and it would be professionally irresponsible to start treating me. This added to the hopelessness, something horrible had happened and no one could help. I didn't have my driving licence.

Incidents like these are why I ended up suicidal. I would use almost all my energy to get somewhere, be in great pain and arrive only to be rejected. I sometimes ended up stranded for an hour, waiting for my legs to work well enough to get me back to a bus home. I eventually got referred to an NHS Cognitive Behavioural Therapy (CBT) psychologist. I had waited around a year to see her. This was prior to *Achieving Better Access to Mental Health Service by 2020* (NHS England; Department of Health, 2014) and the guidelines *Improving Access to Psychological Therapies* (NHS England, 2015). I was so relieved to see her, I told her everything. She then told me, 'You don't remember anything because you don't want to remember anything' and that I'd just had

---

8   She thought that a woman who had depression since the age of 15 and who had been told by six independent professionals that she had PTSD would confuse the worst experience of her life for a depressive episode. I disagreed and wish I'd asked for a second opinion. I hadn't realised you could do that with mental health.

an extreme depressive episode, not PTSD.[8] She didn't want to help me. I've chosen to believe that this woman simply hadn't come across Ostrow (2016) who concluded it's possible to get PTSD from family trauma. Rather than purposefully misdiagnose me, she minimised it. Her medical autonomy over me ensured her discharge effectively blocked my access to other services in the region.

During these times, I couldn't remember what had happened to me the previous day, the previous week. I had almost no concept of time, what I did or what I was going to do. My memory loss was probably my biggest tormentor, and her words kept me awake at night. That 1-hour session with this woman was deeply influential, because it was nearly 7 years before I spoke to a new counsellor or tried to get help. I remember her name. She wrote up everything I told her in detail and sent it to my GP. I believed she'd just write a summary. That letter is still in my medical records. As a disabled woman, I need to see many medical professionals and I live in fear of them reading it. They all have access to it. Somewhere a secretary or two has read my story and knows what happened to me. I have tried to since to get it removed from my medical records, but my GP practice at the time refused because 'it could potentially inform diagnostic practice' despite me withdrawing my consent. Further clarity around the parameters of consent and guidance for areas outside of treatment would be welcome. There is no absolute right to consent leading to what I see as a failure in my care (Selinger, 2009). These doctors ignored withdrawn consent, and kept information about me without my permission in the event I would ever come to them for help. Unlikely. Who would trust a doctor who doesn't care about what you want? It felt like an abuse of medical power.

I was vulnerable because I was at the mercy of professionals who minimised what had happened to me. Politically, my race played into it. Black people have a harder time accessing mental health services (Memon *et al.*, 2016; Omonira-Oyekanmi, 2014). We are seen to be more resilient, vulnerability and delicacy are not attributes afforded to us under white supremacy and we are expected to deal with more because black bodies are not valued. None of the professionals I encountered told me about survivors' organisations. My abuse experience doesn't fit the stereotype. I didn't walk home with clothes dragged off my body. I don't quite fit the victim profile, I didn't scream like you're supposed to. I didn't react until years later. I was totally fine until it was discovered and by then I was alone.

Independent support: survivors' organisations

Once I accepted a mental health diagnosis, I felt I would not be believed. I regularly doubt my perception and sanity during high stress times. The services I received that were NHS funded pushed me away. The National Institute for

Health and Clinical Excellence standards recommend timely access to treatment for 15 per cent of those who could benefit (NHS England, n.d.), meaning 85 per cent of people are likely to have difficulty accessing appropriate services. Without the endorsement of NHS professionals, I struggled to get the opinions of my counsellors recognised or taken seriously. Without a diagnosis, I feel I wouldn't have been treated with such disrespect. Had the time been taken it would have been very clear that I was experiencing PTSD. Unfortunately, I felt like my symptoms made me less believable as though I were an undesirable patient. My concentration problems aggravated by pain medication, my hypervigilance leading me to lock doors behind me without even noticing, my insomnia, my constant feelings of guilt, my reckless behaviour and particularly my inappropriate personal relationships: these were the things that I felt made me undeserving of help.

Would this psychologist have dismissed me so quickly if I didn't have a history of mental health? I struggle to imagine my white able-bodied peers receiving the same treatment. Had I never had depression, insomnia, anxiety before, if my interactions with health services were infrequent, would I have been treated differently? She treated me as though I were a hypochondriac and as I sat there alone – I could well have been. The evidence of my disability was used against me. I wasn't pinned down by a man twice my size but I had the same amount of power in that room. When I told her everything, I was prepared to be sectioned under the Mental Health Act. I was not prepared to be discarded. Knowing I physically cannot fight made me defeatist. Knowing I would be dismissed (or run the risk of it) made me learn to try to handle things myself. When approaching health services, I learned an institution is only as good as it's gatekeeper and my trust in strangers diminished.

I already knew the power of a doctor. At 18 years old, a disagreement in front of a doctor with my mother about a surgery date translated to me not wanting the surgery due to the appearance of scarring. Entirely not true, but that is in my medical notes forever. If called upon, a doctor will trust the doctor's account of events rather than mine. Will I be considered a shallow person, unable to make decisions? What kind of capacity do I have left, and will it be taken away?

As the years went by some of the more problematic symptoms calmed. It became difficult to live without addressing all that happened and following a positive encounter with CBT I felt ready to trust professionals. Media coverage of high-profile historic sexual abuse cases made it easier, for example Jimmy Saville and Operation Yewtree (Halliday, 2014), it felt as though the atmosphere had changed. I looked up my nearest survivor's organisation and self-referred.

They were very discreet and I had confidence in them. I had a month wait until my assessment and on the day of my assessment, I had a big anxiety attack – I knew it was big because I don't often vomit uncontrollably before getting on with my day. At the appointment, the therapist opened by saying something like, 'You're here because you've experienced child abuse and rape'. My hands clenched, I broke whatever I was holding and she went to get me a drink. She acknowledged that it was a huge step, because it was. She asked me a question but before I answered I asked her to explain their documentation and retention policies because I've been burned before.

I needed assurances before I handed anything over. Information is power and I was about to give them notable information. My negative experiences with professionals before were so devastating because I had given damning information while I was in a position of vulnerability. I have ended up deeply guarded and I don't know if that will ever go away.

For years, I have been tortured with flashbacks to the abuse or reminders of people and places linked to the event. The frequency has been increasing. I cooked a traditional meal and had heavily intrusive thoughts relating to the abuse. I whitewash the experiences, and minimise them to make it easier to deal with. I took a selfie while at the cinema and my hair was styled differently that day. I became upset because my own face reminded me of people linked to the abuse. It is one thing to avoid triggers when they are external because you can always move or get away. My own face being a trigger is a betrayal I cannot escape.

I now have weekly sessions. During one of them, I wondered why my mind was so mean to me – constantly attacking me when I least expected it. I did not even recognise my symptoms as PTSD and only thought of them as intrusive thoughts or bad days. I told my counsellor and she offered to bring in resources to help me. When the resources all related to PTSD I finally felt validated. It felt like someone telling me I had been right all along and my sanity confirmed.

Conclusions

I used to wonder if I have been seeing a different world to everyone else. Just like I can't imagine what it's like to wake up in the morning and not be depressed or to never know what it's like, some women will go their whole lives and never be raped. Others will be brutalised, even murdered during acts of sexual violence. I fell somewhere between the two, as though the lack of physical violence delegitimised my experience.

Key messages from this chapter

- My abuse had such a powerful impact over me because I was so isolated, my abuser had access to me because of heteronormative assumptions dictating gender roles within the family.
- Professionals missed opportunities to help me because they prioritised medical notes over my patient experiences.

- My abuse being regularly minimised led to me doubting my sanity and hindered my chances of getting help.

References

Allnock, D., 2010. *Children and Young People Disclosing Sexual Abuse: An Introduction to the Research*, London: NSPCC.

Alriksson-Schmid, A. I., Armour, B. S. and Thibadeu, J. K., 2010. Are Adolescent Girls with a Physical Disability at Increased Risk for Sexual Violence? *Journal of School Health*, 80(7), pp. 361–367.

Assemblies of God Incorporated, 2017. Who We Are: AOG Great Britain. [Online] Available at: www.aog.org.uk/about-us/who-we-are [Accessed 1 August 2017].

Cho, S., Crenshaw, K. W. and McCall, L., 2013. Toward a Field of Intersectionality Studies: Theory, Applications, and Praxis. *Signs Journal of Women and Culture in Society*, 38(4), pp. 785–810.

Crenshaw, K., 1991. Mapping the Margins: Intersectionality, Identity Politics and Violence Against Women of Colour. *Stanford Law Review*, 43(6), pp. 1241–1299.

Dagon, D., 2012. Preventing Sexual Exploitation. *Children and Young People Now*, 36(March), pp. 6–19.

DiLillo, D., 2001. Interpersonal Functioning among Women Reporting a History of Childhood Sexual Abuse: Empirical Findings and Methodological Issues. *Clinical Psychology Review*, 21(4), pp. 553–576.

El-Bushara, J. and Sahl, I. M. G., 2005. *Cycles of Violence: Gender Relations and Armed Conflict*. London: Agency for Co-operation and Research in Development.

Goodyear-Brown, P., ed., 2012. *Handbook of Child Sexual Abuse: Identification, Assessment and Treatment*. Hoboken, NJ: Wiley.

Halliday, J., 2014. Jimmy Savile: Timeline of His Sexual Abuse and its Uncovering. [Online] Available at: www.theguardian.com/media/2014/jun/26/jimmy-savile-sexual-abuse-timeline [Accessed 1 September 2017].

Harris, J. H., 1990. Practicing Liberation in the Black Church. *Christian Century*, 13–20 June.

Hendricks, J., 2012. Considering Life Course Concepts. *The Journals of Gerontology: Series B*, 67B(2), pp. 226–231.

Henerey, C., 2017. Black Women, Police Violence, and Mental Illness. [Online] Available at: www.aaihs.org/black-women-police-violence-and-mental-illness/ [Accessed 1 September 2017].

Kendall-Tackett, K., 2001. *The Long Shadow: Adult Survivors of Childhood Abuse*. Oakland, CA: New Harbinger.

Krause, N. and Wulff, K. M., 2009. Church-Based Social Ties, A Sense of Belonging in a Congregation, and Physical Health Status. *The International Journal for the Psychology of Religion*, 15(1), pp. 73–93.

Manion, I.G., McIntyre, J., Firestone, P., Ligezinska, M., Ensom, R. and Wells, G., 1996. Secondary Traumatization in Parents Following the Disclosure of Extra-familial Child Sexual Abuse: Initial Effects. *Child Abuse Neglect*, 20(11), pp. 1095–1109.

Memon, A., Taylor, K., Mohebati, L.M., Sundin, J., Cooper, M., Scanlon, T. and de Vissa, R., 2016. Perceived Barriers to Accessing Mental Health Services among Black and Minority Ethnic (BME) Communities: A Qualitative Study in Southeast England. *BMJ Open*, 6(11).

Mertz, E. and Lonsway, K. A., 1998. Power of Denial: Individual and Cultural Constructions of Child Sexual Abuse. *Northwestern University Law Review*, 92(4), pp. 1415–1457.

NHS England; Department of Health, 2014. *Improving Access to Mental Health Services by 2020*. London: Derpartment of Health.

NHS England, 2015. *Improving Access to Psychological Therapies (IAPT) Waiting Times and Guidance FAQs*. London: NHS England.

NHS England, n.d. Service Standards. [Online] Available at: *www.england.nhs.uk/mental-health/adults/iapt/service-standards/* [Accessed 1 September 2017].

Omonira-Oyekanmi, R., 2014. Black and Dangerous? Patient Experiences of Mental Health Services in London. [Online] Available at: https://lacuna.org.uk/politics/black-and-dangerous-patient-experiences-of-mental-health-services-in-london/ [Accessed 1 September 2017].

Ostrow, R., 2016. Family Trauma Can Trigger Complex PTSD. [Online] Available at: www.theaustralian.com.au/life/health-wellbeing/family-trauma-can-trigger-complex-ptsd/news-story/d7674b0f5115326c269b9ba6e3983a51 [Accessed 1 September 2017].

Pemberton, C., 2016. Sexual Exploitation: Disturbing Signs. [Online] Available at: www.eani.org.uk/_resources/assets/attachment/full/0/41537.pdf [Accessed 1 September 2017].

Platt, L., Powers, L. and Leotti, S., 2017. The Role of Gender in Violence Experienced by Adults With Developmental Disabilities. *Journal of Interpersonal Violence*, 31(1), pp. 101–129.

Redmond, S. A., 1989. Christian 'Virtues' and Recovery from Child Sexual Abuse. In: J. C. Brown and C. R. Bohn, eds. *Christianity, Patriarchy and abuse: A Feminist Critique*. New York: Pilgrim Press, pp. 70–88.

Reid, M. A., 1993. Family Film: Black Writers in Hollywood. In: *Redefining Black Films*. London: University of California Press.

Reid, S., Rheddock, R. and Nickenig, T., 2014. Breaking the Silence of Child Sexual Abuse in the Caribbean: A Community-Based Action Research Intervention Model. *Journal of Child Sexual Abuse*, 23(3), pp. 256–77.

Reynolds, T., 2004. *Caribbean Families, Social Capital and Young People's Diasporic Identities*. London: Families & Social Capity ERSC Research Group, London South Bank University.

Reynolds, T., 2006. Family and Community Networks in the (Re)Making of Ethnic Identity in Caribbean Young People in Britain. *Community, Work and Family*, 9(3), pp. 273–290.

Rhimes, S., Nowalk, P. and Listo, M., 2014. *Mama's Here Now*. Series 1 ed. s.l.: ABC Studios.

Selinger, C. P., 2009. The Right to Consent: Is it Absolute? *British Journal of Medical Practitioners*, 2(2), pp. 50–54.

Sivakumaran, S., 2010. Lost in Translation: UN Responses to Sexual Violence against Men and Boys in Situations of Armed Conflict. *International Review of the Red Cross*, 92(877), pp. 259–277.

Smethers, S., 2015. 'What are the Issues Affecting Grandparents in Britain Today?', Quality in Ageing and Older Adults. *Emerald Insight*, 16(1), pp. 37–43.

UNICEF Jamaica, 2006. Parenting In Jamaica. [Online] Available at: www.unicef.org/jamaica/parenting_corner.html [Accessed 1 September 2017].

West, K. and Cowell, N. M., 2015. Predictors of Prejudice Against Lesbians and Gay Men in Jamaica. *The Journal of Sex Research*, 52(3), pp. 296–305.

Williams, L. M., 1995. Recovered Memories of Abuse in Women with Document Child Sexual Victimization Histories. *Journal of Traumatic Stress*, 8(4), pp. 649–673.

Part 3

Older life

Chapter 8

Elder abuse, ageing and disability

A critical discussion

Bridget Penhale

Introduction

From the latter decades of the last century, there has been increasing global recognition of the abuse and neglect of older people who might be at risk of such forms of harm, as a social problem in need of attention. Specifically, over the last two decades, the issue of elder abuse has gained importance at international level and European Union levels. The World Health Organization (WHO) and the International Network of the Prevention of Elder Abuse (INPEA) have recognised the abuse of older people as a significant global problem (United Nations 2002; WHO 2002). Elder abuse is a human rights violation resulting in suffering, decreased quality of life and even hastening mortality. Moreover, it is an infringement of Article 25 of the EU Charter of Fundamental Rights, which recognises and respects the rights of older people to lead lives of dignity and independence, and to participate in social and cultural life.

The proportion of older people is increasing in most societies and in 2050, over a quarter (26 per cent) of the population in Europe will be 65 years old or older (Organisation for Economic Co-Operation and Development (OECD), 2010). There is a growing proportion of older people in many societies and concern has been raised that violence against older persons is likely to increase in 'incidence, prevalence and complexity' (United Nations Economic Commission for Europe, 2013, p. 1).

A number of national and international organisations have been established to promote knowledge, understanding and awareness of such abuse and a number of countries globally have been working in this area but are at different stages of development. Education and training for professionals has been increasing regarding recognition of abuse and skills in intervention are in development. However, identification of elder mistreatment remains problematic and strategies and techniques for intervening in such situations are in comparatively early stages of development, although some recent progress has been made. One essential future element of the process is the involvement of the public and in particular older service users themselves, including those who experience different impairments, in discussion about the issues of relevance to them; public education and awareness-raising are also very important in order to try and address this critical problem.

Background

Situations encompassing elder abuse and neglect are found across the world and as yet we have not found a country where some form of abuse and/or neglect does not exist. Considering historical perspectives, there are references to abuse and neglect of older people in documents and literature dating back over several centuries. For example, the Shakespeare play, *King Lear*, which concerns the relationships between an elderly father and his adult daughters, could be seen as an example of psychological and emotionally abusive behaviour towards the old man, as well as dysfunctional familial relationships. Nevertheless, the phenomena of abuse and neglect of older people have really only been recognised comparatively recently. In many countries it is only in the last 30 years, or less in some places, that there has been recognition of the problem, while it is clear that there has been growing concern about the issue since that time. Reasons for this increasing recognition and concern include the following:

- systems of de-institutionalisation of care and care provided in the community for older adults in need of support;
- demography and an ageing population;
- medical advances, technology and improvements in public health leading to more people living longer, even with complex health conditions/ disabilities;
- a comparatively recent focus on advocacy and rights (human and citizenship rights);
- changing social structures, for instance patterns of mobility and changes in family structures and support systems for elders.

It is important here to recognise the significance of professional recognition of the issue as a problem area and one in need of attention. This is similar to the situation of child abuse/protection, where in the late 1960s and early 1970s medical clinicians first raised concerns about this form of abuse; however, in the 1970s it was activists in the feminist movement who initially identified violence and abuse directed towards (younger) women, specifically in relation to domestic and intimate partner violence. This resulted in a more political 'grass-roots' approach to the apparent problem that directed attention towards this issue. Moreover, concerning elder abuse and neglect it was not until the 1980s, within a European context, that professionals began to draw attention to the phenomenon, although this occurred some years earlier than this in the North American region. Recognition of these processes of identification is important, as this has had an influence on the development of responses to elder abuse and neglect and is also related to the comparative lack of awareness by the wider public of the issue (Penhale 2008).

Nevertheless, over the past two decades there has been a growing body of international research concerning elder abuse. A number of countries have undertaken nationally representative studies on self-reported elder abuse and neglect among community-residing older persons (Acierno *et al.* 2010; Eisokovits *et al.* 2005; Naughton *et al.* 2012; O'Keeffe *et al.* 2007). Specific research concerning violence against older women has also been carried out (Luoma *et al.* 2011; Zink and Fisher 2006). However, when considering estimates of prevalence rates for violence against women, in many studies the populations studied have tended to exclude women older than, for example, 60 years.

Additionally, it is difficult to accurately compare the results of studies because of variations in research designs. Definitions and concepts of violence, mistreatment and abuse used; measurements, together with sample sizes, time periods for prevalence and age limits used may all vary between studies (Bonnie and Wallace 2003; De Donder *et al.* 2011a; Nerenberg 2007). Therefore, there is a wide range of results concerning the nature and scope of the problem.

General points

There are a number of general points that need to be made that relate to the whole area of elder abuse and neglect. First, there are a number of definitional issues of relevance. Up until now, there has been no agreement on a universal or standardised definition. Different stakeholders, for example legal and policy-makers, practitioners and researchers, may use different definitions, although ideally these should be explicit and acknowledged by the different constituent parties (Penhale 1993). However, there is still some debate about definitions, indicators of mistreatment and different aspects of neglect.

Second, in many countries there is also a general lack of awareness of abuse and this can lead to difficulties in detection and identification of abuse and neglect. This lack may occur for practitioners as well as the wider public and older people themselves. Until comparatively recently, elder mistreatment has been very much a taboo and unrecognised topic, particularly in relation to certain forms such as sexual abuse, and in general, the concept of abuse and neglect is both under-developed and under-researched. And as might be expected given the global diversity of societal and cultural variations, recognition of the phenomena has followed different pathways and histories in different countries and contexts. A number of non-governmental organisations (NGOs) working in this area have been established in recent years and in many places important work is being undertaken in raising awareness and lobbying for change to existing practices. One example of an international (and global) initiative is INPEA, which was set up in 1997 (see www.inpea.net). The organisation, a virtual network, has done much to raise awareness about the issue and was instrumental in the establishment of World Elder Abuse Awareness Day – celebrated on 15 June annually and ratified as such by the United Nations (UN) since 2011. As an example at a national level, in the UK the charity Action on Elder Abuse has been operating since 1993 (see www.elderabuse.org.uk) and has undertaken much work to raise awareness of the general public and of relevant professionals about the mistreatment of older people. It also acts to lobby government across the UK for change, including legislation, in this area. Nevertheless, there is still an important need for more education, training and awareness-raising at a range of different levels: for the general public, as well as for practitioners and students in the fields of health and care.

Third, when considering the term vulnerability, there is a need to acknowledge that there are issues that relate to visibility and invisibility in terms of what is recognised as mistreatment or not, as well as such aspects as marginalisation and exclusion of those who may be considered vulnerable, or at risk of mistreatment. From current understanding, vulnerability appears to be largely situational; it is not solely the characteristics of an individual that results in assignment of the status 'vulnerable' but it is, rather, the interaction with other, situational and circumstantial factors that lead to a vulnerable state developing for the individual (Penhale and Parker 2008). It seems that often those individuals who are most at risk of harm from abuse and/or neglect are likely to be people who are acknowledged to be from 'hard to reach' or 'seldom heard' groups and who may experience life on the margins of society due to a number of reasons. This will likely have adverse effects on individuals' health and well-being, but we must recognise that this is not just in relation to physical health but also states of mental well-being. In addition, older individuals who have impairments, either due to a physical or cognitive related illness or disability (or even more complex conditions, combining both aspects) may also be 'hard to reach' as their needs may mean that they are not fully addressed by current service structures. This may be particularly relevant in relation to such individuals' experiences of abuse and violence as existing provision may not serve intersectional interests appropriately.

Then again, the nature of public policy and service provision and the changing nature of relationships between the individual and the state, and perhaps particularly the welfare state (and the residualisation of welfare) in many countries needs further exploration in relation to mistreatment. This is especially germane, irrespective of whether a situation consists of violence, abuse, neglect or exploitation or indeed combinations of these (mistreatment is the term used to encompass these aspects, as suggested by O'Keeffe *et al.* 2007).

Furthermore, a number of additional issues appear to be linked with family relations and familial matters. During the last century, there were a number of changes to family structures, particularly in western and more industrialised countries. As a result of such changes, family types and patterns have changed and developed; examples of these can be seen in the rise in levels of lone parenting and increases in the number and extent of re-constituted families following divorce and separation. In many countries, there have also been increases in multi-generational families, some of whom share accommodation and family life; this is due at least in part to the demographic changes already referred to and the rising number of people living into late old age (Antonucci 2007). Socio-demographic factors such as gender, marital status, education and income have also resulted in changes. There have been significant effects from these and other factors on patterns of familial relationships in the twenty-first century and on the nature of caregiving in later life.

Within this field, however, it is important that various forms of differentiation occur. It is necessary, for example, to differentiate between the different types of abuse, neglect and exploitation that exist. Within many typologies that have been developed, these types generally include: physical abuse, sexual abuse, psychological and emotional abuse, financial abuse and exploitation, and neglect. However, in certain societal contexts, there may be differences in the typologies that have been developed and are used. For example in France, societal abuse exists as a distinct category, whereas in England due to recent changes instigated by the Care Act, 2014, several additional types have been included, although societal abuse is not one of them. Importantly, however, this revised framework, introduced in England from April 2015, includes self-neglect as a distinct category of what is now referred to as adult safeguarding and includes other adults who might experience abuse and/or neglect (not only older people). Other categories that have been included in the revised policy framework are domestic violence and abuse, which includes situations of honour-based violence, organisational abuse (also referred to institutional abuse in some countries), and modern slavery, which includes human trafficking, domestic servitude and forced labour. These latter categories have been included as the legal and policy framework that has been developed in England also relates to younger adult populations who may be considered to be at risk of harm. This includes individuals who may have specific needs in relation to physical or intellectual disability and severe and enduring mental health difficulties (i.e. those people who may be likely to come into contact with health and social care organisations and their services) as well as older people; what is less clear is whether those people who are at the intersections of age, disability and violence are covered effectively within such a framework.

There are also different levels at which mistreatment may arise: at individual, community and societal levels (also termed: micro, meso and macro levels: Bennett *et al.* 1997). This differentiation also relates to ecological frameworks that have been developed at international level, notably by WHO in their work on violence prevention (see for example: www.who.int/violenceprevention/ approach/ecology/en/ and Dahlberg *et al.*, 2002). The framework has previously been used in consideration of risk factors for elder abuse (Schiamberg and Gans 1999)

Use of an ecological framework allows for a broader exploration of the associated risk factors as it suggests that violence can be understood as a result of human behaviour on individual, relational, community and societal levels. A combination of characteristics at individual, relational and community levels can be employed to identify the most important factors for increased likelihood of victimisation from violence. This then allows for the development of appropriate interventions on a societal level that goes beyond a normative design of interventions.

In addition, there are a number of different locations and settings in which abuse may happen. For instance, these incorporate domestic, and familial settings, as well as a variety of institutional and community settings. And there are a number of possible different participants in abusive situations; not solely at the level of victim and abuser, but also in terms of potential witnesses within situations, who may provide valuable testament about what they may perceive the situation to consist of and think should be done in terms of potential responses to such situations.

Theoretical perspectives

Although the remit of this chapter does not allow for a comprehensive consideration of either theoretical or conceptual frameworks, causative factors or indicators of risk for individuals, several key points need to be taken into account when discussing abusive situations. While some aspects of theories relating to family violence may be of use when developing a theoretical framework of elder mistreatment, it is important to recognise that the phenomenon of elder abuse is not just a sub-type of family violence. As observed earlier in this chapter, elder abuse does not just occur in familial or domestic settings. Within the continuum of elder abuse and neglect are found many different types of behaviours, actions and lack of actions. Additionally, the spectrum covered by the term 'abuse' is far wider than that which is generally ascribed to violence, where a general perception of physical violence tends to prevail.

From the evidence to date, elder abuse appears to be a complex and multi-causal phenomenon. However, there are several problems with interpretations of existing evidence. A number of the causal factors that have been suggested as relevant to elder abuse seem to focus more on micro, individual factors. This means that the macro, structural factors are not fully taken into account and that, in addition, there often appears to be an ascription of pathology to older people, perhaps particularly those with some form of disability, whether this is physical or mental in nature. A clear example of this is when an older person who is dependent on others for care and support is seen as a source of stress and is therefore in some way held responsible for abuse that arises from such situations. Such perceptions of pathology have a tendency towards confirmation of some existing societal views of older people as dependent and powerless, which is not helpful. And despite attempts to promulgate the social model of disability as widely as possible across societies, this is comparable to existing and quite prevalent societal perceptions of disabled people as helpless and dependent and unable to care for themselves or to live independently. Thus, individuals who are both disabled and older may actually be more likely to be perceived in this way and to experience an increase in vulnerability, due to this intersectionality. Such situational vulnerability, compounded by inter-sectionality, also includes exposure to violence, abuse and neglect so that older disabled individuals (perhaps in particular women) are more likely to experience violence in their daily lives. However, such positioning (of older and disabled people as dependent and powerless) also fails to take account of the potential role of other factors (such as neighbourhood and community (Buffel *et al.* 2009) in acting as protective factors against the development of abusive situations.

It is unlikely that any one theoretical perspective will be developed which can account for every type of mistreatment that happens to older people. And there is a history of different theoretical perspectives in this field (Phillips 1986; Pillemer 1993; Steinmetz 1993). The aim is surely to more accurately reflect what is likely to be: 'A complex and multi-layered structure' (Sprey and Matthews 1989 p. 57). If this is so, then a variety of different conceptual frameworks and explanations will be necessary to develop a theoretical model that accounts for specific but different phenomena that constitute the continuum as a whole. This is especially so in considering the intersectional issues of age, disability, violence and gender raised above and ensuring that these are included in the frameworks that are developed. The particular aim here would be to try and counter the perception that elder abuse is 'Elusive, ambiguous and multi-dimensional' (Filinson 1989 p.26). Developing the concept of intersectionality in order to locate older individuals who are disabled and have been abused alongside alliances of oppression, discrimination and power, will highlight the complex nature of such abuse experiences for individuals and emphasise the inadequacy of the responses which have been developing (both professional and otherwise), that tend to leave women without sufficient support and protection where this is needed. Moreover, in general terms, the whole area of theoretical issues has been perceived as difficult and problematic. Such perceptions also have a bearing on the develop-ment and implementation of interventions and responses to mistreatment.

Risk factors

In relation to existing understandings of risk factors, a number of issues are pertinent. From what is known, mental health problems, alcohol and/or substance misuse, a past history of violence or abuse (within the family), dependency, stress and isolation are important factors to take account of when exploring allegations and situations in which abuse (and/or neglect) may occur. In relation to social isolation, it would seem that there are significant risks arising from being socially isolated from welfare agencies or other forms of community support as well as from wider family, relatives and friends. Overall, such risk factors should be considered in any comprehensive assessment of a potentially abusive situation and may contribute to both the genesis and perpetuation of abuse. However, it is important to note that it is not possible for professional practitioners to predict or determine levels of risk of abuse with certainty simply on the basis of identifying these factors.

In addition to the more established knowledge about risk factors there are a series of points that have emerged from both the work of Lachs et al. (1997) and the National Center on Elder Abuse, (1998). Lachs et al. suggest:

> In summary, poverty, minority status, functional disability, and worsening cognitive impairment were risk factors for reported elder mistreatment . . .
> (Lachs et al. 1997, p. 474)

The National Center on Elder Abuse study (1998) also determined the issue of worsening cognitive ability and the development of impairment as factors of relevance. The findings from that study showed that older people who were unable to care for themselves, or who were depressed or mentally confused, were more vulnerable to abuse and neglect as well as to situations in which self-neglect develops. Comparable to the risk from dependency, this factor has been re-iterated in more recent studies (for example, Görgen et al. 2009; Iborra 2008). As stated above, older people who are disabled, whether this is physical, intellectual or incorporates a mental health component – or indeed those who may have complex health conditions combining a number of impairments – are more vulnerable to risk of violence or neglect. Although an early paper (Smith 2007) indicates younger age as a variable increasing the likelihood of intimate partner violence, since gender and disability also feature as variables of relevance it is important to investigate intersectional conjunctions further in order to extend understanding of this area.

The implication from this information is that risk of abuse should be assessed at a range of different levels. Structural factors including environmental issues and social factors and divisions need to be taken into account in conjunction with particular family histories and individual characteristics. Consideration of micro, meso and macro levels of risk would seem to be necessary within any comprehensive assessment of an individual and their situation. This is clearly important when trying to decide what interventions would likely be most effective for an individual and their situation.

There appear to be several risk factors found across the prevalence studies that have been undertaken in Europe over the past decade (De Donder et al. 2011b; Eisikovits et al. 2005; Görgen et al. 2009;, Görgen 2010a, 2010b; Iborra 2008; Luoma et al. 2011; O'Keeffe et al. 2007; Siegel-Itzkovitch 2005). These are: gender (older women more at risk overall); age (those of increasing age more at risk of neglect and/or financial abuse). In relation to interpersonal abuse, family members living together and relationships between health status and dependency (including poor health of the care giver) also appear to be relevant. It is also apparent that more research needs to be undertaken to determine this area more fully.

Critical factors

There are a final set of important factors that we need to acknowledge when considering mistreatment of older people and developing interventions and responses to abusive situations. First, we must take into account societal, social, relational and cultural contexts concerning situations that occur (Penhale and Parker 2008). The phenomena of abuse and mistreatment are socially con-structed, so it is imperative that the meanings and understandings that are ascribed to situations by individuals are fully considered (Biggs et al. 1995). However, we also need to develop our knowledge and understanding of issues relating to both gender and power relations (Brandl et al. 2003, Whittaker, 1995 and 1996) and their respective roles in both the development and maintenance of abuse and abusive situations. The conjunctions that occur and inter-relate between age, disability and violence are also of increasing interest and concern and to these further intersections of gender and race might also be usefully added.

Moreover, within the continuum of elder mistreatment, it is evident that there is a range of actions and behaviours (including some lack of actions and some failures to act) that need to be considered as indicative of abuse. When considering the spectrum of mistreatment, it is also apparent that it is not just familial and interpersonal relationships and violence that are pertinent, but that other aspects such as institutional forms of mistreatment are of importance and need to be taken account of (Stanley et al. 1999). This is of particular concern when considering the individuals who are most likely to be at risk of such harms: older disabled women – who are also more likely to be admitted to institutional care.

Mistreatment can happen at different levels and therefore we need to recog-nise the personal, cultural and social structural levels at which mistreatment can occur (following ideas originally developed by Thompson 1998) and develop ability to act at the different levels. These levels are comparable to the micro, meso and macro levels already discussed. In addition, the overall context in which mistreatment occurs is one of societal ageism. This structural context is the backdrop in which, elder mistreatment is both accepted and somehow seen as behaviour that is permitted within society. To this degree, ageism appears to act as a 'master category' in the power relationships that affect older people (Penhale et al. 2000). However, other intersectional interests such as gender and disability are also of relevance and need to be taken into account here.

In general, the links between disability and violence have been under-examined until now and this has led to the marginalisation of disabled women who experience violence. It was identified several years ago that this side-lining occurred across the spheres of politics, theory, and practice (Thiara *et al.* 2011). This is even more apparent in the context of the topic(s) covered by this chapter and emphasises the evident need for intersectional approaches that cover the nexus of age, disability, gender and violence. Within a life course approach it is clear that so far less attention has been paid to the latter stages of life, particularly in comparison to the consideration given to the earlier stages of childhood, adolescence and young adulthood.

Issues in responding to mistreatment

In determining decisions about responding to mistreatment, there are several additional aspects to consider. First, are elder abuse and neglect issues that relate only to ageing? Do these phenomena only occur because of ageing processes? From what is known so far, this would seem unlikely to be the case. For example, domestic violence that occurs in later life may be a continuation of very long-standing problems within a relationship (Brandl and Horan 2002; Fisher and Regan 2006; Sev'er 2009) rather than something that only occurs due to the ageing process or in later life. Risk of violence relating to disability and impairment is also germane in this respect, with risk relating more to perceived dependency (due to disability) than to age. It is also apparent, however, that there are several different forms of elder mistreatment, and some of these, for example neglect, may be more related to ageing processes than others.

Second, does elder abuse principally arise as a complication of caregiving? Since it is clear that situations of abuse and neglect can happen beyond a caregiving context, this also does not appear to provide a satisfactory answer. Further, there does not seem to be any direct causal link between caring and abuse and/or neglect. If this were the case, then all caregiving situations would likely be abusive, and as work on the satisfactions of caregiving demonstrates, this is evidently not the case (Nolan 1997).

Moreover, if we take a family violence perspective, which is relevant in this area (Browne 1989; Browne and Herbert 1997; Gelles 1987; Lowenstein 2009), then our focus for interventions may be on systems of prevention, protection and punishment. Yet even within this situation, it seems that there are some apparent tensions between service and welfare perspectives on the one hand and an orientation towards justice and criminalisation, on the other. The implication of this is that an orientation towards prevention of mistreatment happening may be quite different from one that is premised on either protection or punishment. The latter of these perspectives may mean that there is an emphasis on criminal justice approaches rather than on the provision of welfare, care and treatment, which may be more likely to be found in systems that are concerned with prevention (or at times also protection). In addition, the types of interventions that have been developing in relation to elder abuse need to take into account different types of violence and abuse that may happen.

The decision concerning which intervention(s) to use will depend on the context, the situation and the type of mistreatment that has taken place. For example, provision of practical assistance to support the individuals involved may be used effectively in situations in which the abuse and/or neglect is due to caregiver stress, but this type of intervention may not work in situations related to financial abuse and exploitation of older people. Furthermore, we do not know enough yet about which strategies of intervention work best and are most effective for which situation to be able to state categorically that a specific intervention is best for a particular type of mistreatment. This is particularly likely to be the case in under-researched areas like the abuse of older disabled women, and work in this area also needs to include determining the perspectives of individuals on their situations, incorporating their views about the impacts of mistreatment. Such aspects as these are likely to require much greater attention in future. Clearly the intersections between age, disability, gender and abuse are crucial here, and ascertaining which perspective(s), preventive strategies and interventions will best meet the needs and situations of individuals whose needs fall within these intersections is fundamental to this endeavour.

Key messages from this chapter

- Elder abuse is a worldwide phenomenon; in general, older women are at more risk of experiencing abuse than men.
- The intersections of age, gender, and disability are essential components when considering violence.
- Different strategies for prevention and intervention are likely to be needed for different types of abuse and settings in which abuse occurs.

References

Acierno, R., Hernandez, M. A., Amstadter, A. B., Resnick, H. S., Steve, K., Muzzy, W. and Kilpatrick, D. G. (2010) Prevalence and Correlates of Emotional, Physical, Sexual, and Financial Abuse and Potential Neglect in the United States: The National Elder Mistreatment Study. *American Journal of Public Health*, 100(2), 292–297.

Antonucci, T. (2007) *Elder Abuse and Family Structures*. Presentation at Third World Elder Abuse Awareness Day Conference, WHO, Geneva.

Bennett, G., Kingston, P. and Penhale, B. (1997) *The Dimensions of Elder Abuse: Perspectives for Practitioners*. Basingstoke, UK: Macmillan.

Biggs, S., Phillipson, C. and Kingston, P. (1995) *Elder Abuse in Perspective*. Buckingham, UK: Open University Press.

Bonnie, R. J. and Wallace, R. B. (Eds) (2003) *Elder Mistreatment: Abuse, Neglect, and Exploitation in an Aging America*. Washington, DC: National Academies Press.

Brandl, B., Hebert, M., Rozwadowski, J. and Spangler, D. (2003) Feeling Safe, Feeling Strong: Support Groups for Older Abused Women. *Violence Against Women*, 9(12), 1490–1503.

Brandl, B. and Horan, D. (2002) Domestic Violence in Later Life: An Overview for Health Providers. *Women and Health*, 35(2/3), 41–54.

Browne, K. (1989) Family Violence: Elder and Spouse Abuse in K. Howells and C. R. Hollins (Eds) *Clinical Approaches to Violence.* Chichester, UK: John Wiley and Sons.

Browne, K. and Herbert, M. (1997) *Preventing Family Violence.* Chichester, UK: John Wiley and Sons.

Buffel, T., Verte, D., De Donder, L., Dury, S. and De Witte, N. (2009) *Conceptualizing the Neighbourhood as a Dynamic Social Space: Recognizing Older People as Actors in Placemaking,* European Sociological Association Conference, Lisbon.

Dahlberg, L. L. and Krug, E. G. (2002) Violence – A Global Public Health Problem in Krug, E., Dahlberg, L. L., Mercy, J. A., Zwi, A. B. and Lozano, R. (Eds) *World Report on Violence and Health.* Geneva, Switzerland: World Health Organization.

De Donder, L., Luoma, M. L., Penhale, B., Lang, G., Alves, J-F., Santos, A. J., Tamutiene, I., Koivusilter, M., Enzenhoffer, E., Perttu, S., Savola, T. and Verté, D. (2011a) European Map of Prevalence Rate of Elder Abuse and Its Impact for Future Research. *European Journal of Ageing*, 8(2), 129–143.

De Donder, L., Lang, G., Luoma, M-L., Penhale, B., Alves, J-F., Tamutiene, I., Santos, A., Koivusilter, M., Enzenhoffer, E., Perttu, S., Savola, T. and Verte, D. (2011b) Perpetrators of Abuse against Older Women: A Multi-national Study in Europe. *Journal of Adult Protection*, 13(6), 302–314.

Eisikovits, Z., Winterstein, T. and Lowenstein, A. (2005) *The National Survey on Elder Abuse and Neglect in Israel.* Haifa, Palestine: The Center for Research and Study of Aging, the University of Haifa and ESHEL.

Filinson, R. (1989) Introduction in Filinson, R. and Ingman, S. R. (Eds) *Elder Abuse: Practice and Policy.* New York: Human Sciences Press.

Fisher, B. and Regan, S. (2006) The Extent and Frequency of Abuse in the Lives of Older Women and Their Relationship with Health Outcomes. *The Gerontologist*, 46(2), 200–209.

Gelles, R. J. (1987) *Family Violence* (2nd edition), Sage Library of Social Research, No. 84. Beverly Hills, CA: Sage.

Gelles, R. J. and Loseke, D. R. (1993) (Eds) *Current Controversies in Family Violence.* Newbury Park, CA: Sage.

Görgen, T. (2010) (Ed.) *Sicherer Hafen oder gefahrvolle Zone? Kriminalitäts- und Gewalterfahrungen im Leben alter Menschen* [Safe Haven or Dangerous Zone? Experiences of Crime and Violence in Older People's Lives]. Frankfurt, Germany: Polizeiwissenschaft.

Görgen, T. (2010) *Dimensions of Elder Abuse: Current State of Research and Perspectives.* Presentation to Conference on High Quality Care, Essen (March 2010).

Görgen, T., Herbst, S., Kotlenga, S., Nagele, B. and Rabold, S. (2009). *Kriminalitäts- und Gewaltgefährdungen im Leben älterer Menschen – Zusammenfassung wesentlicher Ergebnisse einer Studie zu Gefährdungen älterer und pflegebedürftiger Menschen* [Experiences of Crime and Violence in Older People's Lives: Summary of Key Results of a Study on Hazards to Older People and Care Recipients]. Berlin: Bundesministerium für Familie, Senioren, Frauen und Jugend [Federal Ministry for Family Affairs, Senior Citizens, Women and Youth].

Iborra, I. (2008) *Elder Abuse in the Family in Spain*. Valencia, Spain: Queen Sofia Centre

Lachs, M. S., Williams, C., O'Brien, S., Hurst, L. and Horwitz, R. (1997) Risk Factors for Reported Elder Abuse and Neglect: A Nine-year Observational Cohort Study. *The Gerontologist*, 37(4), 469–474.

Lowenstein, A. (2009) Elder Abuse and Neglect – 'Old Phenomenon': New Directions for Research, Legislation, and Service Developments. *Journal of Elder Abuse and Neglect*, 21(3), 278–287.

Luoma, M. L., Koivusilta, M., Lang, G., Enzenhofer, E., De Donder, L., Verté, D., Reingarde, J., Tamutiene, I., Ferreira-Alves, J., Santos, A. J., and Penhale, B. (2011) *Prevalence Study of Abuse and Violence against Older Women: Results of a Multicultural Survey in Austria, Belgium, Finland, Lithuania, and Portugal* (European Report of the AVOW Project). National Institute for Health and Welfare (THL), Helsinki.

National Center on Elder Abuse. (1998) The National Elder Abuse Incidence Study, www.aoa.gov/abuse/report/default.html (Accessed March 2017).

Naughton, C., Drennan, J., Lyons, I., Lafferty, A., Treacy, M., Phelan, A., O'Loughlin, A., and Delaney, L. (2012) Elder Abuse and Neglect in Ireland: Result from a National Prevalence Survey. *Age and Aging*, 41(1), 98–103.

Nerenberg, L. (2007) *Elder Abuse Prevention: Emerging Trends and Promising Strategies*. New York: Springer.

Nolan, M. (1997) Sustaining Meaning: A Key Concept in Understanding Elder Abuse in Decalmer, P. and Glendenning, F. (Eds) *The Mistreatment of Elderly People* (2nd edition). London: Sage.

O'Keeffe, M., Hills, A., Doyle, M., McCreadie, C., Scholes, S., Constantine, R., Tinker, A., Manthorpe, J., Biggs, S. and Erens, B. (2007) *The UK Study of Abuse and Neglect of Older People*. London: National Centre for Social Research, 1305

Organisation for Economic Co-Operation and Development. (2010) *Health Status*. Retrieved from http://stats.oecd.org/Index.aspx?DatasetCode=HEALTH_STAT (accessed March 2017).

Penhale, B. (2008) Elder Abuse in the UK. *Journal of Elder Abuse and Neglect*, 20(2), 151–168.

Penhale, B. (1993) *The Abuse of Elderly People: Considerations for Practice. British Journal of Social Work*, 23(2), 95–112.

Penhale, B. and Parker, J. (2008) *Working with Vulnerable Adults*. London: Routledge.

Penhale, B., Parker, J. with Kingston, P. (2000) *Elder Abuse: Approaches to Working with Violence*. Birmingham, UK: BASW/Venture Press.

Phillips, L. R. (1986) Theoretical Explanations of Elder Abuse: Competing Hypotheses and Unresolved Issues in Pillemer, K. A. and Wolf, R. S. (Eds), *Elder Abuse: Conflict in the Family*. Dover, MA: Auburn House.

Pillemer, K. (1993) The Abused Offspring are Dependent: Abuse is Caused by the Deviance and Dependence of Abusive Caregivers in Gelles, R. J. and Loseke, D. R. (Eds), *Current Controversies in Family Violence*. Newbury Park, CA: Sage.

Schiamberg, L. B. and Gans, D. (1999) An Ecological Framework for Contextual Risk Factors in Elder Abuse by Adult Children. *Journal of Elder Abuse and Neglect*, 11(1), 79–103.

Sev'er, A. (2009) More than Wife Abuse That Has Gone Old: Violence against the Aged. *Journal of Comparative Family Studies*, 40(2), 279–292.

Siegel-Itzkovitch J. (2005) A Fifth of Elderly People in Israel are Abused. *British Medical Journal*, March 5; 330.7490.498c.

Smith, D. (2008) Disability, Gender and Intimate Partner Violence: Relationships from the Behavioral Risk Factor Surveillance System. *Sexuality and Disability*, 26(1), 15–28.

Sprey, J. and Matthews, S. H. (1989) The Perils of Drawing Policy Implications from Research: The Case of Elder Mistreatment in Filinson, R. and Ingman, S. R. (Eds), *Elder Abuse: Practice and Policy*. New York: Human Sciences Press.

Stanley, N., Manthorpe, J. and Penhale, B. (1999) *Institutional Abuse. Perspectives across the Life Course*. London: Routledge.

Steinmetz, S. K. (1993) The Abused Elderly are Dependent: Abuse is Caused by the Perception of Stress Caused by Providing Care in Gelles, R. J. and Loseke, D. R. (Eds) *Current Controversies in Family Violence*. Newbury Park, CA: Sage.

Thiara, R., Hague, G. and Mullender, A. (2011) Losing Out on Both Counts: Disabled Women and Domestic Violence. *Disability & Society*, 26(6), 757–771.

Thompson, N. (1998) *Promoting Equality*. Basingstoke, UK: Macmillan.

United Nations. (2002) *Political Declaration and Madrid International Plan of Action on Ageing*. Second World Assembly on Ageing, Madrid, Spain.

United Nations Economic Commission for Europe. (2013) *Abuse of Older Persons* (UNECE Policy Brief on Ageing No. 14). www.unece.org/fileadmin/DAM/pau/age/Policy_briefs/ECE-WG-14.pdf (Accessed March 2017).

Whittaker, T. (1995) Violence, Gender and Elder Abuse: Towards a Feminist Analysis and Practice. *Journal of Gender Studies*, 4(1), 35–45.

Whittaker, T. (1996) Elder Abuse in Fawcett, B., Featherstone, B., Hearn, J. and Toft, C. (Eds) *Violence and Gender Relations: Theories and Interventions*. London: Sage.

World Health Organization (2002). *The Toronto Declaration – On the Global Prevention of Elder Abuse*. Geneva, Switzerland: WHO.

World Health Organization (WHO). Violence Prevention Alliance: The Ecological Framework. Available from: www.who.int/violenceprevention/approach/ecology/en/ (Accessed September 2017).

Zink, T. and Fisher, B. (2006) The Prevalence and Incidence of Intimate Partner and Interpersonal Mistreatment in Older Women in Primary Care Offices. *Journal of Elder Abuse & Neglect*, 18(1), 83–105.

Chapter 9

Violation of human rights and elder abuse among older persons with disabilities

A policy review from Europe

Anne-Sophie Parent, AGE Platform Europe

Introduction

AGE Platform Europe (AGE) is a European network of more than 120 organisations which represent together more than 40 million people aged 50 and over in Europe. AGE aims to voice and promote the interests of the 190 million inhabitants aged 50+ in Europe and to raise awareness of the issues that concern them most in European Union (EU), United Nations (UN) and Council of Europe (CoE) institutions. AGE's mission is to give a voice to older and retired people in relevant EU and international policy debates. To achieve its mission AGE supports the active participation of older people's organisations in its work, so as to inform EU, UN and CoE policy development with the input of a hugely diverse representation of grass root older persons living in EU.

AGE policy work is co-funded by the EU and focuses on a wide range of policy areas that impact on older women and men's lives. These include issues of anti-discrimination and human rights, active ageing, social protection, pension reform, social inclusion, healthy ageing, research, accessibility issues, standardisation and new technologies. AGE works in close cooperation with other EU non-discrimination non-governmental organisations (NGOs) to raise awareness of issues linked to the intersection of ageing with gender, disability and other grounds of discrimination such as ethnic origin, religion and sexual orientation.

Since AGE was established in 2001, its members' representatives have been reporting great concerns about a pervasive form of human rights violation: elder abuse that affects a significant number of older persons, in particular those who have become frail and dependent on others as a result of age-related functional limitations. As highlighted during AGE Annual Conference in June 2017, elder abuse, violence and neglect are among the most serious violations of older persons' human rights and a global societal challenge. Furthermore, the selection of this societal challenge as one of the two topics for discussion at the 8th session of the UN Open-ended Working Group on Ageing (OEWG) in July 2017 was an acknowledgement that further action is needed worldwide to tackle elder abuse. In his statement to the OEWG, AGE President Ebbe Johansen stressed:

> elder abuse is the reflection of ageist attitudes towards older persons, seen as a burden, as inevitably frail and undeserving of dignified treatment. When it comes to older persons in need of care, elder abuse is also the result of the underdevelopment of care services and the lack of support for family and informal carers.
>
> (AGE Platform Europe, 2012b)

Discussion

Why focus on elder abuse?

While violence against women and children has rightly gained a high level of awareness among the public and policy makers in the last decades and is no longer tolerated, violence against older persons often remains unnoticed or even taboo, and is highly underreported. It is therefore difficult to find data that is collected in a systematic and comparable way on violence against older persons, let alone older disabled women. Yet elder abuse is not a new phenomenon and has been defined already more than decade ago by the World Health Organization (WHO) as 'a single, or repeated act, or lack of appropriate action, occurring within any relationship where there is an expectation of trust which causes harm or distress to an older person' (WHO, 2017b).

Elder abuse is a widespread phenomenon that affects significant numbers of older people, in particular the very old and dependent. In an updated fact sheet published in June 2017 (WHO, 2017b), WHO reported that:

- Around 1 in 6 older people experienced abuse in the past year.
- Rates of abuse may be higher for older people living in institutions than in the community.
- Elder abuse can lead to serious physical injuries and long-term psychological consequences.
- Elder abuse is predicted to increase as many countries are experiencing rapidly ageing populations.
- The global population of people aged 60 years and older will more than double, from 900 million in 2015 to about 2 billion in 2050.

All too often older persons in situations of dependency and with high care needs suffer abuse in silence, both at home and in residential care settings. In their 2017 updated factsheet on elder abuse, WHO refers to a recently published study on elder abuse based on evidence compiled from a wide range of studies worldwide (WHO, 2017b). The research team concludes that:

Over the past year, 15.7% of people aged 60 years and older were subjected to some form of abuse. This is likely to be an underestimation, as only 1 in 24 cases of elder abuse is reported, in part because older people are often afraid to report cases of abuse to family, friends, or to the authorities. Consequently, any prevalence rates are likely to be underestimated.

(WHO, 2017b)

The gender face of elder abuse

According to Eurostat, in 2016 19.2 per cent of people living in the EU were aged 65 and over, and two third of those aged 85 and over were women as a result of their longer life expectancy (Eurostat, 2016). Since the risk of elder abuse increases with the level of dependency and old age, older women are overrepresented among the victims of elder abuse and, as the above 2017 study reports, 'older women may face higher risk of persistent and severe forms of elder abuse compared to men' (Eurostat, 2016).

Elder abuse in long-term care for dependent older persons

Elder abuse can be intentional or unintentional and covers not only physical abuse, but also psychological and emotional, sexual, financial, pharmaceutical abuse and neglect. The denial of civic rights, discrimination on the ground of age and ageist attitudes are also considered to be forms of elder abuse. Unlike financial and sexual abuse that are always intentional, unintentional abuse often results from a lack of understanding of the older person's needs and feelings and the carer's difficulty in reconciling the older person's needs and wishes with one own private and professional demands.

There are huge discrepancies among the providers, conditions and types of eldercare services across EU countries. However as documented by EUROCARERS (2017),

today in the European Union around 80 per cent of older dependent people are still cared for by informal carers (i.e. relatives, friends, neighbours). Informal carers often face a high risk of burn-out and social exclusion due to the physical and psychological demands put on them. Professional carers are also put under huge pressure and are not always offered the training and support they need to perform their work under good conditions.

As anticipated by WHO, today's austerity measures combined with rapid demographic ageing are putting pressure on home and residential care systems, creating higher risks of elder abuse towards dependent older persons. For that reason, it was important for AGE to bring the issue of elder abuse on the EU, UN and CoE's agendas.

Putting elder abuse on the EU agenda

Although the EU has no real competency in fighting elder abuse which falls under national or local authorities' duties, with the support of the European Parliament and European Commission, AGE managed after a few years of hard work to bring the issue of elder abuse on the EU agenda. As a result, elder abuse has become a growing concern in recent years as European countries face irreversibly transformed age pyramids. Eurostat projections expect the number of people over the age of 65 to double and the number of people over the age of 80 to triple by 2060. The oldest old are more exposed to social isolation and poverty, which means they have fewer opportunities to access quality health care and social assistance, both key elements in preventing elder abuse (Eurostat, 2016).

Over the last decade, public awareness of this issue has been improving as a result of higher mediatisation of severe cases of elder abuse and greater attention paid by national and local policy makers. A Eurobarometer study on 'Health and Long-term care in the European Union' published by the European Commission in 2007 (European Commission, 2007) showed that nearly half of those surveyed consider maltreatment, neglect and even abuse of older people to be widespread in their country. Among all respondents 67 per cent felt that older people, especially older women, are financially exploited and receive inadequate care, and most felt that this vulnerable group is at risk of mental and physical abuse. Building on the outcomes of the Eurobarometer, in 2008 the European Commission also organised a conference on how elder abuse could be prevented by promoting high quality long-term care for older people.

The European Charter on the rights and responsibilities of older persons in need of care and assistance (2010) and the European Quality Framework for long-term care

At the same time awareness increased at EU level and AGE decided to start working on a European strategy to combat elder abuse and submitted a project proposal under the European DAPHNE programme which aimed to combat violence against women and children (European Commission, 2017b). With a group of 11 member organisations, AGE proposed to develop a European Charter of the rights and responsibilities of older persons in need of care and assistance (AGE Platform Europe, 2010). The European Strategy to combat Elder Abuse against Older Women (EUSTACEA) project was selected for funding and after 2 years, in 2010, we published a commonly agreed European Charter outlining nine rights and one chapter on the responsibilities of older dependent persons. The Charter was developed as a tool to combat elder abuse and neglect affecting so many older persons who need care and assistance, whether they are cared for at home, in the community or in institutional settings and is available in 13 EU languages. We also issued an accompanying guide or 'toolkit' addressing each of the rights expressed in the Charter, explaining what they concretely mean and how they can be enforced in practice (see Box 9.1).

BOX 9.1

AGE members and the EUSTACEA project partners stressed that advancing age should not result in any reduction of a person's rights, duties and responsibilities, including when a person is in either a permanent or temporary state of incapacity and unable to protect their own rights.

The EUSTACEA project adopted a broad-ranging definition of abuse encompassing intentional violence and mistreatment but also neglect. The Charter does not focus exclusively on older women and addresses issues that are relevant to both sexes. Yet the Charter recognises that the vast majority of frail and vulnerable older people are women: today two out of three people aged 80+ in Europe are women. Women may have a longer life expectancy than men but they spend many more years in old age suffering from frailty, disability and functional limitations. More than one-third of very old persons suffer from Alzheimer's disease or dementia, making them even more vulnerable to abuse. The gender dimension is thus crucial when tackling elder abuse. Younger groups can also benefit from the Charter: prevention and awareness-raising of potential victims must start at a much younger age and everyone should be empowered as early as possible to protect themselves against abuse.

The project attempted to cover all forms of elder abuse drawing on the expertise of partners in tackling abuse in institutions, community and home care settings, financial crimes and scamming for instance. Since then, we have heard from our member organisations and public authorities that financial abuse among older people is on the rise and requires specialised prevention to deal with this new form of crime that strives in our increasingly digitalised environment. Again, older women seem to be at higher risk than men due to the fact that they may not be so used to managing the household finances.

Situations of dependency on others and vulnerability are complex: the older people themselves, their families, and professional and voluntary caregivers, should all respect the stated rights. The Charter aims to enable everyone to facilitate older people's access to their fundamental rights. It seeks to complement and support charters and other measures that are already implemented in some countries of the EU and not to replace them. The Charter also raises awareness among a wider public, to promote the rights of the increasing number of people receiving long-term care, and to foster best practices in Member States and beyond. These rights are not fully respected today but our ambition is to fulfil them. The EUSTACEA Charter was developed with the clear objective to become a reference document setting out the fundamental principles and rights that need to be respected for the wellbeing of all those who are dependent on others for support and care due to age, illness or disability. Its accompanying guide clarifies what is meant in the Charter and provides examples of how the human rights of older people who depend on others for care and assistance can be protected and enhanced.

The European Quality Framework for long-term care

The EUSTACEA project ended in December 2010 but AGE successfully applied for funding for a new EU project to prevent elder abuse through improving quality care, the so-called WeDO projecta European Partnership for the Wellbeing and Dignity of Older People (AGE Platform Europe 2012c). The WeDO project (2010–2012) was aimed at creating a lasting and growing cross-border partnership of organisations and public actors committed to improve the wellbeing and dignity of older people at grass root level in ten countries. The WeDO project developed an EU quality framework for long-term care services based on the Charter of Rights and Responsibilities of Older People in need of care and assistance. Together these documents have since inspired some national and regional legislation on long-term care and are used as reference material in some key EU documents. Although the EU funding of the WeDO project stopped in 2012, work has continued since with the networks of stakeholders it set up in various EU countries and, with the support of AGE, its impact keeps growing.

AGE toolkit on dignity and wellbeing for older persons in need of care

To help a wider range of older citizens build their capacity to claim their rights and prevent elder abuse, in 2016 AGE launched an online toolkit on the dignity and wellbeing of older persons in need of care which was updated recently (AGE Platform, 2012a). This interactive online tool aims to help both policymakers and care professionals to adopt a rights-based approach to care policies and daily practice. It does so by providing evidence on the need to develop quality services that protect the dignity of older persons in need of care. The toolkit also lists the available international and European legal and policy frameworks, and the elements that need to be part of a comprehensive policy for long-term care. The latter include developing an adequate legal framework to enforce the rights of older persons, providing adequate social protection for long-term care, implementing a rights-based approach to monitoring of eldercare services, and preventing and fighting elder abuse.

The European Network of National Human Rights Institutes' (ENNHRI) project on the rights of older persons in care

With the support of the European Commission, in 2015 the European Network of National Human Rights Institutes (ENNHRI) launched a project called 'The Human Rights of Older Persons and Long-term Care' in which AGE participated. Running until June 2017, the aim of the project was to improve the human rights protection of older persons in long-term care, with particular emphasis on residential care. Their main findings are:

> The human rights framework governing long-term care in Europe is comprehensive. An analysis of the relevant binding United Nations, Council of Europe and European Union conventions shows that we can talk of approximately twelve rights with regard to the protection and promotion of the rights of older persons either in or seeking long-term care. Protecting and promoting the rights of older persons either in or seeking long-term care includes the following:
>
> • The Right to Life
> • Prohibition of Torture, Degrading or Inhuman Treatment
> • Freedom of movement, including freedom from restraint
> • The Right to Autonomy
> • The Right to Dignity
> • The Right to Privacy and Family Life
> • The Right to Participation and Social Inclusion
> • Freedom of Expression
> • The Right to the Highest Attainable Standard of Health
> • The Right to an Adequate Standard of Living
> • Equality and non-discrimination
> • Access to Justice, and the Right to an Effective Remedy.
>
> (European Network of National Human Rights Institutes, 2017)

The project concludes that

> several rights are not adequately protected. For example, there is no automatic right to receive long-term care services, nor to choose the provider or care setting. Recipients of long-term care are not automatically entitled to immediate treatment or healthcare if they require it — they only have the right to the same equal access to available services, which may mean being placed on a waiting list.

Many rights are interpreted differently by different treaty bodies and courts. For example, the European Court of Human Rights (EctHR) has stated that it is acceptable for 'persons of unsound mind' to be deprived of their liberty under certain conditions both because they may be a danger to public safety and also because their own interests may necessitate their detention (CoE/ EctHR, 2014).

On the other hand, the UN's Committee on the Rights of Persons with Disabilities has stated that all individuals have legal capacity to make decisions affecting their daily lives, including all persons with disabilities. Anyone who has impaired decision-making skills, often because of a cognitive or psychosocial disability, still retains the power to make decisions and should not have this power taken away from them. Instead, states have an obligation to offer support to help individuals exercise their legal capacity. Moreover, even when a person makes a decision that is considered to have negative consequences, their legal capacity must continue to be respected.

Elsewhere they have argued that forcing someone to go and live in an institution on the grounds of disability alone is incompatible with the Convention on the Rights of Persons with Disabilities (CRPD), and have criticised a number of states for continuing with this practice. As domestic courts in Europe have to apply the CRPD, the different interpretation seems like a denial of the rights of older persons who may be denied the right, and the support they need, to make decisions. However, the EctHR is now frequently referring to the CRPD in its judgements and is seeking to give disabled people as much legal autonomy as possible'(European Network of National Human Rights Institutes, The Human Rights of Older Persons and Long-term Care project, 2015–2017, 2014).

Other EU institutions initiatives

Fortunately, recent developments show an increasing interest of European institutions to work on long-term care. The European Commission organised peer reviews on quality of care in 2011 (European Commission, 2011) and 2013 (European Commission, 2013), and the Council of the EU has adopted several times conclusions promoting dignified ageing. Recent important developments include also a European Commission Staff working document on long-term care (European Commission, 2011) published within the 2013 Social Investment Package and the joint European Commission-Social Protection Committee report on Adequate social protection for long-term care needs published in 2014 (European Commission, 2014).

Most importantly, in its proposal for a European Pillar of Social Rights issued in May 2017, the European Commission recognises the right to long-term care in Principle 18: 'Everyone has the right to affordable long-term care services of good quality, in particular home-care and community-based services' (European Commission, 2017a). Once the European Pillar of Social Rights will be proclaimed by all EU Member States in November 2017, this will introduce the right to quality long-term care as a key principle that should be respected across the EU, and will constitute a major step forward in the protection of the human rights of older persons in need of care and assistance.

Further initiatives from the UN, WHO and CoE

In 2009, the CoE adopted a Recommendation on disability and ageing stressing,

> Ageing people with disabilities and older people who develop disabilities as they age, wish to live their lives with the maximum degree of freedom and autonomy, in human and physical environments and with support services that facilitate rather than hinder this style of life.
>
> (CoE, 2009)

The Recommendation also called on Member States to protect older disabled persons from violence and abuse, and to provide services and legal protection on an equal basis to all individuals, regardless of their lifestyle, origin, type or degree of disability, age, social or family origin, financial capacity and philosophical or religious convictions.

International organisations such as the Organisation for Economic Co-operation and Development (OECD), the International Labour Organization and WHO are also increasingly involved in fighting elder abuse and developing access to quality long-term care.

In 2015, in their World Report on Ageing and Health, WHO stressed that various factors such as being a woman and having a physical and/or a mental or cognitive disability are factors that have a strong on the risk of elder abuse (WHO, 2015). In October 2016 to mark the International Day of Older Persons, WHO launched a campaign to combat ageism stressing:

> Negative attitudes about ageing and older people also have significant consequences for the physical and mental health of older adults. Older people who feel they are a burden perceive their lives to be less valuable, putting them at risk of depression and social isolation. Recently published research shows that older people who hold negative views about their own ageing, do not recover as well from disability and live on average 7.5 years less than people with positive attitudes.
>
> (WHO, 2016)

Initiatives around the World Elder Abuse Awareness Day

For several years, AGE has co-organised a series of annual conferences on the topic of fighting against elder abuse with the support of the European Commission, CoE and ENNHRI, to mark World Elder Abuse Awareness Day (15 June). Each year, these events have helped update each other on what should and could be done to prevent elder abuse, moving step by step towards a better acknowledgement that although elder abuse is an issue falling under the competency of national authorities, action is also needed at European and international level.

On the occasion of the World Elder Abuse Awareness Day 2016, AGE alerted policy makers at the EU, UN and CoE levels about the growing risk of cherry picking in access to long-term care that results in excluding some of the most severely dependent from long-term care facilities. The trend to cut in publicly funded long-term care means that waiting lists are growing and service providers increasingly tend to exclude older persons with severe forms of dementia whose behaviour or needs are considered 'too heavy' for the structure. This denial of care is a severe form of elder abuse and a denial of their human rights to have access to the care one needs to live in dignity. The phenomenon of cherry picking in long-term care is not new but seems to be growing. While they may be aware of it, it is not addressed yet by those responsible for ensuring that everyone who needs care and assistance can have access to a choice of services responding to their needs. The needs and dignity of older persons with severe forms of dementia are ignored, and the only option they are offered is heavy sedation to keep them 'manageable' within the limited human and financial resources available, when they are not kicked out of the daycare or residential facility for disturbing the other care beneficiaries.

Currently the UN CRPD has a limited impact for older persons with disabilities. The UN CRPD is supposed to protect anyone living with a disability regardless of their age. Yet AGE members report that in most EU countries there exist age limits in access to disability benefits, mobility allowance and personal assistance, which put older people in need of support in a disadvantaged position compared to younger disabled people, and may lead to elder abuse.

While not all older people are disabled, the likelihood of acquiring a disability increases with age. In the EU, people at the age of 65 are expected to live more than half of their remaining years with a frailty or disability (European Commission, 2013). Many of these older people require support in their everyday living, but in practice there are several barriers to accessing the support they need. In several EU countries there is little to no right to social protection covering the care needs of older people (Social Protection Committee and European Commission, 2014). Due to gaps in coverage, older disabled people often have to pay out of their pocket for part or all of their needs for long-term assistance. Many countries offer only means-tested support, which in some cases require older people to sell all assets, including their own homes, before public systems intervene (OECD, 2017). Moreover, home care is not a statutory right for older people in all EU countries, which means that they may have access to less support if they decide to remain in their own homes. In addition, in most EU countries there exist age limits in access to disability benefits, mobility allowance and personal assistance, which put older people in need of support in a disadvantaged position compared to younger persons with disabilities (30).

One of the trends induced by the aim to support independent living in accordance with Art. 19 of the CRPD and reinforced by the recent crisis, is that older people are taken out of residential care because it is costly and are forced into home care, without any assessment of their care needs nor sufficient support. This increases the risk of unmet needs, elder abuse, isolation and declining health.

CoE Report on the impact of austerity

Under similar considerations, the CoE Commissioner for Human Rights stated in a report on the impact of austerity in 2012:

> Many families are reportedly withdrawing older persons from residential care centres and taking them home in order to benefit from additional income in the form of their pensions. While de-institutionalisation is a welcome process, if carried out as part of comprehensive policies and with additional support for the elderly persons and families concerned, it may result in higher levels of abuse, including violence and neglect, when it takes place without sufficient control and adequate support from the state.
>
> (CoE, 2012)

The UN OEWG tackles elder abuse

Each year the OEWG meets to discuss issues around older people's human rights, including the potential need for a new UN instrument to protect the rights of older persons, as there are already such UN instruments for women, children and disabled people. In 2012, AGE was asked to play an active part in four out of five working sessions in the OEWG as the UN secretariat and the Bureau considered it crucial to have the voice of civil society from Europe heard, to raise issues of concern to older people in the continent. They were interested in particular to hear more about the work we had done on elder abuse through the EUSTACEA and WeDO projects, the Charter of Rights and responsibilities of older people in need of care and assistance and the European Framework on quality for long-term care.

In July 2017, the UN OEWG discussed two themes: equality and non-discrimination, and violence and abuse. Ms Kornfeld-Matte, the UN Independent on the Enjoyment of All Human Rights by Older Persons, explained that the prohibition of age discrimination lacks legal basis in international law. This creates great challenges in eradicating discrimination, marginalisation and exclusion of older persons. She also stressed that institutional culture tolerates the aggression and abandonment of older persons and called for appropriate preventive and monitoring mechanisms to tackle this problem, including support for caregivers and specialised training for professionals. AGE warmly supported the points raised by the independent expert and stressed that gaps in legislation and policies are numerous. Today the vast majority of countries lack a definition of elder abuse in their legislation, which hinders the ability and undermines the willingness of governments to prevent and tackle it. This also means that older persons and their specific needs are not adequately included in existing policies and laws on violence and abuse, and this lack of awareness extends to law enforcement bodies, police and services to support victims, which are unable to offer victims of elder abuse the support, redress and protection they need and to which they are entitled.

Where are we today?

Thanks to the European Charter on the rights and responsibilities of older persons in need of care and assistance and the European Quality Framework for long-term care, the issue of elder abuse has gained greater visibility at global and EU level in the last few years. Yet millions of older persons continue to suffer abuse and neglect across Europe and worldwide. And this situation may get worse in particular for those needing health and long-term care services as a result of the growing demand for care due to demographic ageing and the current austerity cuts in publicly funded services.

Mistreatment and neglect in old age are the consequences of negative perceptions of old age and ageist stereotypes, which remain deeply rooted in behaviours and attitudes, but are also reflected in many laws, policies and practices underlying the functioning and structure of our societies. This so-called 'structural ageism' has been revealed by our members and is described in a position paper AGE published in 2016 on structural ageism (AGE Platform Europe, 2016a). Ensuring dignity in later life and access to quality care services would be a key step towards addressing elder abuse in Europe (see Box 9.2).

BOX 9.2

For 15 years now, AGE has been stressing that human dignity is inviolable. Our members feel that age and dependency cannot be the grounds for restrictions on any inalienable human right and civil liberty acknowledged by international standards and embedded in democratic constitutions. Everybody, regardless of gender, age or dependency is entitled to enjoy these rights and freedoms and everybody is entitled to defend their human and civil rights.

The EU recognises and respects the rights of older people who are more likely to come to depend on others for care, to lead a life of dignity and independence and to participate in social and cultural life (European Charter of fundamental rights, art. 25.). Any restriction of these rights, if caused by age and dependency, must rest on clear legal grounds and transparent legal proceedings, must be proportionate, reviewable, and above all, considered in the best interest of the party concerned. Disregard of and contempt for these rights must be considered unacceptable. Member States should develop policies that promote these rights at home and in institutional care settings, and support individuals asserting them.

Tackling elder abuse

Tackling elder abuse includes adequately addressing the needs of informal carers and respecting their right to decide not to become an informal carer. AGE fully shares EUROCARERS' view that 'there are only few examples of good practice that take on board carers' needs and the difficult challenges faced by formal and informal carers who devote significant parts of their lives to care for dependent elders, as their needs and the challenges they face constitute important risk factors. Yet it is the duty of public authorities – together with the care providers – to protect all those who become dependent on others for their daily needs and to enable them to live a dignified life until the very end of their lives. Such measures must go hand in hand with measures to protect and support both formal and informal carers by offering them decent working and living conditions and acknowledging and valuing the huge contribution they make to the community

Health and long-term care, including prevention and early intervention, should be considered not as a cost but as an investment that benefits all age groups. EU health care and long-term care services should be based on solidarity between generations, to reflect the provisions of the Lisbon Treaty which state that the EU 'shall combat social exclusion and discrimination, and shall promote social justice and protection, equality between women and men, solidarity between generations and protection of the rights of the child'.

Need for specific legislation to protect older persons from elder abuse

On the occasion of the World Elder Abuse Awareness Day on 15 June 2017, the European Commissioner for Justice acknowledged that demographic ageing may increase the risk of elder abuse. Despite such acknowledgement and the gravity of the situation, we observe that there is overall a clear lack of governmental action in the EU. Gaps in legislation and policies are numerous. Today the vast majority of countries lack a definition of elder abuse in their legislation, which hinders the ability and undermines the willingness of governments to prevent and tackle it.

This also means that older persons and their specific needs are not adequately included in existing policies and laws on violence and abuse, and this lack of awareness extends to law enforcement bodies, police and services to support victims, which are unable to offer victims of elder abuse the support, redress and protection they need and are entitled to.

Currently AGE works on these matters with the input of its Task Force on Dignified Ageing and develops policy positions with its members around quality long-term care and elder abuse. AGE is also part of a coalition of European organisations that advocate for quality long-term care services across the EU, with a focus on respect for human rights, dignity and integration. Our dialogue with other European NGOs and with European institutions aims at producing a real impact on the development of quality long-term care services and the fight against elder abuse at grass root level across EU Member States

AGE members continue to contribute to the debate building the case for a UN initiative on the rights of older people and action to prevent and combat elder abuse as well as to protect the dignity of older people in need of care and assistance, including in the final stages of our lives. We also call for investment in long-term care services, in order to guarantee access to quality care to all those older persons who need it in the type of settings they chose.

Elder abuse increasingly recognised as a form of domestic violence

According to a study performed by the AVOW project (European Commission, 2011a) led by the Finnish National Institute for Health and Welfare, 28 per cent of older women in a 2011 sample taken in five EU countries had suffered abuse and violence in the previous 12 months. Older women face a double discrimination resulting from the interaction between sexism and ageism. Whereas elder abuse affects both women and men, women are overrepresented among victims as a result of this intersection.

Thanks to the WeDO project and further work on elder abuse we have done with our members and partners, the need to include violence faced by older women who need care and assistance in the scope of domestic violence is finally recognised at EU level, and in a few European countries elder abuse is now tackled by the services in charge of providing support to victims of domestic violence against women and children.

On the occasion of the 2017 International Women's Day on 8 March, AGE Platform Europe joined forces with 27 other NGOs and civil society organisations to call on the EU for further action to end violence against women. The joint statement supported by AGE highlights the urgency of taking action to stop this ongoing human rights violation. The statement highlights the fact that sexism is coupled with racism, xenophobia and homophobia as well as discrimination based on age, disability, ethnicity, migrant status or religion. These intersecting discriminations prevent women from accessing justice and the support and protection services they need (European Women's Lobby and 27 other NGOs, 2017).

Conclusions

The next steps for AGE are to:

- ensure that older Europeans' voice will be heard in the debate on age discrimination and elder abuse at the UN OWEG;
- continue to build the capacity of our members to press for local and national bodies responsible for providing support to victims of crime in the framework of the 2012 European Union Directive on Victims' Rights to protect older persons equally through a wide and comprehensive implementation of the rights and guarantees introduced by this new EU legal instrument.

This should ensure a level playing field for the protection of victims of crime in EU countries, and contribute to the wellbeing and protection of vulnerable citizens, including older persons with disabilities. However, many efforts are still needed to make this Directive relevant to victims of elder abuse since most victims do not report nor seek redress.

It is crucial for services responsible for protecting victims of violence to understand that elder abuse is not a minor or anecdotal phenomenon, but a widespread violation of the human rights and dignity of older persons, especially those in situations of dependency and with care needs. Persistent ageist attitudes, demographic ageing and increasing financial pressures on care systems are very likely to make elder abuse even more prevalent in the near future in Europe.

Given the very high levels of underreporting, there is an urgency to ensure that victim protection mechanisms can become more effective and reflect the realities faced by older persons who are victims of violence, abuse and exploitation. The implementation of the 2012 Directive provides an excellent opportunity in that regard. It can serve as a new platform to facilitate the exchange of information and practices between victim support services, police and court practitioners and older persons and their organisations.

Key messages from this chapter

- Elder abuse is a widespread phenomenon which affects significant numbers of older people, in particular the very old and dependent. Elder abuse, violence and neglect are among the most serious violations of older persons' human rights and a global societal challenge. Intersection of ageing with gender, disability and other grounds of discrimination such as ethnic origin, religion and sexual orientation increase the risk of elder abuse.

• As anticipated by WHO, today's austerity measures combined with rapid demographic ageing are putting pressure on home and residential care systems, creating higher risks of elder abuse towards dependent older persons.

• There is an urgent need to reinforce the existing international human rights framework to offer adequate protection against elder abuse and respect for dignity in old age.

References

AGE Platform Europe (2010), EUSTACEA Project: European Charter of the rights and responsibilities of older persons in need of care and assistance, www.age-platform.eu/images/stories/22204_AGE_charte_europeenne_EN_v4.pdf.

AGE Platform Europe (2011), Contribution to Social Protection Committee Peer Review: On closing the gap – in search of ways to deal with expanding care needs and limited resources, http://ec.europa.eu/social/BlobServlet?docId=8231&langId=en.

AGE Platform Europe (2012a), Dignity and wellbeing of older persons in need of care WeDO Toolkit, http://publications.age-platform.eu/opcare-toolkit.

AGE Platform Europe (2012b), Elder abuse and neglect in the European Union, UN Open-ended Working Group on Ageing 21–24, https://social.un.org/ageing-working-group/documents/ElderAbuseNGOEWG2012.pdf.

AGE Platform Europe (2012c), WeDO Project, http://wedo.tttp.eu.

AGE Platform Europe (2016a), Elder Abuse Awareness Day 2016: AGE calls for strengthening older people's rights in the access to care, www.age-platform.eu/special-briefing/elder-abuse-awareness-day-2016-age-calls-strengthening-older-people%E2%80%99s-rights-access.

AGE Platform Europe (2016b), Response to OHCHR consultation on article 5 of the UNCRPD, www.ageplatform.eu/sites/default/files/AGE_input_CRPD_article_5_Jun2016.pdf

AGE Platform Europe (2017a), EUSTACEA Project Charter and accompanying guide, www.age-platform.eu/project/daphne-eustacea.

AGE Platform Europe (2017b), Quality and long-term care against elder abuse, www.age-platform.eu/policy-work/quality-long-term-care-fight-against-elder-abuse.

AGE Platform Europe (2017c), Statement on violence, abuse and neglect for the 8th Session of United Nations Open Ended Working Group, https://social.un.org/ageing-working-group/eighthsession.shtml.

Council of Europe (2009), Recommendation CM/Rec (2009)6, art. 1, p. 4, https://rm.coe.int/16806992fc.

Council of Europe (2012), Report on Impact of Austerity Measures, p. 2 Summary. https://wcd.coe.int/com.instranet.InstraServlet?command=com.instranet.CmdBlobGet&InstranetImage=2134231&SecMode=1&DocId=1919090&Usage=2.

Council of Europe/European Court of Human Rights (2014), Article 5(1)(e), European Convention on Human Rights, www.echr.coe.int/Documents/Guide_Art_5_ENG.pdf.

EUROCARERS (2017), Leaflet, www.eurocarers.org.

European Commission (2007), Special Eurobarometer 283: Health and long-term care in the European Union, https://data.europa.eu/euodp/data/dataset/S657_67_3_EBS283.

European Commission (2011a), Prevalence study of violence and abuse against older women, www.thl.fi/en/web/thlfi-en/research-and-expertwork/projects-and-programmes/avow-study.

European Commission (2011b), Report on Social Protection Committee Peer Review on Long-Term Care, Social Protection Committee and European Commission, https://ec.europa.eu/social/BlobServlet?docId=11905&langId=en.

European Commission (2013), Staff working document on long-term care in ageing societies – challenges and policy options, based on data from 2009 for EU27, Social Protection Committee and European Commission, https://ec.europa.eu/social/BlobServlet?docId=12633&langId=en.

European Commission (2014), Adequate social protection for long-term care needs in an ageing society, Social Protection Committee and European Commission, http://ec.europa.eu/social/main.jsp?catId=738&langId=en&pubId=7724.

European Commission (2017a), Communication from the Commission to the European Parliament, the Council, the European Economic and Social Committee and the Committee of the Regions Establishing a European Pillar of Social Rights, http://eur-lex.europa.eu/legal-content/EN/ALL/?uri=CELEX:52017DC0250.

European Commission (2017b), DAPHNE Programme, http://ec.europa.eu/justice/fundamental-rights/programme/daphne-programme/index_en.htm.

European Network of National Human Rights Institutes (2017), The Human Rights of Older Persons and Long-term Care project, quotes from ENNHRI website.

European Network of National Human Rights Institutes (2017), Project on Human Rights of Older Persons in Long-Term Care 2015–2017, www.ennhri.org/-rights4elders-.

European Women's Lobby and 27 other NGOs (2017), Violence against women and girls, will Europe rise up in 2017, ILGA-Europe, www.ilga-europe.org/resources/news/latest-news/joint-statement-8-march-2017.

Eurostat (2016), Population structure and Ageing, http://ec.europa.eu/eurostat/statistics-explained/index.php/Population_structure_and_ageing.

Muir, T. (2017), Measuring social protection for long-term care. OECD Health Working Papers.

Organisation for Economic Co-operation and Development (OECD) (2017), Health Working paper. Measuring Social Protection for Long-term Care.

Social Protection Committee and European Commission (2014), Adequate social protection for long-term care needs in an ageing society.

World Health Organization (2015), World Report on Ageing and Health, http://apps.who.int/iris/bitstream/10665/186463/1/9789240694811_eng.pdf.

World Health Organization, Campaign Stop Ageism (2016), Discrimination and negative attitude about ageing are bad for your health, www.who.int/mediacentre/news/releases/2016/discrimination-ageing-youth/en/.

World Health Organization (2017a), Ageing and life-course: Elder abuse, www.who. int/ageing/projects/elder_abuse/en/.

World Health Organization (2017b), Fact sheet on elder abuse updated in June 2017, www.who.int/mediacentre/factsheets/fs357/en/.

Yon, Y., Mikton, C., Gassoumis, Z. and Wilber, K. (2017), Elder abuse prevalence in community settings: a systematic review and meta-analysis. *The Lancet Global Health*, 5(2), pp. e147–e156.

Conclusion
Reflections of the editors

Caroline Bradbury-Jones and Sonali Shah

We are extremely excited about this book and its contribution to understanding the intersectionality of disability, gender and violence over the life course. At its heart is the issue of human rights and this has been reflected across the chapters, incorporating as we would expect, reference to the Convention on the Rights of People with Disabilities (United Nations 2006) and in the early chapters, the Convention on the Rights of the Child (United Nations 1989). Bringing the book to a close provides opportunity for us to reflect on the rich insights provided by the contributors and to consider where this leaves us in relation to the problems and issues raised, and potentials pathways ahead.

Stigma, discrimination and marginalisation

What comes over powerfully in the chapters is the significant stigmatisation, discrimination and marginalisation experienced by disabled people across the life course. The global context of the book has highlighted this in a cultural context. Karen Soldatic sets the scene in Chapter 1, by laying out how the act of giving birth to a disabled child in indigenous mothers in Australia, results in racialised stigmatisation of being a 'bad mother'. In Chapter 4, Freyja Haraldsdóttir brings an Icelandic perspective, arguing that experiencing oppression over a lifetime can lead to internalised oppression for disabled women, where messages about being inferior and abnormal or belonging to a group that is stigmatised. Similarly, in the following chapter, Aizan Sofia illuminates the impacts of Malaysian culture on the disabled women who took part in her study. They were culturally influenced by discourses that led to them internalising messages that impairment is defective and actions should be taken to eliminate it.

Throughout the book we can trace this strong theme of marginalisation. Concluding with the spotlight on older people, Bridget Penhale in Chapter 8, reports that individuals who are most at risk of harm from abuse and/or neglect are likely to be people who are acknowledged to be from 'hard to reach' or 'seldom heard' groups. She describes this as 'life on the margins of society' and being disabled is one risk factor for being in that place. Anne-Sophie Parent and AGE Platform Europe echo these risks in our final chapter, and highlight the significant challenges in eradicating discrimination, marginalisation and exclusion of older people.

Intersectionality and multiple forms of discrimination

We are really pleased that so many of the contributors have highlighted the issue of intersectionality; how the multiple forms of discrimination coalesce. Aizan Sofia talks of the intersection between impairment- and gender-based prejudice that lead to simultaneous oppression and multiple discrimination. As Freyja Haraldsdóttir, points out, internalised sexism is a subtle but almost inevitable part of girls' and women's lives and it can intersect with many other forms of oppression, for example, racial, ableist and ageist oppression. Similarly, Ashley Thompson and Mridul Wadhwa, in Chapter 3, draw out the intersectionality of racism, sexism and disablism, arguing that the consistent marginalisation due to racism along with sexism has empowered the patriarchal control of women within Black Minority Ethnic (BME) communities, especially of disabled women and girls. In Chapter 6, Theresa Lorenzo and Harsha Kathard report on an empirical study from South Africa where disabled women's stories highlight violence and impairment intersect with poverty.

Importantly, the life course perspective has allowed us to look across the age spectrum and again, the final chapters emphasise how ageing intersects with other issues. The intersection of ageing with gender, disability and other grounds of discrimination such as ethnic origin, religion and sexual orientation increase the risk of elder abuse (AGE Platform Europe). As Bridget Penhale points out, individuals who are both disabled and older may be more likely to experience an increase in vulnerability, due to this intersectionality. Such situational vulnerability, compounded by intersectionality, also includes exposure to violence, abuse and neglect so that older disabled individuals (perhaps in particular women) are more likely to experience violence in their daily lives.

Organisational and structural disempowerment

The chapters highlight the extent of organisational and structural disempowerment experienced by disabled women and children. As we have found in our own work, access to services can be a significant issue (Bradbury-Jones et al. 2015a; 2015b; Breckenridge et al. 2014; Shah et al, 2014). Karen Soldatic talks of 'deep structural inequalities' and this issue pervades the content of this book. In Chapter 2, Christine Jones and Julie Taylor explore the complexities of disclosure of abuse among disabled children and highlight a myriad of structural issues that hamper disclosure and reporting. These and other chapter authors, reveal how the interplay of structural and individual factors perpetuate the silence around the abuse of disabled children and adults in different social and cultural contexts. In the context of exploring forced marriage, Ashley Thompson and Mridul Wadhwa highlight how forced marriage of girls with learning difficulties needs to be viewed as a human rights issue instead of a cultural practice. Professionals are concerned that they may come across as racist or culturally insensitive and frequently accept a particular format of arranging a marriage in a family as acceptable without appropriate probing, thus failing to protect victims of forced marriage. In the context of our own research, this kind of fear among professionals is something that we have reported ourselves (Bradbury-Jones *et al.* 2014). The risk is of course, that silence, either through non-disclosure and/or not being heard when trying to disclose (Shah *et al.*, 2016) coupled with pervasive fear and avoidance among professionals, serves to perpetuate marginalisation, inequality and risks of further abuse.

Vulnerability and survivorship

So far, we have problematised the intersectionality of disability, gender and violence across the life course, bringing to the fore the inherent issues of discrimination, marginalisation, lack of voice and inequitable access to services with which it is associated. We didn't ask contributors to put forward messages of survivorship, resilience, resistance and strategies for change – but they all discussed them. A useful viewpoint is that vulnerability is not a weakness. We like the distinction that Theresa Lorenzo and Harsha Kathard make regarding the women in the study in South Africa. The women experienced vulnerability, but vulnerability did not necessarily mean low self-esteem. Experiencing vulnerability as strength seemed to depend on the nature of support systems and access to resources that made the difference between fragility and resilience. Similarly, in discussing the building up and working at Tabú, a feminist disability movement in Iceland, Freyja Haraldsdóttir explains an 'intersectional feminist space', where 'we don't have to separate our disability from our gender; where we can be vulnerable and strong together'.

Empowerment and agency

Many contributors have emphasised the issues of empowerment and agency. For example, Theresa Lorenzo and Harsha Kathard argue that pivotal to any success in the process of social change, women must feel empowered and sure of their own value. We have learned a great deal about different approaches through which such empowerment might be achieved, such as disability advocacy as an enabling possibility (Karen Soldatic) and feminist therapy (Freyja Haraldsdóttir): an approach that listens to, and privileges, the voices and experiences of women and other persons who have been perceived as 'other'. Given the structural and organisational barriers to the equal inclusion of disabled people, perhaps unsurprisingly, training and support for professionals to deal more effectively with disability and violence is a repeated call (AGE Platform Europe, Aizan Sofia, Ashley Thompson and Mridul Wadhwa). We are optimistic about the potential impact of some of the proposed models presented in the book, that of Christine Jones and Julie Taylor for example. As they suggest, this 'emergent international model' to facilitate disclosure of abuse among disabled children, has considerable potential in supporting professional practice.

Stories of survivorship

A powerful element of this book is that it captures the voice of disabled women and children survivors of abuse, either through qualitative data that reports their experiences, or through the personal reflections of chapter contributors. So far, we haven't mentioned Chapter 7, written under the pseudonym of Lois Llewellyn. Lois's account of surviving what she calls a 'quiet black British sexual abuse' tells of 'the most secretive and closeted of all types of sexual abuse', that of female perpetration. Her account speaks to so many of the issues covered in the other chapters. She tried to tell – to disclose – but she was silenced and ignored by those in her family who should have believed her and protected her. She was marginalised and ignored; viewed as a problem. Lois was failed also, by professionals who missed opportunities to help her. Fitting with the life course narrative, Lois stories a pattern of abusive relationships that take her from childhood to womanhood. The long-term impacts of abuse are evident in the enduring control and power of the abuser (and hence the need for the pseudonym) and the detriments to her emotional health in the form of Post-Traumatic Stress Disorder (PTSD). Just like all the other contributors, Lois ends with a powerful message regarding survivorship and the importance of counselling. Reflecting on the impact of the therapeutic relationship and diagnosis of PTSD, she writes 'I finally felt validated. It felt like someone telling me I had been right all along and my sanity confirmed'. This quote from Lois's personal story is an appropriate ending to our book as one that not only emphasises the complexities, challenges and vulnerabilities for women when disability, gender and violence intersect, but also the potential for survivorship, ability to find a voice and the possibility of experiencing real empowerment. These are of course, contingent upon being listened to, being believed and being in receipt of appropriate help and support where needed.

References

Bradbury-Jones C., Taylor J., Kroll T. and Duncan F. (2014) Domestic abuse awareness and recognition among primary healthcare professionals and abused women: a qualitative investigation. *Journal of Clinical Nursing*, 23(21–22), 3057–3068.
Bradbury-Jones, C., Breckenridge, J., Devaney, J., Duncan, F., Kroll, T., Lazenbatt, A. and Taylor, J. (2015a) Priorities and strategies for improving disabled women's access to maternity services when they are affected by domestic abuse: a multi-method study using concept maps. *BMC Pregnancy & Childbirth*, 15, 350.

Bradbury-Jones, C., Breckenridge, J., Devaney, J., Kroll, T., Lazenbatt, A. and Taylor, J. (2015b) Disabled women's experiences of accessing and utilising maternity services when they are affected by domestic abuse: a critical incident technique study. *BMC Pregnancy & Childbirth*, 15, 181.

Breckenridge, J., Devaney, J., Kroll, T., Lazenbatt, A., Taylor, J. and Bradbury-Jones, C. (2014) Access and utilization of maternity care for disabled women who experience domestic abuse: a systematic review. *BMC Pregnancy & Childbirth*, 14, 234.

Shah, S., Tsitsou, L. and Woodin, S. (eds). (2014) Access to specialised victim support services for women with disabilities who have experienced violence. Retrieved 16 August 2016: http://women-disabilities-violence.humanrights.at/resources/national-report-united-kingdom-empirical-report.

Shah, S., Tsitsou, L. and Woodin, S. (2016) 'I can't forget': experiences of violence and disclosure in the childhoods of disabled women. *Childhood*, 23(4), 521–536.

United Nations (1989) *Convention on the Rights of the Child.* New York, United Nations General Assembly. Retrieved 12 February 2018: www.cirp.org/library/ethics/UN-convention/.

United Nations (2006) *Convention on the Rights of People with Disabilities.* New York: United Nations.

Index

Note: Entries marked with an 'f' refer to figures.

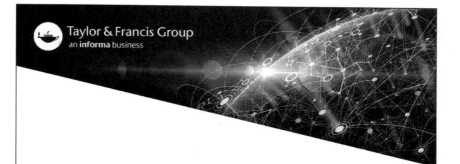